The
Arom
Bible

The Aromatherapy Bible

Gill Farrer-Halls

THE DEFINITIVE GUIDE TO USING ESSENTIAL OILS

Bounty Books

First published in Great Britain in 2005 by Godsfield Press,
a division of Octopus Publishing Group Ltd
Revised edition published in 2009

This edition published in 2011 by Bounty Books,
a division of Octopus Publishing Group Ltd
Endeavour House, 189 Shaftesbury Avenue, London WC2H 8JY
www.octopusbooks.co.uk

An Hachette UK Company
www.hachette.co.uk

A CIP catalogue record for this book is available from the British Library.

Printed and bound in China

ISBN: 978-0-75372-122-3

Contents

PART ONE

INTRODUCING AROMATHERAPY

History of aromatherapy

Although the contemporary practice of modern aromatherapy originated within the last hundred years, the use of essential oils to heal mind, body and spirit can be traced back to all the major ancient civilizations of the world. Aromatic plants played a central role in the healing arts of early humankind.

Our ancestors learned – through trial and error, and through observing which plants sick animals ate – that eating certain roots, berries and leaves helped to alleviate the symptoms of different ailments. Other plants had little (if any) effect; and a few plants aggravated symptoms, caused vomiting and even occasionally death. This highly prized healing wisdom was passed down from one medicine man or woman to the next, together with new discoveries and innovations. This knowledge was eventually transmuted into the herbal medicine we know today.

Early civilizations also discovered that burning twigs and leaves from certain plants could produce interesting effects. Some of these smoky aromas made people drowsy, while others cured ailments; some stimulated the senses, and a few gave rise to mystical, religious experiences. The precious, magical nature of aromatic plants was honoured by burning them and offering the smoke to the gods of these early civilizations.

We can see this principle at work today in the temples of the East, where incense is still ritually burned on the altars of Hindu and Buddhist deities. The modern Catholic Church also continues its tradition of burning frankincense during church services.

Clouds of incense smoke ascend towards the heavenly realms as an offering to the gods.

Into the modern era

Now, in the modern world, a renewed interest in natural, plant-based healing led to the development of modern aromatherapy. In the 1920s a French chemist, René Gattefossé, experimented with essential oils and realized their great healing potential.

After burning his hand in a laboratory accident, he plunged his arm into some lavender essential oil. The miraculous effectiveness of lavender in healing his burn led him to further research essential oils, and to use the term *aromathérapie* for the first time in a scientific paper in 1928. This heralded the arrival of contemporary aromatherapy as we know it today.

Aromatherapy as a healing art

Gattefossé's research into essential oils was taken up by another Frenchman, Dr Jean Valnet, who used essential oils to heal soldiers' burns and wounds during the First World War. He then successfully treated psychiatric patients with essential oils, demonstrating their emotional and psychological healing qualities. Marguerite Maury subsequently pioneered their use in beauty and revitalization therapy, thereby establishing another aspect of the healing powers of essential oils.

Combining essential oils with intuitive and Swedish massage techniques in the 1960s led to the contemporary practice of aromatherapy as a healing art. Aromatherapy is an holistic, complementary health-care discipline. The main treatment is full body massage, using essential oils diluted in a base of vegetable oil. When you visit a qualified aromatherapist, she or he will take a detailed case history covering your medical history, lifestyle and emotional wellbeing, before selecting appropriate essential oils for you.

Drinking herbal teas is often recommended by aromatherapists.

The healing power of touch

Although there are other important uses of essential oils, it is human touch and essential oils that hold the essence of the healing art of aromatherapy. The healing power of touch is instinctive in human nature: we express affection, sexuality and other forms of non-verbal communication using touch. We naturally

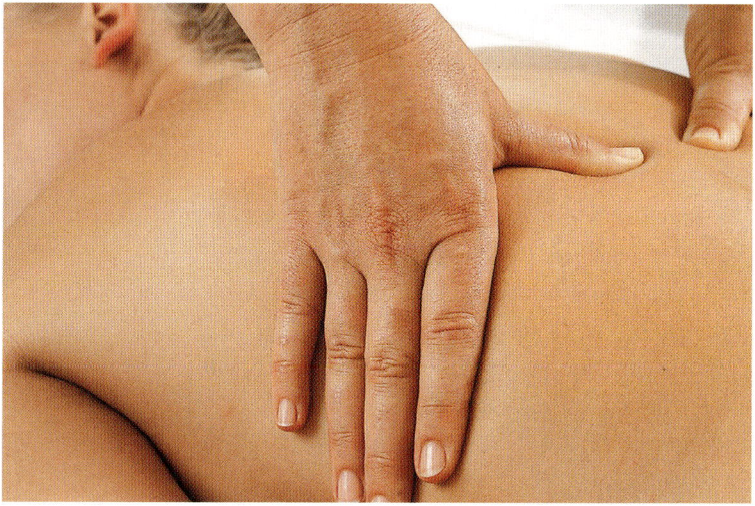

Massage using essential oils diluted in a base oil is the main application of aromatherapy.

rub our body for pain relief when we hurt ourselves. And when we formalize that instinctive touch into massage, it becomes a powerful healing tool.

One of the most important aspects of aromatherapy is that essential oils are only applied by external means. It is illegal for a qualified aromatherapist to suggest that a client ingest essential oils by mouth. Although in France some medical doctors are trained to prescribe the internal use of essential oils, this is a highly specialized aspect of aromatherapy.

It has been scientifically demonstrated that the external application of essential oils is in most cases more effective, and considerably safer, than taking them internally. Thus the healing art of aromatherapy lies in the hands of the therapist working in synchronicity with the judicious choice of essential oils.

An holistic approach

The principle behind allopathic, or orthodox, medicine is that illness is seen as something to be treated by suppression of the symptoms, often using quite harsh, synthetic drugs. This is in stark contrast to the holistic approach used in aromatherapy, which aims to treat the whole person: mind, body and soul (or spirit). Symptoms of illness – or 'dis-ease' – are seen as an imbalance of energies, and treatment with essential oils works in conjunction with the body attempting to heal itself.

This holistic framework involves the aromatherapist doing far more than simply choosing essential oils from the narrow perspective of treating symptoms. The essential oils themselves are complex, with many different qualities. So part of the skill of the therapist lies in selecting the right combination of essential oils to help the client regain mental, physical and spiritual health and balance.

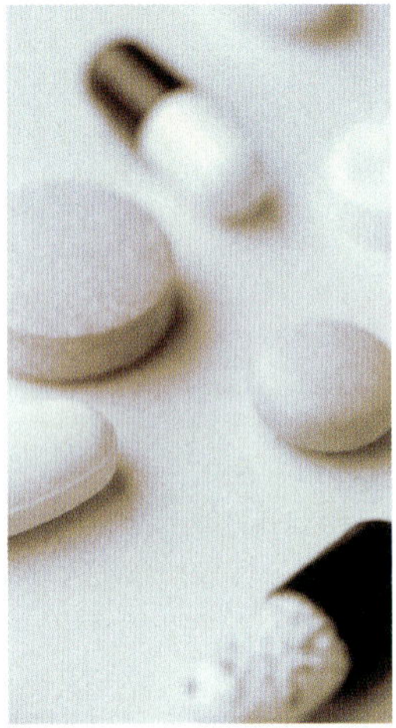

Although being prescribed medicine by your doctor is sometimes necessary, you can use aromatherapy to help keep you healthy.

What a treatment includes

A full aromatherapy treatment involves far more than simply giving a massage. The therapist will also make suggestions to assist the client to help himself or herself. Advice on lifestyle issues, diet, exercise and so on all form part of an holistic aromatherapy session.

For example, if a client presents with symptoms of insomnia, instead of simply giving a panacea (like a doctor prescribing sleeping pills), the therapist will treat the client holistically. This includes giving advice on reducing caffeine intake, checking whether the client's bedroom is sufficiently dark and quiet to promote sleep, and asking if there is some emotional problem troubling the client – all before selecting the essential oils for the aromatherapy treatment.

In this way, the holistic approach seeks to address the causes of the dis-ease, and not simply suppress the symptoms. By removing the causes, the desired effect of health and wellbeing is brought about as naturally as possible. Of course there are times when allopathic medicine is invaluable and life-saving. A truly holistic approach to health care means using all medical systems, and complementary therapies as and when they are appropriate.

During an aromatherapy consultation you may be offered different blends of essential oils to choose from.

The benefits of aromatherapy

There are many different benefits of aromatherapy that help people find health and wellbeing. Perhaps the most important are the completely natural qualities of aromatherapy, the emphasis on preventative measures and on clients learning to take responsibility for their own health care.

Essential oils are a precious gift from Nature, derived with only minimal human intervention, as you will discover in the following section (see page 18). The vegetable base oils used to dilute essential oils before massage are also natural. Both base and essential oils work in harmony with the human body, minimizing any risk of adverse reactions.

In the modern world there are many chemicals and synthetics in common use, to which increasing

Lavender fields in full bloom during summer are an inspiring sight in the Grasse region of France.

numbers of people suffer allergic reactions, such as asthma, skin rashes, digestive upsets, and so on. Aromatherapy's natural qualities help to redress the problems caused by excessive use of these unnatural substances.

A blend of your favourite essential oils mixed into a base of vegetable oil makes a wonderful perfume.

Focus on prevention

The emphasis of aromatherapy can be summed up as 'Prevention is better than cure'. In practical terms, this means that an aromatherapist will look at a client's lifestyle holistically and suggest simple changes that can prevent illness or dis-ease arising in the first place.

For example, one of the most common problems that clients present with is backache. Aromatherapy massage reduces pain and dispels the stress and tension that are a major cause of back pain. However, there are many other potential causes of backache. The aromatherapist will go through these with the client to see if physical causes such as an uncomfortable work chair, a sagging mattress or an unsupportive car seat might be contributing to the problem. Redressing such causes will alleviate some, if not all, of the problem.

Prevention leads naturally into the arena of self-responsibility. The aromatherapist will encourage clients to look after themselves, to be involved in, and take responsibility for their own health care. In this way clients can actively seek their own health and wellbeing, with assistance from the aromatherapist.

Essential oils

What are essential oils?

Aromatic plants produce fragrant essences in secretory cells, using nutrients from the soil and water, and light and warmth from the sun in a process called photosynthesis. These naturally occurring plant essences attract beneficial insects, such as bees, to help pollination and deter less friendly insects that would otherwise eat or damage the plant.

In many aromatic plants the secretory cells are near the surface, located in flowers and leaves. When you walk past these plants and brush against them, this releases the fragrance into the air. The beauty and magic of these essences are often described as the aromatic heart, life force or energy, and soul or spirit of the plant. When aromatic plants are distilled (usually by steam distillation), the essences undergo subtle chemical changes and turn into essential oils.

These lovely, fresh-smelling organic lemons are suitable fruits for expressing essential oils.

The term 'essential oil' is generally applied to all the aromatic oils used in aromatherapy, although strictly speaking this is not technically correct. Oils extracted from citrus fruits using simple expression of the rinds are still the plant essence. Some floral oils,

Waving a bottle of essential oil below your nose is the best way to appreciate its fragrance.

such as jasmine, are obtained by a process called enfleurage or solvent extraction. This produces a 'concrete', which then undergoes further solvent extraction to produce an 'absolute'. However, for ease and simplicity, the term 'essential oil' is often used generally to mean all aromatherapy oils.

Main characteristics of essential oils

Many essential oils are light, clear and non-greasy, although a few are viscous and some are coloured. However, they all share one important characteristic: they will only dissolve in fatty oils, such as almond or sunflower oil, or in alcohol. They will not dissolve in water, and this has implications for the way they are used.

Essential oils are very concentrated and powerful, and are greatly diluted before use in aromatherapy. In a massage oil, for example, the dilution of essential oil in base oil is around 2 or possibly 3 per cent. Essential oils are only rarely used undiluted, and in very specific instances. They are also highly volatile and evaporate quickly when exposed to the air, so they are best kept in airtight, dark glass bottles.

How are essential oils used?

Essential oils are the main 'tools of the trade' for an aromatherapist, and in her or his hands they become a powerful, yet subtle instrument of healing. In this context, the most valuable use of essential oils lies in professional aromatherapy massage treatments.

Such a treatment consists of two parts. The first part is a consultation, during which the aromatherapist will establish the best way to treat the client, and which essential oils will be most beneficial. This is followed by blending the massage oil and giving a full body massage.

Mixing a few drops of essential oils into a base face cream is a simple way to make your own moisturizer.

Sometimes a shorter treatment of a back, head, neck and shoulder massage is offered, which may be conveniently fitted into a lunch hour. Some aromatherapists also offer facials, lymphatic drainage massage and other specialized aromatherapy treatments.

After an aromatherapy massage, the aromatherapist may suggest that the client uses essential oils at home to reinforce the treatment and to maintain an ongoing beneficial effect. The aromatherapist may then make up a body oil or bath oil for the client, or suggest specific essential oils for the client to purchase and use for themselves at home.

Add a few drops of essential oil to your bath water just before getting in, to make a relaxing bath.

Enjoying essential oils at home

There are several ways to use essential oils at home, with or without the specific advice and support of an aromatherapist. So long as you stick to the guidelines and instructions, such as those given in this book, using essential oils at home can be both fun and rewarding.

Perhaps the most common way to use them at home is by adding a few drops to a bath. However, there is far more to this than simply choosing a bottle of essential oil at random and adding a few drops to your bath water!

Other home uses of essential oils include steam inhalations, hot and cold compresses, blending them into face creams and body lotions, using them in hair care, and as room fragrances and personal perfumes. Specific instructions, recipes and suggestions for all these methods are given later on.

How do essential oils work?

Essential oils are volatile, which means that they evaporate as soon as they come into contact with the air. So whichever method of applying essential oils is used, a certain amount is always inhaled. Because body massage is the main method of applying essential oils, this suggests that the lungs and the skin are both of prime importance in the way essential oils get into the body and do their work.

In the lungs

When we inhale air during an aromatherapy massage, bath or other treatment, we also breathe in particles of essential oil. This air/essential oil mix travels down the trachea (windpipe) into the bronchial tubes and then into the lungs. Within the lungs are tiny balloon-shaped air sacs known as alveoli, around which lie minute blood vessels that carry out the exchange of gases. This means that waste products – mainly carbon dioxide – are exchanged for oxygen and particles of essential oil.

Flower waters sprayed on your face make refreshing and gentle skin toners.

On the skin

During a body massage, the skin becomes covered with a base oil (such as sweet almond) containing a small amount of essential oil. Because the skin is semi-permeable – which means that it can absorb and excrete certain

substances with a small molecular structure – the oils are drawn into the body through the skin.

If you follow the safety guidelines given in this book, it is quite safe to use aromatherapy treatments during pregnancy.

Within the body

Once inside the body, the particles of essential oil circulate around the bloodstream and travel to the different organs and body systems. Most essential oils have a therapeutic affinity with particular organs or body systems. For instance, essential oil of rose has a purifying, regulating and tonic effect on the uterus. Once inside the body, the particles of rose will travel to the uterus and have a beneficial effect upon it.

In the mind

Essential oils also have powerful mental, emotional and psychological effects. Staying with the example of rose, it is also an anti-depressant, nerve tonic and aphrodisiac. So an aromatherapist would be likely to include rose in a massage blend for a woman experiencing problems in conceiving. Rose would have an overall beneficial effect on this woman physically, emotionally and psychologically.

Families of essential oils

There are several ways of classifying essential oils into groups or families. The directory of essential oils at the end of this book (see pages 268–385) uses a fairly common method of classification according to the type of plant (such as a herb) and the part of the plant from which the essential oil is derived (such as the flowers).

The classification of essential oils according to botanical family is less commonly used in practical lists, but nonetheless gives valuable insights into the quality of essential oils. These are not used exclusively in aromatherapy; the flavouring, perfumery and pharmaceutical industries also use essential oils. However, the oils used in these industries do not require the same level of purity and authenticity that essential oils for aromatherapeutic use must have.

Chamomile essential oil may be distilled from one of several different varieties of the chamomile species.

A botanical overview

It is important that you must know that your essential oils are botanically pure for use in aromatherapy. Botanical purity and authenticity can usually be determined by the retailer supplying the plant's botanical name, and not just its common name. For example, the common

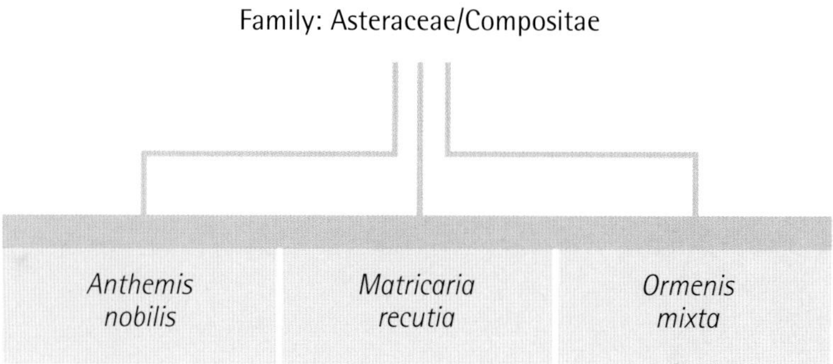

You can see clearly from this diagram that the Asteraceae/Compositae botanical family produces three different essential oils.

name 'chamomile' could mean one of three different essential oils: roman chamomile (*Anthemis nobilis*), german chamomile (*Matricaria recutia*) or moroccan chamomile (*Ormenis mixta*). Although in this instance all three belong to the same botanical family – Compositae (also called Asteraceae) – each of the three chamomiles has distinct properties and should not be confused with the others.

It is also important to know the part of the plant used. For instance, there are two different essential oils distilled from the juniper tree *Juniperus communeris*. The essential oil distilled from the berries is considerably finer than that distilled from the leaves and twigs, and this is the one you should use in aromatherapy.

Alongside knowing the true botanical name of the essential oil and which part of the plant it is derived from, it is useful to know the source and country of origin of the oil, as well as the extraction method used. In this way you can be confident that your essential oil is pure and authentic.

Methods of extraction

There are three principal methods of extracting essential oils from aromatic plants. These are: expression processes; distillation processes; and extraction using volatile solvents.

Expression

This method is only used for citrus fruit. The essential oils in citrus fruits are situated close to the surface of the peel and are easily obtained by squeezing and scarification (finely puncturing the peel). Expression methods include the sponge method and machine abrasion, the former being more traditional and producing a very pure essential oil.

You can experiment at home with hand expression and produce small quantities of your own citrus essential oils. Wash and dry the fruit and cut off segments of peel. Using your fingers, squeeze the peel over a small bowl to collect the drops of essential oil. Store them in a small, dark glass bottle with a dropper insert, and use them as you would any other citrus oil.

Distillation

Distillation processes involve heating the plant material until a vapour is formed, then cooling the vapour until it becomes liquid. In water distillation, the plant material is covered in water and heated in a vacuum-sealed container. This method is slower and sometimes inferior to steam-distillation, because certain delicate components of essential oils are

damaged by exposure to heat. The more efficient steam-distillation uses steam under pressure to swiftly extract the essential oil.

Solvent extraction

For the most delicate plant material, such as flowers, and for those containing only a small amount of essential oil, solvent extraction processes are used. The main advantage is that this method is gentle, but the resulting essential oils include non-volatile waxes and plant dyes, as well as the essential oil itself. Nonetheless, these essential oils are considered by many authorities to be fine for use in aromatherapy. The main solvents used in modern production are volatile hydrocarbons (such as hexane).

A recent innovation is a process called hypercritical carbon dioxide. This is reputed by some authorities to produce essential oils of very high quality and purity, though others are critical of oils produced in this way. The process requires very expensive equipment, so essential oils produced in this manner are difficult to obtain and expensive.

This is an example of a professional and commercial still used to steam-distill essential oils from plant material.

How to use essential oils safely

Essential oils are highly concentrated, as you can deduce from the fact that it takes thousands of rose petals to produce a single drop of rose essential oil. This potency must be respected, and the way you handle and use essential oils is important. Following the guidelines given below (and elsewhere in this book) will ensure that you use essential oils safely and effectively.

Because these oils are powerful and highly concentrated, they can be toxic if used incorrectly. However, if you handle the oils carefully and follow a few simple safety tips, they are safe and beneficial.

Safety guidelines

- As already mentioned, you should never take essential oils orally. Avoid all contact between essential oils and the delicate mouth area, and avoid placing them in or near your eyes.

- Some essential oils can cause irritation if they are applied undiluted to the skin, so this is recommended only occasionally and in specific circumstances with selected oils. Otherwise, apply only properly diluted essential oils to the skin, and follow the recipes and methods carefully. Do not increase the amount of essential oils used in the recipes.

• Certain essential oils, such as spices, may cause skin irritation on those with sensitive skin. Occasionally a slight redness or itchiness might occur from using these or other essential oils. If this happens, put some base cream or base oil, such as sweet almond oil, on the affected area and then apply a cold wet flannel until the redness or itchiness disappears.

• If you accidentally splash a drop of essential oil in your eyes, use a small amount of base oil to dilute the essential oil, and absorb this with a soft cloth, before rinsing your eyes with cold water. If there is a serious incident, seek medical attention.

• A few essential oils, such as bergamot and other citrus oils, are phototoxic. This means that they might cause skin discoloration in bright sunlight, even when diluted. It is therefore best to avoid using bergamot and other citrus oils on exposed skin if the weather is sunny.

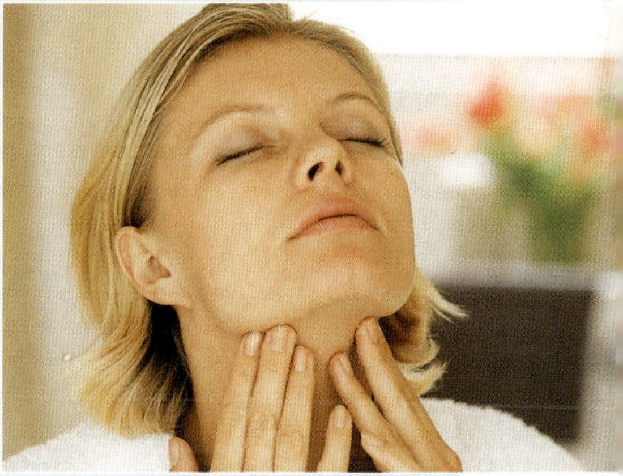

The art of blending

The magic art of combining essential oils into different blends is creative, rewarding and fun.

Essential oils can work well on their own for therapeutic purposes, and are often individually aesthetically pleasing. However, the real essence – and fun – of aromatherapy lies in creating blends of essential oils. The extensive range of oils and the different proportions you can use means that each blend you make has a unique quality.

A blend is more than just a collection of essential oils mixed together. Blending is an art and, like other art forms, it is an intuitive, creative process. When you mix essential oils into a blend you create more than the sum of its parts. This is a concept called 'synergy', which reflects the way the oils interact with each other, how they subtly change over time and how the blender responds to the blend.

In other words, blending essential oils is like magic or alchemy, and the blend itself evolves and subtly changes as time passes. We can say that a blend of essential oils is a living, organic process rather than a static, inert object or substance.

Finding your own preferences

Essential oils are blended together for their therapeutic and medical qualities and to create fragrances. However, these two aims are not exclusive; there is no point in making up a blend of essential oils for a headache, only to discover that you don't like the smell. People tend to be attracted to essential oils that will be of benefit to them, and personal likes and dislikes often change over time.

How do you know which essential oils will blend together well and which should not be mixed? Some basic guidelines are given on the next few pages, but this is also very much down to individual taste and preference. There are no hard-and-fast rules – just a few general principles. For example, many women like sweet, floral scents, while most men prefer woody, herby or spicy fragrances.

Each essential oil has its own individual character. As you become familiar with the different oils, you will intuitively learn and understand which oils blend well with which others. Experimentation and experience are key to the art of blending.

Top, middle and base notes

The blending of essential oils into perfumes is an ancient art that shares with music the concept of 'scales'. This means that just as musical notes in a scale range from low through middle to high, so a good blend of essential oils has top, middle and base notes. A good blend is therefore harmonious, balanced and well rounded.

The scale of notes

- Top notes are those that are most volatile and are the first that we smell. They are light and fresh, and tend to dissipate quickly.
- Middle notes then appear, representing the heart and bulk of the fragrance, and some of them will linger for a while.
- Base notes are rich and heavy, and last a long time. In perfumery, base notes are called 'fixatives' – they literally 'fix' a perfume and hold it together, helping to prevent the lighter notes dispersing too quickly.

As you will learn from reading the descriptions of the individual essential oils, each one is composed of different notes. These evaporate at different rates, so that we smell different parts at different times, according to their volatility. When several oils are blended together, this creates a complex fragrance that subtly changes as each aromatic particle in its own time releases its fragrance into the atmosphere.

Ornate glass bottles like these make attractive perfume bottles to hold your home-made perfumes of essential oils.

Classic blends

As blending is an art and not an exact science, it comes as no surprise to learn that there are differences of opinion as to where on a scale each essential oil belongs. Some are easier to categorize than others; for example, citrus oils are almost always designated as top notes, while patchouli, benzoin and myrrh are usually designated as bottom notes. Below is a short list of blends, using top, middle and base notes, of some commonly used essential oils. These give a few examples of some simple, classic and harmonious blends.

Top	Middle	Base
Lemon	Geranium	Cypress
Bergamot	Neroli	Frankincense
Sweet orange	Lavender	Patchouli
Eucalyptus	Rosemary	Sandalwood
Basil	Rosewood	Myrrh

Evaporation rates and odour intensities

The art of blending using top, middle and base notes leads naturally into a look at evaporation rates and odour intensities. These are similar to the scale of notes, but offer extra useful information.

This professional perfumer has a huge range of aromatic material to choose from.

Rates of evaporation

Evaporation rates, on a scale of 1 to 100, determine how long an odour will last, and this information can help you establish whether an essential oil is a top, middle or base note. However, you will notice from the following examples that this is not always the case; for example, basil is generally classified as a top note, yet it has an evaporation rate of a middle-note essential oil.

Eucalyptus	5	Bergamot	55	Ylang ylang	91
Melissa	17	Frankincense	75	Cedarwood	97
Marjoram	40	Basil	78	Rose	99
Chamomile	47	Lavender	85	Patchouli	100

Odour intensities

The odour intensity of essential oils, on a scale of 1 to 10, reveals more surprises, because not all the base-note essential oils have an intense odour, while some of the top-note essential oils do. Although these anomalies may seem confusing, they simply demonstrate the complex nature of essential oils and their aromas.

Bergamot	4	Clary sage	5	Geranium	6	Basil	7
Cypress	4	Juniper	5	Rosemary	6	Jasmine	7
Benzoin	4	Neroli	5	Ylang ylang	6	Frankincense	7
Lavender	4	Sandalwood	5	Fennel	6	Peppermint	7

If you know which note, evaporation rate and odour intensity an essential oil has, this is helpful information when you are creating a blend. Eventually your intuition and your sense of smell will assist you, but these tables are useful when you are starting out, to help you create harmonious, well-rounded and aesthetically pleasing blends of essential oils.

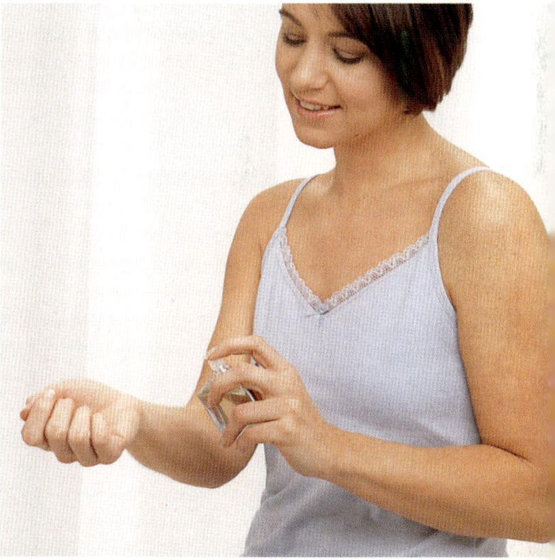

Once you know the basic facts about evaporation rates and odour intensities, you can blend your own perfumes.

Perfume families

This professional perfumer is creating a new commercial perfume.

The perfume industry has a great deal of specialized expertise in creating commercial fragrances, and we can learn some tips on blending essential oils from some of the classic perfume families. Although the perfume industry also uses animal aromatics, such as civet, musk and ambergris (which aromatherapists obviously never use), essential oils do play a major role in perfumes.

The heart of the perfume industry is in Grasse in southern France, an area that grows huge fields of lavender, other flowers and herbs. Essential oils are distilled locally for use in making perfumes. Opposite are some descriptions of perfume families, which include useful information for blending essential oils.

Family traits

Each perfume family has its own specific character and scent.

- Floral is the largest family and the scent is best described as feminine, delicate and romantic. Floral essential oils, such as lavender, ylang ylang, geranium and rose, form the base of these perfumes, but other oils are also used (for example, citrus oils are included in floral/fruity blends).
- Green fragrances evoke summer meadows and freshly mown grass. A typical green perfume includes essential oils from herbs such as basil and rosemary, and mosses, and might also include florals, woods and citruses.
- Chypre fragrances are elegant, formal and sophisticated, and typically include clary sage, oak moss and patchouli blended with rich, deep florals and fresh citruses.
- The citrus family is based on citrus oils and the perfumes are fresh, clean, light and youthful. Other essential oils in citrus perfumes include lemongrass, verbena and palmarosa.
- Spicy fragrances are sharp, clean and deep, somewhat unconventional and outgoing. The spice essential oils, such as clove, black pepper, cardamom, cinnamon and nutmeg, form the base of spicy perfumes. Individual spice oils are used surprisingly often in other perfumes.
- Amber-oriental perfumes are deep, heavy, mysterious, seductive and exotic; they tend to be warm and long-lasting. Typically these perfumes include sandalwood, cedarwood, frankincense, myrrh, patchouli, vanilla and ambrette seed. Amber-oriental perfumes tend to suit both men and women.

These 'tears' of hardened resin extracted from the myrrh bush are steam-distilled to produce essential oil.

Blending techniques

When you create a blend of essential oils for yourself or someone else, you need to take into account any dis-ease or disorder, the underlying causes of the symptoms, psychological and emotional factors, and an overall aesthetic consideration. Even if you are just blending a perfume, the therapeutic action of the essential oils you select will still be present, so you need to bear this in mind.

To create a pleasing blend of essential oils you need to smell quite a few to decide which oils to use.

There is a strong association between scent and memory, and certain essential oils may summon up elusive memories or quite specific recollections. Avoid any essential oil that conjures up unpleasant memories – or that you simply dislike on first smelling – because scents that you find unpleasant will not have a beneficial effect, and may even cause an adverse emotional reaction.

Blending tips

• When you first start creating your own blends, stick to a maximum of four essential oils in any one blend. Even using just three oils allows you to create blends with a top, middle and base note (see pages 32–33). If you make a mistake and create a blend that you find unpleasant, it is easy to discover what went wrong if there are only a few oils involved.

• A useful tip is to select the essential oils that you wish to use in your blend, and before mixing them into a base of sweet almond oil, skin lotion or other base, put a drop or two of each essential oil onto a separate cotton wool bud. By holding the three or four buds a little way from your nose and waving them around, you will get a good sense of what the blend will smell like.

• By taking one bud away, or by adding another one with a different essential oil, you can fine-tune your blend before actually making it up into an aromatherapy product. This prevents expensive waste, and is a useful way of helping you learn about the complexity of blending. The blending process has been described as 'learning to listen through your nose', which offers an interesting insight into the art of blending.

To assess a potential blend, sniff together the different essential oils on cotton buds.

Using essential oils

There are several different ways of using essential oils, which are described on the following pages.

Baths

After massage, aromatic bathing with essential oils is the most effective and enjoyable aromatherapy treatment. The therapeutic effects of water and bathing are well known, but adding essential oils makes the experience special.

Aromatic baths offer simplicity and versatility. A bath with essential oils can be relaxing, stimulating, refreshing or aphrodisiac. You can treat skin conditions and relieve aching muscles. However, aromatic baths are most commonly used to promote relaxation and dispel stress.

Adding essential oils to your bath

- Fill the bath with water, sprinkle 4–8 drops of essential oil on top and – because essential oils don't dissolve in water – agitate the bath water to disperse the oils. Don't add essential oils beforehand or much of the highly volatile oils will be lost.

- You can make a moisturizing bath oil using a dispersant bath oil base, or a base oil such as sweet almond. To 5 ml (1 tsp) of base oil, add 4–8 drops of essential oils of your choice, then add this mixture to the bath, as described above. A classic relaxing bath blend is 2 drops of lavender, 2 drops of geranium and 2 drops of chamomile.

Vaporizers and diffusers

A delightful and natural way to perfume a room is to diffuse essential oils into the atmosphere. Essential oil burners offer a convenient way to vaporize essential oils. They are usually constructed of pottery or stone, and have a lower chamber for a tea-light candle and a top bowl for water and essential oils.

Also available are electric aromatic diffusers and light-bulb rings, which work in a similar way to burners. Even placing a small bowl of hot water on a radiator creates a simple device for vaporizing oils.

Using a burner

- Light the tea light, and pour some warm water into the top bowl to half-fill it. Then sprinkle on 8–10 drops of essential oil. As the water heats, the essential oils vaporize and fragrance the air.

- Lemongrass will keep insects at bay, while geranium and bergamot will deodorize and neutralize cigarette smoke and pet smells. To prevent infection spreading, use ti-tree, rosemary or eucalyptus, and to create a relaxing atmosphere, try frankincense and sandalwood.

Room sprays

If using a burner or an electric diffuser is inconvenient or not to your taste, then you can make up room sprays instead, using water and essential oils. The effect is less powerful than when you vaporize essential oils, but some people prefer a less intense aroma. Room sprays also have an instant effect.

Do not use plastic bottles, as essential oils can chemically react with the plastic. It is important to remember that essential oils do not dissolve in water, so you must shake the bottle vigorously every time before spraying.

Making a room spray

- Take a glass bottle with a spray attachment and almost fill it with cold water. For each 5 ml (1 tsp) of water, use 3 drops of essential oils. For instance, a 100 ml ($3\frac{1}{2}$ fl oz) bottle will take 60 drops of essential oils.

- A room freshener might include lavender, rosewood, bergamot and sweet orange. For a bathroom or toilet, a suitable blend could be cedarwood, juniper, pine and lemon. To create a sensuous evening atmosphere you could try rose, patchouli, mandarin and sandalwood.

In cooking

Although it is not recommended to use essential oils internally, when they are incorporated into foods and drinks in tiny amounts, they are heavily diluted and unlikely to cause an adverse reaction. The flavourings industry uses essential oils to flavour food, drink and toiletries such as toothpaste, so we already ingest tiny amounts of essential oils.

Using essential oils as flavourings

- Make fruit syrups by boiling 100 g (4 oz) of sugar with 600 ml (1 pt) of water for five minutes. Cool, then add 1 drop of lemon, orange, grapefruit or lime essential oil. Stir thoroughly. Add a tablespoon or two of fruit juice before pouring the syrup over ice cream, fruit or sponge cake.

- Make a hot punch using 1 litre (1¾ pt) of red wine mixed with a pot of strong tea made with four teabags. Add a tablespoon of brown sugar, slices of orange and lemon, and a small glass of brandy. Five minutes before serving, add 1 drop each of cinnamon, clove, cardamom and ginger essential oils, and stir well.

Scent for paper and linens

It is very romantic to receive a perfumed letter from a loved one. Scented note paper used to be popular before e-mails drastically reduced the number of letters that we write, so making your own scented note paper might inspire you to write more letters. Alternatively, try scenting your bed linen or even your underwear!

Scenting items

- Take half a dozen paper tissues and place 1 drop of essential oil onto the corners and centre. Interleave the tissues between sheets of paper in a box of quality writing paper. After two days the paper will be delicately scented, but not stained with essential oil. The most romantic fragrance is rose, while lavender is suitable for your mother, grandmother or aunt.

- Place paper tissues scented with essential oils in the linen cupboard between sheets, to gently perfume your bed linen. Try a mixture of lavender, ylang ylang and bergamot.

Scent for cleaning products

Most cleaning products that you can buy have synthetic fragrances. However, some biodegradable, unscented cleaning products are available, and adding essential oils to these perfumes them pleasantly and naturally. Unfragranced liquid clothes wash, fabric softener, floor cleaner and toilet cleaner are all suitable products.

Perfuming your cleaning products

- Keep an old bottle of cleaning fluid, and half-fill it from a new bottle of the same product. After adding essential oils, shake the bottle vigorously so that the oils are thoroughly mixed in. A 1/2 per cent dilution is achieved by adding 1 drop of essential oil to 10 ml (2 tsp) of cleaner, so a 500 ml (17 fl oz) bottle of cleaner will take 50 drops of essential oil. Lavender, lemon and pine are traditional scents for cleaning fluids.

- When vacuuming carpets, put 4–6 drops of essential oil onto a cotton wool ball and place it in the dust bag. This freshens and perfumes the room while you are cleaning.

PART TWO

USING AROMATHERAPY

How to use aromatherapy

In this part you will read about how to use aromatherapy in different ways. We begin with the way in which aromatherapy contributes to beauty and skin care (see pages 50–89). This important dimension of aromatherapy will help you learn about your skin and how to care for it. Once you have established your skin type, there are instructions and recipes to enable you to create suitable aromatherapy face and skin-care products.

A fascinating aspect of aromatherapy is experiencing the powerful effects that essential oils have on people, both psychologically and emotionally. You

will learn how to create individually tailored perfumes to suit different moods and emotions (see pages 90–131). In addition, there are aromatherapy techniques and remedies to help alleviate a range of negative emotions, such as sadness and fear. A brief introduction to personality types will assist you in creating your own personal perfume that reflects who you are.

Although visiting a professional aromatherapist for a full body massage cannot be surpassed, you can nonetheless learn some basic aromatherapy massage strokes and techniques (see pages 132–181). These enable you to practise self-massage, and to offer simple massage to friends and family. The relaxing benefits of aromatherapy massage are enhanced by choosing appropriate blends of essential oils, and some classic blends are suggested.

Healing body, mind and spirit

The physical healing qualities of essential oils are introduced with a practical first-aid and home remedies section (see pages 182–217). You will learn, for example, how to make a compress; which essential oils can help with digestive problems; and how to treat minor cuts and abrasions. This section also gives instructions on how to use aromatherapy with babies, children, pregnant women and the elderly.

In ancient times, aromatic plants were used to honour the divine. In a contemporary context, we can use essential oils during meditation to connect with our inner being or spirit (see pages 218–267). Simple instructions for various meditations are given, together with appropriate essential oils. Included in this section are ideas for using essential oils with crystals and chakras, and tips on creating perfumes according to astrological star signs.

Make sure that you have everything you will need close to hand before you begin giving a massage to someone.

Aromatherapy for beauty

Essential oils and skin care

The judicious use of essential oils in skin care helps to rejuvenate and beautify the face and body. We can call this 'cosmetic aromatherapy' – a natural way to enhance the skin's condition and maintain it in good health. However, following the holistic approach of aromatherapy, we need to look further than our faces.

Beauty is more than skin deep, because what you eat and drink, how you cleanse your skin and your overall general health are all reflected in your face. Taking an holistic approach to caring for your skin helps to ensure that you face the world looking as good as possible. This means examining what you eat and making changes to help your skin from within.

Lifestyle checklist

Some people can eat cream cakes and chips and still have lovely skin, but they are in a tiny minority. Most of us need to eat sensibly to keep our skin in good condition. This means drinking lots of spring water, substituting herbal teas for tea and coffee, and eating lots of fresh fruit and vegetables, together with whole grains. Eliminating or reducing salt, alcohol, fried foods, red meat and sugars will help the skin to retain its natural bloom.

Fresh air and sufficient exercise, avoiding smoking (or passive smoking) and reducing stress complete the lifestyle checklist for healthy, beautiful skin. Once skin care has been tackled from the inside, it is time to consider how essential oils can be used to improve your complexion, treat specific skin conditions and generally care for your skin.

Essential oils have been used for cosmetic purposes for centuries, notably by the Egyptians, who included frankincense and cedarwood in embalming procedures. Scientific studies have revealed that certain essential oils, such as

Drinking lots of spring or mineral water helps to keep your complexion clear and glowing.

rose, frankincense, neroli and lavender, stimulate the regeneration of healthy new skin cells. Some essential oils also have a rejuvenating effect on the skin, restoring vitality and regulating capillary activity. Essential oils are, therefore, of great value in skin care.

What is the skin?

The skin is the largest organ of the body, and its functions include temperature regulation and the manufacturing of vitamin D as well as protecting the body beneath. The skin is divided into three main layers, with each layer having specific characteristics.

The layers of the skin

- The first, outer or top layer is called the epidermis and is also known as the *stratum corneum*. This is what we see when we look at the surface of the skin. The epidermis is composed of essentially dead cells of a flat appearance.
- The second, middle layer is called the dermis, and is considerably thicker than the epidermis. It contains blood and lymph vessels, hair follicles, sensory nerve endings and sebaceous and sweat glands. The dermis manufactures new, living skin cells, which gradually emerge onto the surface epidermis.
- The third and bottom layer of the skin is known as the subcutaneous layer. This is where the tiny muscles that keep the skin toned and firm are located, along with fatty tissue that supports the skin.

How aromatherapy can help

The epidermis is the area that you concentrate on with your skin-care regime, although its condition is interdependent with the two lower layers and the rest of the body. The appearance of the skin is conditioned by how quickly the dead surface cells are replaced by new cells from the dermis. The more rapidly this process occurs, the softer, smoother and healthier the skin appears.

When dead skin cells collect on the surface of the skin, the complexion appears lifeless, dull and lacklustre. This is one of the functions of cleansing the skin: not only do you remove dirt from the surface and dirt trapped in

the pores, but you also remove dead skin cells. In this way gentle exfoliation can improve a dull complexion.

As we age, the natural process of cell renewal slows down, and the youthful elasticity of the skin diminishes. Rejuvenating aromatherapy skin products stimulate rapid regeneration of cells in the dermis to help retain a beautiful complexion as you age.

Using aromatherapy products to look after your skin will help to keep it looking youthful and beautiful.

Normal skin

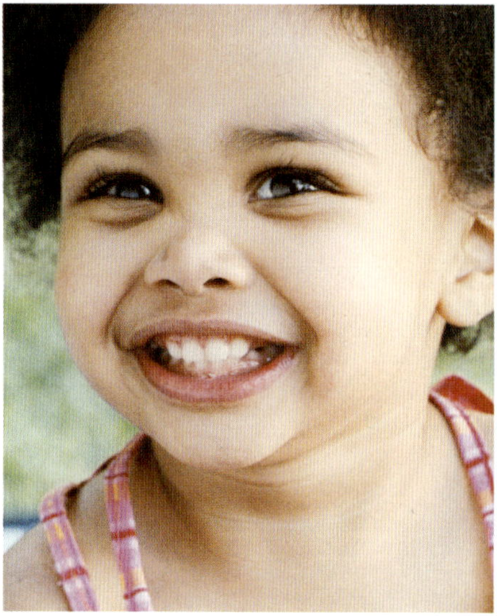

Children have naturally lovely skin and are one of the few lucky groups of people to have a normal skin type.

So called 'normal' skin is rare beyond puberty, and therefore – other than in children – not really normal at all! For the lucky few, normal skin is characterized by good hydration, muscle tone, a balanced metabolism and good circulation.

Normal skin has an attractive, natural bloom and colour, and looks soft and supple. The surface of the skin is free from blemishes and has a fine texture with no wrinkles, no crow's-feet around the eyes and no enlarged open pores.

Caring for normal skin is just as important as caring for other skin types, although in this instance the aim is to preserve the skin condition, rather than compensate for any deficiencies. As with other skin types, normal skin must be cleansed thoroughly, first thing in the morning and last thing at night before going to bed. Toning and moisturizing after cleansing completes the basic daily skin-care regime.

Occasional exfoliation – perhaps once a fortnight – using a facial scrub is recommended, and using a face mask or pack once a week is also a good way

Suitable aromatherapy products

• If you have normal skin, you can use almost any essential oil you like in your skin-care products, with the exception of essential oils that might cause irritation, such as the spice oils. However, the following essential oils are particularly recommended for normal skin care: german chamomile, rose otto, rose absolute, neroli, lavender, geranium, palmarosa and rosewood.

• Flower or floral waters (also known as hydrosols) are by-products of distillation of essential oils, and are valuable in skin care alongside essential oils. Suitable flower waters for normal skin include rose water, chamomile water, orange-flower water, cornflower water and linden-blossom water.

to keep normal skin healthy. Specific recipes and instructions for incorporating essential oils into base creams and other skin-care bases are given for all skin types later on in this section (see pages 78–89).

A home-made moisturizer with appropriate essential oils will keep your complexion looking good.

Dry and sensitive skin

Dry skin is caused by insufficient production of sebum, the skin's natural moisturizer or lubricant, which is manufactured by the sebaceous glands. Dry skin is also often dehydrated, which is not quite the same condition. Dehydrated skin lacks moisture generally (and even oily skin can be dehydrated). However, the lack of sebum in dry skin diminishes the skin's ability to retain moisture, so dry and dehydrated skin often accompany each other.

Dry skin frequently looks delicate, fine and thin, with tiny pores. It is heavily affected by sun, wind and rain and wrinkles easily. It needs a lot of protection and moisturizing to maintain it well. Sensitive skin is usually fair and delicate, and shares with dry skin the need for lots of protection and moisturizing.

Check the condition of your skin to make sure you choose the most appropriate skin-care products.

Suitable aromatherapy products

- The best essential oils to use for dry skin include german chamomile, roman chamomile, rose otto, rose absolute, geranium, lavender, neroli, jasmine and sandalwood. For sensitive skins, essential oils include rose otto, rose absolute, melissa, neroli, helichrysum (also called 'everlasting' and 'immortelle'), german chamomile and roman chamomile. For sensitive skins, always use a very low percentage of essential oil, such as 1 or even ½ per cent, and if any reaction occurs, stop using that particular essential oil.

- Suitable flower waters for both dry and sensitive skin include chamomile water, rose water, orange-blossom water, rose geranium water and lemon-balm (melissa) water.

Sensitive skin easily reddens and itches, and only gentle, plant-based natural cosmetics should be used. It is also prone to allergic reactions caused by the alcohol and chemicals used in many commercial cosmetics and skin-care products, so these should be avoided.

Both dry and sensitive skins need more attention than normal skin. They should be moisturized several times a day, using a light base cream rather than a rich, heavy moisturizer. Cleansers and toners need to be very gentle, and plain flower waters make excellent toners. Gentle, hydrating face packs that include honey should be used once a week.

Mature skin

There is no need to panic about losing your youthful bloom if you look after your skin.

Mature skin is something we will all have one day. This brings up an interesting point about skin types: they change, according to age, health, environmental circumstances, diet and other lifestyle factors. It is therefore important to reassess your skin type from time to time, because you may find that your once-lovely normal skin has become dry or sensitive, or has simply aged into mature skin. Ageing is, however, a normal part of life and with proper skin care, mature skin can still look good for its time of life.

As we age, the body's functions slow down, cells are not replaced as quickly, and skin elasticity gives way to a gradual drooping. A mature skin is characterized by wrinkles and crow's-feet (those fine lines around the eyes), and thread veins, blemishes and age spots start to appear. The skin loses the natural bloom of youth, the bone structure underneath the face becomes more noticeable, and creases along the lines of the face muscles become apparent.

Do not despair! This process happens gradually, individual variations occur and for some lucky people the signs of ageing appear only in late life. Good and regular skin-care treatments can even slow down the signs of

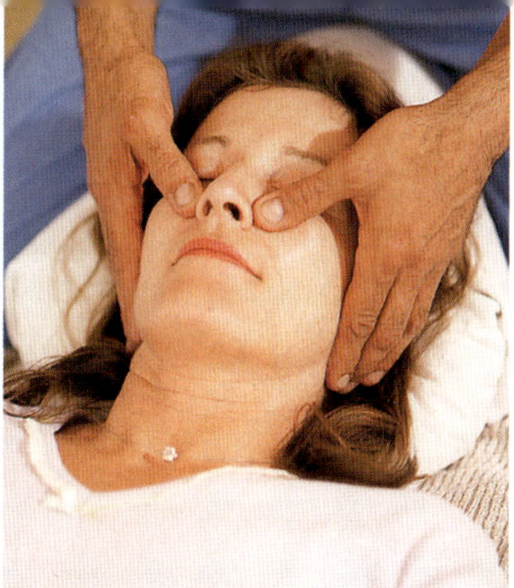

Regular aromatherapy facials are a relaxing treat and maintain the condition of your skin.

ageing. Reducing unnecessary exposure to the sun, assessing your diet and trying to improve it, and eliminating stress and environmental pollution as much as possible all help to delay the signs of ageing.

Regular aromatherapy facial treatments with selected essential oils can help maintain a healthy skin. Facial massage helps tone the sagging muscles and restore some skin tone. Hydrating face masks that include aloe vera, seaweed extracts, honey with propolis and other nutrients are beneficial. Careful twice-daily cleansing, toning and moisturizing remains important.

Suitable aromatherapy products

- Essential oils that have a beneficial effect on mature skin include carrot seed, frankincense, sandalwood, myrrh, patchouli, rose otto, rose absolute, roman chamomile, german chamomile and palmarosa. Carrot seed is especially valuable for revitalization, and frankincense can help to reduce wrinkles.

- Suitable flower waters include rose water, chamomile water, linden-blossom water and angelica-root water.

Oily and combination skin

Oily skin is the bane of many adolescents, with the accompanying acne and blackhead spots. Adolescents tend to have oily skin because their bodies are going through changes and flux after puberty, especially the endocrine system, which is linked to sebum production. At that vulnerable age it is small satisfaction to learn that an oily skin in your early years means that your skin will age more slowly than normal or dry skin.

Oily skin can also affect adults. It is characterized by a dull, neglected appearance, possibly acne, and certainly some blackheads, spots and blemishes. The skin feels oily to the touch and has a shiny look, together with enlarged pores and sometimes a thick, coarse appearance.

The blemishes caused by oily skin can easily be treated by using the appropriate essential oils.

Suitable aromatherapy products

- Essential oils that are beneficial for oily skin include geranium, lavender, cedarwood, palmarosa, niaouli, juniper berry, ti-tree, ylang ylang, cypress, grapefruit. bergamot and myrtle.

- Flower waters for oily skin include verbena water, witch hazel, orange-flower water and cornflower water.

The combination skin of an oily T-shape of forehead, nose and chin with dry skin on the rest of the face is the most common skin type. Aromatherapy treatment is aimed at balancing and reducing sebum production. The patches of dry skin and of oily skin require different essential oils and other skin-care treatments accordingly, so a wide range of products is necessary.

It is important to resist the temptation to use harsh cleansers on oily skin. Although they are effective in temporarily cleansing excess sebum and dirt, such harsh cleansers typically contain alcohol or chemicals that literally strip the skin of sebum. This merely encourages more sebum production and is therefore counter-productive.

The best approach to treating oily skin is gentle, frequent cleansing, toning and moisturizing with a light moisturizer. Essential oils are chosen to balance and reduce sebum production and for their healing, antiseptic qualities. Deep-cleansing treatments weekly are recommended. These include face masks based on green clay, which draws out dirt and excess sebum; and facial steaming to unblock pores and prevent spots from forming.

General toning facial massage

Facial massage relaxes tension, tones muscles, stimulates blood supply, improves skin tone and stimulates lymphatic drainage and the removal of toxins. Although you can do a face massage on yourself, this simple facial massage is easiest to practise on a friend. The person should lie on the floor on a futon or mat, and you should kneel on a cushion behind their head.

How to perform it

YOU WILL NEED

An essential oil and base oil (see the section on base oils on pages 154–157) according to skin type; use a 1 per cent dilution: 1 drop of essential oil in 5 ml (1 tsp) of base oil.

WHAT TO DO

1 Cleanse and tone the face thoroughly, ideally using a cold-cream cleanser and skin toner from the recipes given later (see pages 78–79 and 86–87).

2 Gently hold the head to establish contact. Then oil your fingertips and, with sweeping, stroking movements, lightly draw your fingers from the bottom of the face to the top, avoiding the

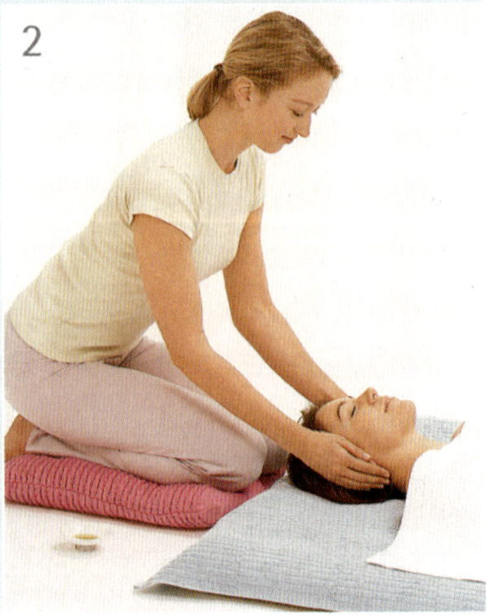
2

eyes. Repeat several times, gently increasing the pressure.

3 Place your fingertips horizontally in the middle of the forehead, using a little more oil if required. Draw them firmly out to the temples several times. You should be able to feel the bones of the forehead through the facial skin and flesh.

4 Now place your fingertips on either side of the nose. Draw them up and out to the sides of the face several times, using a little less pressure than you used on the forehead.

5 Using both index fingers, make small circles all over the nose. Be careful not to block off the air flow. Continue making small circles over the chin and around the mouth area, avoiding the lips.

6 Finish as you started, with gentle sweeping strokes up the face, getting gradually lighter until the contact disappears. Encourage your friend to lie there and relax for few minutes after the massage is finished.

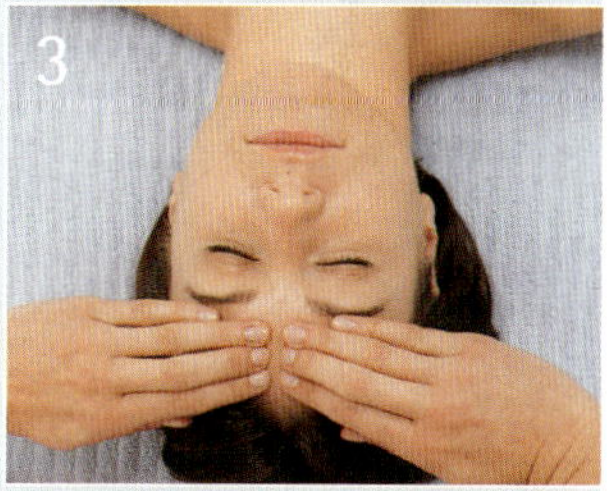

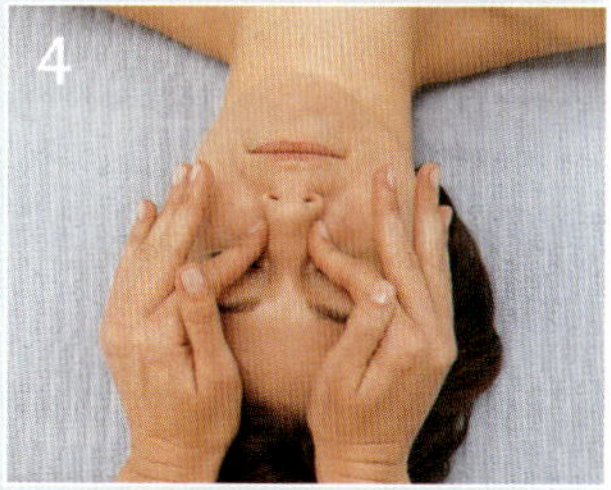

Draining facial massage

If you have a puffy complexion, or a cold, sinusitis, hay fever or nasal congestion that causes headaches, then a draining facial massage can help to relieve the symptoms. Production of excess mucus in nasal and respiratory passages is the body's response to inflammation caused by infection (colds and flu) or irritants (dust and pollen). The nasal passages contract through inflammation, and the mucus becomes trapped in the sinuses, causing pain and congestion.

In addition to draining facial massage, steam inhalations using lavender, eucalyptus or peppermint help to ease pain and congestion. Avoid dairy and wheat products, because these are both mucus-forming.

How to perform it

YOU WILL NEED

An essential oil and base oil (see the section on base oils on pages 154–157) according to skin type; use a 1 per cent dilution of lavender

WHAT TO DO

1 Start the facial massage according to the instructions on page 64. After the firm strokes on the forehead, start the drainage techniques.

2 Using both index fingers, one on each side of the face, place your fingertips on the bony ridge just under the eyebrows at the inner edge. Press firmly upwards, hold for two seconds, then release the pressure and, moving slightly

along the eyebrow, press upwards firmly again. Repeat this procedure until you reach the outermost edge of the eyebrow. Start again at the inner edge, and do it twice more.

3 Now start with your index fingers just above each eyebrow. Using firm pressure, make large circles outwards. Follow the line above the eyebrow, down past the side of the eye (being careful not to get close to the eye), then across the top of the cheekbone and up the side of the nose, until you reach the point where you started. Make a total of six circles.

4 Starting in the same place, do six circles going in the other direction.

5 Finish by completing the rest of the facial massage sequence (steps 4–6, see page 65).

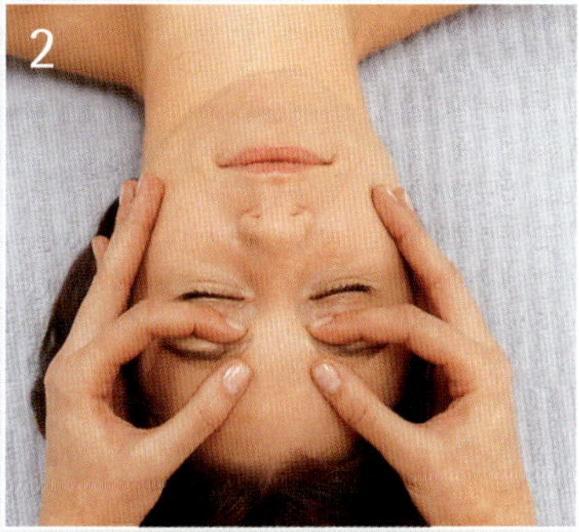

2

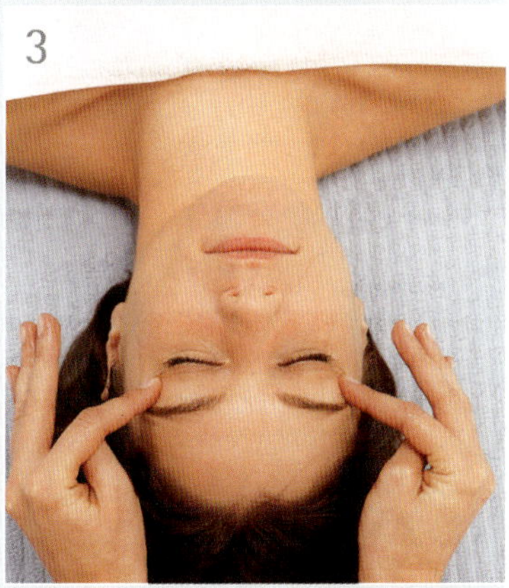

3

Rejuvenating hot-oil treatment

The scalp benefits from aromatherapy massage and treatments just as much as the face. This rejuvenating hot-oil treatment can be given before or after a facial massage, if desired, though it is equally effective on its own and is easy to do to yourself. Hot oil with added essential oils nourishes the scalp and conditions the hair. Scalp massage promotes healthy hair growth, reduces scaling, is deeply relaxing and gently releases tension and dispels headaches.

Suitable base oils for the rejuvenating hot-oil treatment include jojoba, which regulates sebum and is beneficial for dry, itchy scalps; evening primrose oil, which makes a good conditioner for hair; and neem oil, which helps prevent dandruff and itching. Add essential oils as follows: for dark hair, use rosemary; for fair or red hair, use chamomile; for dandruff, use lavender, bergamot or sandalwood.

Regular rejuvenating hot-oil treatments are of great benefit to your scalp and hair.

How to perform it

YOU WILL NEED

An essential oil and base oil, as suggested previously; use a 3 per cent dilution: 3 drops of essential oil for each 5 ml (1 tsp) of base oil • A small cup or bowl • A larger bowl of hot water • Plastic wrap Hot towels • Shampoo and conditioner

---

WHAT TO DO

1 Takc 5–10 ml (1 2 tsp) of base oil, depending on your hair length and thickness. Heat the oil in a small cup or bowl immersed in a larger bowl of hot water or in a microwave. Mix in the essential oil thoroughly.

2 Apply the oil to your hair, making sure that you cover every strand. Give yourself a thorough scalp massage, using small, firm circular movements with your fingertips and covering all of the scalp Make sure you are really moving your scalp and not just skating lightly over the top.

3 Wrap your hair in plastic wrap, and then cover your head with a hot towel. Replace with another hot towel once the first one has cooled, and repeat for as long as you like. Leave the oil in for at least two hours.

4 Shampoo your hair at least twice to wash off the oil, applying neat shampoo for the first wash to ensure that you remove all traces of oil. Condition your hair as usual, but use less conditioner than normal. Your hair will feel soft and glossy, and your scalp relaxed and invigorated.

Facial steam for deep cleansing

Facial steaming with essential oils offers an extra dimension to the cleansing process. A facial steam increases perspiration, deeply cleanses the pores and encourages the elimination of deep-seated wastes and toxins. Steaming also softens and loosens the dead skin cells, making them easier to remove, and hydrates the skin.

Avoid steaming if there are thread veins or broken veins, because steam will aggravate these. If the skin is very sensitive, or if there is sunburn or other inflammation, steaming should also be avoided. All other skin types will benefit from a weekly facial steam with essential oils – especially oily skin.

Special facial saunas are available, some of which are designed for home use. However, you can achieve almost as good an effect using a bowl of boiling water and a towel to cover your head.

A facial steam is a good way to thoroughly cleanse your skin.

How to perform it

YOU WILL NEED

A facial sauna or bowl of boiling water • A large towel • An essential oil appropriate to your skin type (see pages 56–63) • Flower water appropriate to your skin type (see pages 56–63) • A light moisturizer

WHAT TO DO

1 Prepare your facial sauna or bowl of boiling water, making sure that you have a large towel nearby.

2 Add 5–10 drops of essential oil, according to the strength of aroma desired.

3 Either place your face in the facial sauna according to the manufacturer's instructions or hold your face a little way above the bowl of boiling water and essential oil, and place the towel over your head.

4 Keep your eyes closed, but be careful not to get your face too close to the hot water. If the initial vapour of the essential oil is very strong, lift your head away for a few moments, until the vapour is less powerful.

5 After steaming for five minutes, wipe your face and allow it to cool. Then spray it with flower water, allowing it to dry naturally. This further cools the face and closes the pores.

6 Finally, apply a light moisturizer.

Daily skin-care regime

Caring for your skin is vital to keep it healthy and looking good. This is especially important for the face. A basic three-step, twice-daily skin-care regime using aromatherapy products is described below. Recipes for cleansers, toners and moisturizers with essential oils are given later (see pages 78–89).

Three steps to healthy skin

• Cleansing is fundamental to good skin care. This is especially important if you live in a city, where airborne toxins readily adhere to your face, causing damage and premature ageing. Cleansing should be done twice: once to remove surface grime and make-up, and once to cleanse the pores thoroughly. Facial skin is delicate, so soap is too harsh and drying to use on your face. Face cleansers, based on a cream or a lotion, are the best way to cleanse your face thoroughly but gently. Cream cleansers are massaged into the face thoroughly, and then washed off with plain water.

The best cleansers to use on your face are made from a base cream or lotion.

• Skin toners are used after cleansing, to refresh the skin

Flower waters offer a natural gentle way to tone and refresh your skin after cleansing.

and tighten the pores. They also remove any traces of cleanser. However, many store-bought toners contain harsh ingredients that dry out the skin, leaving your face feeling uncomfortably tight. Using flower waters on a cotton wool pad as toners – with and without the addition of essential oils – is a natural and gentle way to hydrate and refresh your skin. Spray pure flower water on your face afterwards and allow it to dry naturally.

• Moisturizer is then applied to the cleansed, toned skin. In many ways moisturizers are the most important product in the whole skin-care range. They nourish, hydrate and protect the skin, preventing dehydration and dryness, and keep the skin supple, glowing and healthy. You need to have two moisturizers: a lighter, easily absorbed one to use in the morning, and a richer, nourishing night cream. The area around the eyes is particularly delicate, so you should only use the lighter moisturizer here.

Before-and-after sun-care regime

Currently there are so many warnings about exposure to the sun that knowing how to protect your skin from harmful rays is quite daunting. Despite this mood of alarm, many people still like to sunbathe in moderation, especially on holiday. If you take sensible precautions and avoid excessive exposure to the sun, then a little moderate sunbathing need not be absolutely forbidden.

Wearing a sun hat on holiday protects your skin from the drying effects of the sun.

Great care must be taken when exposing your skin to the sun. The increasing prevalence of skin cancer is a major health caution, but exposing your skin to the sun for long periods of time, or with great frequency, also speeds up the ageing process. People who have sunbathed excessively develop a leathery skin texture, their suntan fades into a sallow yellow colour, and the general appearance of their skin is unattractive.

How to sunbathe safely

• Before sunbathing: to enjoy moderate exposure to the sun, first consider your complexion. If you have fair or red hair you will probably have fair skin, and this can tolerate less sun than a darker complexion. Adjust the time spent in the sun accordingly. A week before starting to sunbathe, you need to start conditioning your skin. Do a couple of exfoliating body scrubs during the week to remove all dead skin cells. Apply a moisturizing body lotion daily with a 2 per cent dilution of essential oils that will nourish and protect the skin. Choose from patchouli, palmarosa, neroli, lavender and frankincense.

• During sunbathing: choose an appropriate-strength sunscreen lotion for your complexion, taking into consideration the strength of the sun in the area of the world where you will be. Avoid sunbathing between noon and 3 pm when the sun is hottest. Drink lots of water, wear a sunhat and above all do not spend too long in the sun, especially at the beginning.

• After sunbathing: cool the skin with a long, cold shower. Liberally apply a rich moisturizing body lotion with 1 per cent dilution of cooling, regenerating essential oils, such as roman chamomile, german chamomile, jasmine, lavender, neroli, carrot seed, rosewood and rose absolute.

Using a rich moisturizing lotion after sunbathing is essential to keep your skin healthy and looking good.

Skin brushing and body scrubs

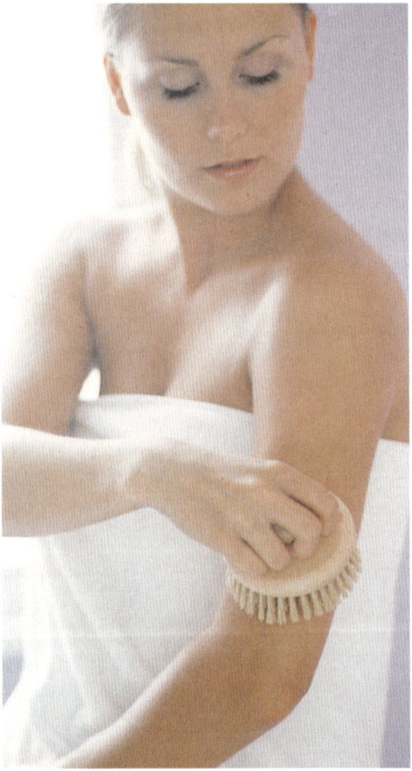

Skin brushing is a great way to stimulate your lymph system and to exfoliate your skin.

Skin brushing and body scrubs are two exfoliating treatments that are of prime importance in looking after your skin. Exfoliation removes dead skin cells and dirt from the body, and afterwards the skin looks and feels vibrant, glowing and healthy. The skin's absorbency is improved, so nourishing moisturizers containing essential oils and other nutrients will soak in easily.

Skin brushing is best done with a dry, natural bristle brush or an abrasive mitt. It is performed with short, brisk movements, always in the direction of the heart, so that the circulation of lymph is encouraged. Skin brushing is ideally done before an aromatherapy massage or the application of body lotion. As part of an aromatherapy lymphatic drainage course of treatments, the client is requested to skin brush every day.

Rejuvenating body scrub

This body scrub is derived from a traditional Indian treatment for brides-to-be. The bride is scrubbed all over with a mixture of finely ground grains, before being massaged with aromatic oils. Doing this body scrub will leave you with invigorated, glowing skin and can be done before an aromatherapy massage. It is best to perform it standing on an old towel as it is a messy procedure.

YOU WILL NEED

1 large handful of finely ground oatmeal • 1 large handful of ground almonds • A bowl • 1 tsp of dried, finely ground orange peel • 1 tsp of rosehip granules • 5 drops of jasmine or rose absolute essential oil • Warm water • A towel • A soft body brush or small towel

---

WHAT TO DO

1 Place the oatmeal and ground almonds in the bowl and mix in the orange peel and rosehip granules.

2 Add the jasmine or rose absolute, together with enough warm water to make a fine, crumbly mixture.

3 Standing on a towel, take a small handful of the body scrub and rub it vigorously with circular movements all over your body. The scrub dries quickly and most of it will fall straight off you.

4 When you have finished, use a soft body brush or small towel to brush off any leftover crumbs.

Making aromatherapy creams and lotions

Making up your own face-cleansing creams, moisturizers, toners and lotions is a rewarding and creative part of cosmetic aromatherapy. The recipes on the next few pages provide a range of cleansers, toners and moisturizers. Included are suggestions for incorporating different essential oils into basic cleansers, toners and moisturizers, so with great simplicity you can personalize all your face-care products to suit your skin type.

Cleanser for normal and oily skin

This cleanser uses a lighter cleansing-lotion base, with no perfume, colour or other additives, and is suitable for normal and oily skins.

YOU WILL NEED

150 ml (5 fl oz) of cleansing lotion • A large glass jar • A chopstick • 10 ml (2 tsp) of orange-flower water • 5 drops each of palmarosa, geranium and lavender • 2 drops each of juniper berry, ylang ylang and grapefruit

---

WHAT TO DO

1 Measure the cleansing-lotion base into the glass jar. Using the chopstick, stir in the orange-flower water.

2 Add the palmarosa, geranium and lavender, then the juniper berry, ylang ylang and grapefruit, and stir well to incorporate them thoroughly into the cleanser.

Cleanser for dry, sensitive and mature skin

This recipe is based on the original Galen's Cold Cream, which is thousands of years old. This rich cream sets firm, but liquefies on contact with the natural warmth of the skin. Galen's Cold Cream is a good cleansing cream for mature, sensitive and dry skins, with the benefit of containing rose essential oil.

YOU WILL NEED

6 g ($^1/_7$ oz) of beeswax or beeswax pellets • 2 heat-resistant glass bowls • A pan of hot water • 120 ml (4 fl oz) of sweet almond oil • 60 ml ($2^1/_4$ fl oz) of rose water • A hand whisk or electric beater with a low setting • 10 drops of rose absolute • A large glass jar

---

WHAT TO DO

1 Melt the beeswax or beeswax pellets in one of the glass bowls, placed inside a pan of hot water over a gentle heat. Stir in the sweet almond oil and warm thoroughly.

2 Heat the rose water in the other bowl, until the contents of both bowls are thoroughly warmed.

3 Now add the rose water, drop by drop, into the oils, beating steadily all the time – just like making mayonnaise.

4 Once all the flower water has been beaten into the oils, remove the pan from the heat, stirring until the mixture has cooled. Then add the rose absolute, mixing it in thoroughly, and pour into the glass jar.

Rich moisturizer for dry, sensitive and mature skin

Here is a recipe for a rich face cream. It is particularly suitable if the face has been exposed to the drying effects of cold, wind, rain, sun or central heating, and the skin has become very dry and perhaps a little red or flaky. The recipe contains both essential and base oils that have a deeply moisturizing effect on the skin.

YOU WILL NEED

4 g (1/9 oz) of beeswax • 2 heat-resistant glass bowls • A pan of hot water • 20 g (3/4 oz) cocoa butter • 15 ml (3 tsp) each of sweet almond and jojoba oils • 10 ml (2 tsp) of rosehip-seed oil • A hand whisk or electric beater with a low setting • 10 ml (2 tsp) of rose water • 5 ml (1 tsp) of glycerine • 8 drops each of rose otto and frankincense • 4 drops each of geranium and carrot seed • A large glass jar

WHAT TO DO

1 Melt the beeswax in one of the glass bowls, placed inside a pan of hot water over a gentle heat. Add the cocoa butter, the sweet almond and jojoba oils, and the rosehip-seed oil, beating the mixture steadily.

2 In the other bowl heat the rose water and glycerine until the contents of both bowls are the same temperature and thoroughly warmed through.

3 Now add the rose-water mixture, drop by drop, into the oils, beating steadily all the time – like making mayonnaise.

4 Remove the pan from the heat and stir until the mixture cools. Mix in thoroughly the rose otto and frankincense, the geranium and carrot seed. Pour into the glass jar.

Rich moisturizer for normal skin

The following recipe uses a moisturizing base cream, which has no fragrance, colour or other additives. One advantage of using a base cream is that home-made moisturizers do not always homogenize completely and the cream may separate a little, although you can still use it. This moisturizer is suitable for normal skins.

YOU WILL NEED

150 ml (5 fl oz) of moisturizing base cream • A large glass jar • A chopstick • 5 ml (1 tsp) each of rose water and avocado oil • 4 drops each of german chamomile, rose absolute, neroli and lavender • 3 drops each of palmarosa and rosewood

WHAT TO DO

1 Measure the moisturizing base cream into the glass jar. Using the chopstick, stir in the rose water and avocado oil.

2 Add the german chamomile, rose absolute, neroli and lavender, and then the palmarosa and rosewood. Stir well to incorporate them thoroughly into the moisturizer.

Light moisturizer for all skin types

This recipe combines the skin regenerative qualities of rosehip-seed oil with the natural moisturizing qualities of sweet almond oil, to make a light but nourishing moisturizer suitable for all skin types. This is an ideal daily moisturizer for use in the morning.

YOU WILL NEED

5 g ($^1/_8$ oz) of beeswax • 2 heat-resistant glass bowls • A pan of hot water • 15 ml (3 tsp) each of sweet almond and rosehip-seed oils • A hand whisk or electric beater with a low setting • 2 vitamin E capsules • A pin • 12 ml ($2^1/_2$ tsp) of rose water • 3 ml ($^1/_2$ tsp) of honey • 4 drops each of neroli, sandalwood and palmarosa • 2 drops of jasmine • A large glass jar

---

WHAT TO DO

1 Melt the beeswax in one of the glass bowls, placed inside a pan of hot water over a gentle heat. Add the sweet almond and rosehip-seed oils, beating the mixture steadily to ensure they are incorporated thoroughly. Prick open the vitamin E capsules with the pin and squeeze them into the mixture.

2 In the other bowl heat the rose water and honey until the contents of both bowls are the same temperature and thoroughly warmed through.

3 Now add the rose-water mixture, drop by drop, into the oils, beating steadily all the time – like making mayonnaise.

4 Remove the pan from the heat and stir until the mixture cools. Mix in thoroughly the neroli, sandalwood and palmarosa, and the jasmine. Pour into the glass jar.

Light moisturizer for oily skin

This moisturizer for oily skin uses antiseptic essential oils that help balance and reduce sebum levels.

YOU WILL NEED

150 ml (5 fl oz) of base moisturizer • A large glass jar • A chopstick • 5 ml (1 tsp) each of orange-flower water and witch hazel • 6 drops each of cypress, geranium and lavender • 2 drops each of grapefruit and ti-tree

WHAT TO DO

1 Measure the base moisturizer into the glass jar. Using the chopstick, stir in the orange-flower water and witch hazel.

2 Add the cypress, geranium and lavender, and the grapefruit and ti-tree. Stir well to incorporate them thoroughly into the moisturizer. An alternative blend of masculine-smelling essential oils to suit an adolescent boy or a man with oily skin or acne, is as follows: 5 drops each of cedarwood, cypress and juniper and 2 drops each of ti-tree, myrtle and lavender.

Simple hand cream

Aromatherapy hand creams moisturize dry skin and help to heal any minor abrasions. This recipe is simple to make because there is no flower water to incorporate. The lemon essential oil gently helps to fade any discoloured skin on the hands, and the benzoin helps to heal paper cuts and so on. This hand cream sets easily because natural, unfractionated (or unrefined) coconut oil is solid at room temperature, but the cream easily liquefies on contact with warm skin. Such hand creams are deeply moisturizing and take a little longer than commercial hand creams to be fully absorbed.

YOU WILL NEED

75 g (3 oz) of unfractionated coconut oil • A heat-resistant glass bowl • A pan of hot water • 25 ml (1 fl oz) of sweet almond oil • 8 drops each of lavender and lemon • 4 drops of benzoin • A large glass jar

---

WHAT TO DO

1 Put the coconut oil in the glass bowl, placed inside a pan of hot water over a gentle heat. Once the coconut oil has melted, add the sweet almond oil and stir until the mixture is thoroughly blended.

2 Remove the pan from the heat and stir in the lavender and lemon, and the benzoin. Mix them in thoroughly, then pour into the glass jar while still warm and liquid.

Hand cream for rough hands

The following hand cream is excellent for those who work outdoors with their hands, such as gardeners, builders and so on. The skin on the hands can easily become hard, dry and chapped or cracked if it is not properly cared for. Calendula is an infused oil with legendary healing properties, while myrrh helps to heal cracked skin.

YOU WILL NEED

5 g ($^1/_8$ oz) of beeswax • A heat-resistant glass bowl • A pan of hot water • 25 g (1 oz) of cocoa butter • 20 ml (4 tsp) of sweet almond oil • 3 ml ($^1/_2$ tsp) each of glycerine and calendula oil • 5 drops each of myrrh and geranium • 3 drops of mandarin • A large glass jar

---

WHAT TO DO

1 Melt the beeswax in the glass bowl, placed in a pan of hot water over a gentle heat. Once the beeswax has melted, add the cocoa butter, sweet almond oil, glycerine and calendula oil, stirring steadily to ensure that all ingredients are incorporated thoroughly.

2 Remove the pan from the heat, stirring until the mixture has cooled. Then add the myrrh, geranium and mandarin, mixing them in thoroughly. Pour into the glass jar.

Skin toner for youthful and oily skin

Making your own aromatherapy skin toners is simple and you only use natural ingredients that are kind to your skin. If you have sensitive skin, use pure flower waters only: once on a cotton wool pad to remove traces of cleanser and then sprayed onto the face to hydrate and freshen the skin. For other skin types, use a toner followed by a suitable flower-water spray. This toner is based on orange-flower water and is slightly astringent, making it ideal for youthful and oily skins, though it is also gentle enough for normal skin. The addition of orange, neroli (orange-flower blossom) and petitgrain (from the wood of the orange tree) utilizes the synergy of the whole tree.

YOU WILL NEED

10 ml (2 tsp) of high-proof vodka • A clean, dry glass bottle large enough to hold at least 300 ml ($^1/_2$ pt) • 3 drops each of neroli, orange and petitgrain • 25 ml (1 fl oz) of witch hazel • 250 ml (8 fl oz) of orange-flower water

---

WHAT TO DO

1 Pour the vodka into the glass bottle. Add the neroli, orange and petitgrain and shake hard to dissolve the oils.

2 Add the witch hazel and shake then add the orange-flower water. Shake the bottle until all the ingredients have blended together well. The essential oils will not completely dissolve, so shake the bottle vigorously each time you use the toner.

Skin toner for dry, sensitive and mature skin

The following toner uses the hydrating, stimulating and anti-inflammatory properties of rose in synergy with rose water. It is especially suited to dry, sensitive and mature skins.

YOU WILL NEED

5 ml (1 tsp) of high-proof vodka • A clean, dry glass bottle large enough to hold at least 300 ml (1/2 pt) • 4 drops each of rose absolute and rose otto • 10 ml (2 tsp) of witch hazel • 270 ml (9 fl oz) of rose-flower water

---

WHAT TO DO

1 Pour the vodka into the glass bottle. Add the rose absolute and rose otto to the vodka and shake hard to dissolve the oils.

2 Add the witch hazel and shake, followed by the rose-flower water. Shake the bottle until all the ingredients have blended together well. The essential oils will not completely dissolve, so shake the bottle vigorously each time you use the toner.

All-purpose body lotion

Body lotions are moisturizers for the body. They are thinner than face creams, so they spread easily over the body and are quickly absorbed by the skin. Body lotions are valuable in the summer when the sun has dried the skin, especially after sunbathing, although the body benefits from moisturizing all year round. This light lotion is suited to all skin types. The recipe uses a base skin lotion, with no colour, fragrance or other additives. Oat-plant milk is a natural moisturizer that is easily absorbed by the skin.

YOU WILL NEED
100 ml (3½ fl oz) of base lotion • A 200 ml (7 fl oz) glass bottle • 50 ml (2 fl oz) of oat-plant milk • 10 ml (2 tsp) of orange-flower water 5 drops each of jasmine, neroli, petitgrain and orange • 3 drops each of bergamot, geranium and rosewood

---

WHAT TO DO

1 Pour the base lotion into the glass bottle. Add the oat-plant milk and the orange-flower water. Shake vigorously.

2 Add the jasmine, neroli, petitgrain and orange, and the bergamot, geranium and rosewood. Shake vigorously again.

Refreshing foot lotion

This stimulating foot lotion revives tired feet and improves their appearance. Apply it after soaking your feet in hot water for ten minutes, then scrubbing off any dead skin with a handful of coarse sea salt.

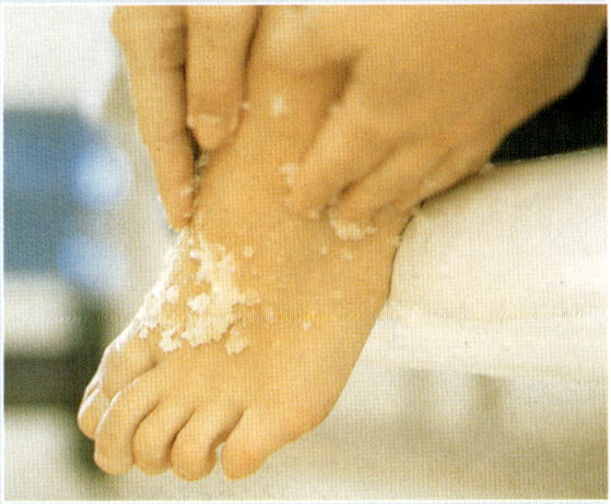

YOU WILL NEED

70 ml ($2\frac{1}{2}$ fl oz) of base lotion • A 100 ml ($3\frac{1}{2}$ fl oz) glass bottle • 5 ml (1 tsp) each of witch hazel and orange-flower water • 5 drops each of peppermint and cypress • 2 drops each of lemon, clary sage and juniper

---

WHAT TO DO

1 Pour the base lotion into the glass bottle. Add the witch hazel and orange-flower water and shake vigorously.

2 Add the peppermint and cypress, the lemon, clary sage and juniper and shake vigorously again.

Aromatherapy for moods and emotions

How essential oils affect your feelings

Essential oils are living and dynamic rather than inert substances because they contain the active life force of the plant from which they come. Experiments with Kirlian photography have revealed this active principle as an aura of light around the plant – similar to our own auras (the aura being the subtle energy field around the physical body, also known as the etheric body). Plants and humans are all children of Nature, sustained by the same life force. The fine, delicate complexity of essential oils cannot be duplicated synthetically with inorganic chemicals. This is why essential oils affect our moods and emotions and synthetic perfumes do not.

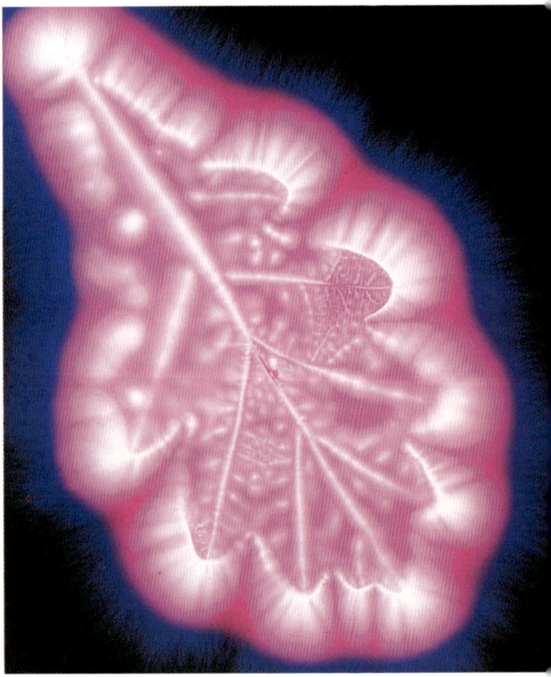

Our ancestors had an acute sense of smell, much like that of dogs. They could smell danger, dinner and a mate because their lives depended on it, and what they smelled caused commensurate feelings of fear, hunger and sexual attraction. Modern humans have lost some olfactory awareness through the evolution of civilization, but we still have a reasonable sense of smell that can be developed through training.

Soothing the mind and balancing the body

Essential oils affect your feelings because they have a dual action. When you smell an essential oil that you find pleasant, this is attractive to and soothes the mind. At the same time as you smell the oil through inhalation, there is a physiological action on your body, independent of the sense of smell. This demonstrates the importance of using essential oils that you find pleasing; if you dislike an oil's aroma, despite its potentially beneficial physical action on your body, the overall effect will be lessened.

The action of essential oils on the mind and feelings is complex and subtle. The oils tend to balance and normalize the body, rather than just stimulate or sedate it, and there is a similar action on the feelings. Essential oils have a complementary affinity with certain parts of the body, mind and emotions.

For example, a person with a 'hard heart', who tends to be harsh and mean, often develops heart problems such as hardening of the arteries. Treating this person with rose has a tonic action on the physical heart, while simultaneously softening the emotions and uplifting the mind.

This Kirlian photograph shows the energy field surrounding a leaf.

Making mood perfumes

A fascinating aspect of working with essential oils is the way their perfume can affect your moods. Each essential oil has an individual character that contributes to the overall fragrance of an aromatherapy mood perfume. Deciding to create a special perfume to help stimulate a particular mood is like opening a box of fragrant spells.

Perfume and scent have always exerted an extraordinary power over the senses and emotions. This subtle side of essential oils – what we can call their

How to make a mood perfume

YOU WILL NEED

A 10 ml (2 tsp) dark glass bottle (a rollette bottle with a roller-ball insert is best) • 10 ml (2 tsp) of sweet almond or jojoba oil • Essential oils of your choice (up to 50 drops)

WHAT TO DO

1 To make up any of the classic mood perfumes on the following pages, take the dark glass bottle and pour in half of the sweet almond or jojoba oil.

2 Add your choice of essential oils and shake well. Then pour in the remaining base oil, shake again, and leave to mature for a few days. In the unlikely event that you develop a rash from using the perfume, dilute it with more base oil.

The fragrance of essential oils has a powerful influence on our moods and emotions, lifting our spirits and inspiring joy.

'psyche' – is mysterious, sacred and magical. The power of scents to move us is reflected in religious ceremonies and rituals, where they are offered to the gods and believed to have their origins in the divine.

We are captivated by scents: they move us emotionally and arouse deep feelings. Perfumes awaken sensual instincts, bring back nostalgic reminiscences and allow the imagination and fantasy to run riot. Poetry and the other arts have always celebrated this evocative power of perfume to move our emotions and bring us into the realm of the senses.

Any application of essential oils affects your moods, because you smell their scent during an aromatherapy treatment. However, when you choose to use essential oils specifically to affect your feelings, their transformative, sensuous power is most evident. Making mood perfumes is one of the most creative ways to unlock the magic potential of essential oils. Try to use some mindful, intuitive ritual techniques when creating mood perfumes to make the experience magical.

Romantic scents

Romance is a special intimate mood which many people would like more of in their lives. Being romantic is different from feeling sexy and erotic and need not be passionate. There is a gentle, wistful quality to romance, which evokes an escapist, fantasy, dreamlike feeling. Women especially watch romantic films and read romantic novels to recreate that special, elusive mood.

We often want our partner to be more romantic, because romantic behaviour tells us that we are loved and cared for. St. Valentine's Day encapsulates the essence of romance, with its traditional gifts of red roses, boxes of chocolates and candle-lit dinners. However, using romantic mood scents can bring a little more romance into your everyday life.

Exotic fantasy

- 15 drops of rose otto
- 15 drops of neroli
- 5 drops of lemon
- 5 drops of verbena
- 3 drops of benzoin
- 3 drops of marjoram
- 2 drops of clove
- 2 drops of mimosa

Deep and mysterious

- 10 drops of rose absolute
- 10 drops of palmarosa
- 10 drops of ylang ylang
- 5 drops of vetiver
- 5 drops of clary sage
- 4 drops of nutmeg
- 3 drops of basil
- 3 drops of violet leaf

Rose is the classic romantic essential oil: both rose absolute and rose otto of any of the different varieties. Marjoram and benzoin are calming when you feel like a romantic cuddle rather than sex. Ylang ylang and rosewood are exotic and sweetly romantic, while clary sage is euphoric and romantic.

Erotic and aphrodisiac perfumes have been used throughout the ages for seduction and to stimulate romantic feelings.

Romantic rose

- 15 drops of rose otto
- 15 drops of rose absolute
- 10 drops of geranium
- 3 drops of bergamot
- 2 drops of patchouli
- 3 drops of rosewood
- 2 drops of ambrette seed

Uplifting scents

Uplifting scents contain some of the most useful essential oils because they help alleviate common psychological symptoms including depression, anxiety, melancholy and apathy. Some of these moods are not entirely psychological and may have physical causes, which you should not attempt to treat. For clinical depression, always seek professional medical advice. Nonetheless, these uplifting mood scents may be of benefit to anyone who is feeling generally low.

Because there are many uplifting essential oils, check carefully how you are feeling before making up a blend. Once you have found a few key words that describe how you feel, read carefully in the directory of essential oils (see pages 268–385) the descriptions of the various

The fragrance of grapefruit is cheering, refreshing and uplifting, and this is a good essential oil to use in an uplifting scent.

Spring blossom

10 drops of rose otto
10 drops of geranium
10 drops of neroli
4 drops of mimosa
3 drops of orange
4 drops of roman chamomile
3 drops of bergamot
3 drops of holy basil
3 drops of sandalwood

essential oils suggested as uplifting, and choose accordingly.

Bergamot, melissa, geranium, rose absolute and rose otto are classic essential oils for creating uplifting mood scents. Basil, holy basil and sandalwood are also good choices. If there is anxiety involved, include neroli, roman chamomile or frankincense; if apathy is a concern, then jasmine, rosemary and patchouli are useful. Orange and mandarin are cheery, smiley oils that enhance uplifting blends.

Summer breezes

10 drops of bergamot
10 drops of melissa
10 drops of neroli
5 drops of lavender
5 drops of petitgrain
7 drops of frankincense
3 drops of juniper

Elixir of life

15 drops of melissa
12 drops of rose absolute
7 drops of cypress
5 drops of rosewood
5 drops of patchouli
3 drops of roman chamomile
3 drops of verbena

Stimulating scents

Stimulating essential oils are enlivening for both body and mind, and almost everyone feels they need a little extra stimulus to get going once in a while. Like all stimulants, these essential oils should not be abused or used too regularly or in large quantities. However, on the odd occasion when you haven't had enough sleep or are feeling especially lethargic, wearing a stimulating mood scent can help you get through the day.

There are also occasions, such as taking an exam, when you want to feel at the peak of your mental powers, and a stimulating mood

Get up and go

- 10 drops of bergamot
- 10 drops of coriander
- 7 drops of jasmine
- 7 drops of petitgrain
- 6 drops of neroli
- 5 drops of black pepper
- 5 drops of lemon-scented eucalyptus

Wearing a stimulating scent and sniffing it frequently can help you stay alert throughout the day.

Spicy sparkler

- 10 drops of grapefruit
- 10 drops of ginger
- 10 drops of ylang ylang
- 10 drops of melissa
- 5 drops of patchouli
- 3 drops of cardamom
- 2 drops of holy basil

Ready to rock

- 10 drops of rosemary
- 10 drops of lemon
- 10 drops of geranium
- 10 drops of juniper
- 5 drops of clove
- 5 drops of basil

scent can assist you. Some of the stimulating essential oils are cephalic, meaning that they actually boost mental activity. These oils are helpful for poor memory and lack of concentration.

The best cephalic essential oil is rosemary, although peppermint, basil and cardamom are all good. Generally stimulating oils include eucalyptus, *Eucalyptus citriodora* – a lovely clean lemon-scented variety – and all of the spice oils. The mood scents above use stimulating oils in aesthetic blends together with other essential oils.

Calming scents

Stress and tension are major problems in today's society and using calming essential oils to relieve their symptoms is one of the major functions of aromatherapy. However, it is not always possible to go for an aromatherapy massage or take a bath with essential oils when you feel stressed out, but calming mood scents can easily be carried in a handbag or pocket and applied when needed.

Stress and tension can easily lead to frustration and even anger if you don't deal with them as and when they arise. All negative emotions are unhealthy and should be calmed as soon as possible. The timely application of a soothing mood scent, and remembering to sniff it frequently in the first few minutes, can release aggravation before it escalates.

One of the most soothing essential oils is frankincense, which actively slows down the breathing process and enables you to take long, deep breaths to calm you down. Lavender is another classic calming favourite, as well as roman chamomile, neroli, marjoram, ylang ylang, clary sage, sandalwood, rose otto, rose absolute, angelica and melissa.

Whenever you feel stressed out, a calming aromatherapy mood scent can help you relax and feel less tense.

Calm tranquillity

- 10 drops of frankincense
- 10 drops of neroli
- 10 drops of sandalwood
- 5 drops of rose otto
- 5 drops of bergamot
- 4 drops of clary sage
- 4 drops of angelica
- 2 drops of jonquil

Provence floral

- 15 drops of lavender
- 15 drops of roman chamomile
- 10 drops of neroli
- 6 drops of ylang ylang
- 2 drops of narcissus
- 2 drops of tuberose

Sweet and gentle

- 12 drops of roman chamomile
- 12 drops of frankincense
- 12 drops of lavender
- 4 drops of marjoram
- 4 drops of melissa
- 4 drops of linden blossom
- 2 drops of vetiver

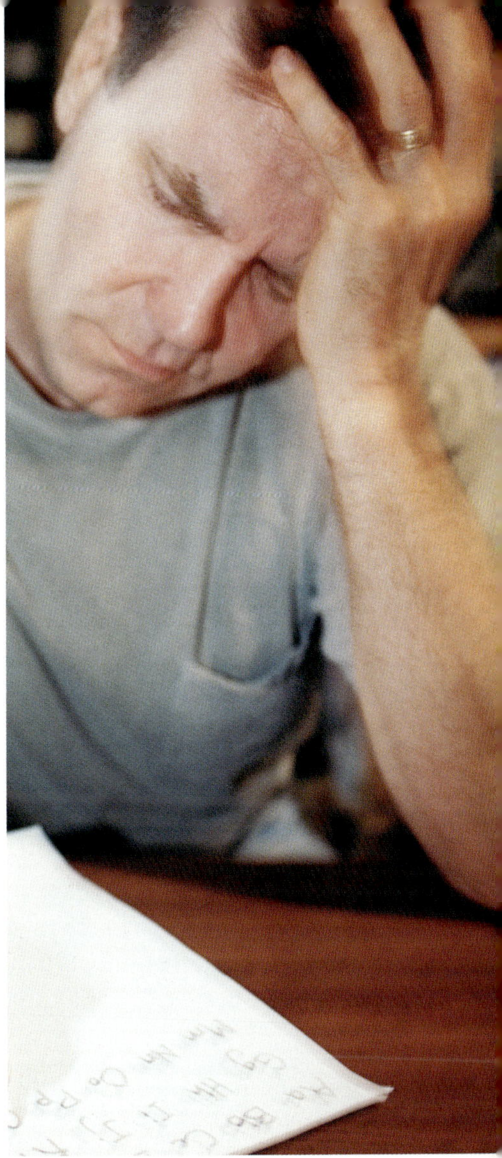

Confident scents

Lack of confidence can be extremely debilitating and can manifest either as feelings of inadequacy on a personal level, such as lack of self-worth, or as a lack of trust in your own ability to accomplish the important tasks at hand. It can also manifest as shyness, not wanting to put yourself in the spotlight and therefore perhaps missing out on life's opportunities.

Confident mood scents can be an effective (although subtle) way to overcome the feelings of lack of confidence. A good way forward is to identify the feelings precisely and try to understand the causes and conditions that bring out your lack of confidence. Once you have a good idea of when and why these feelings sometimes arise, you can be prepared for them and can apply a confident mood scent shortly beforehand.

The shy person's best friend is jasmine. This rich, exotic essential oil is a powerful, relaxing anti-depressant that inspires confidence. If anxiety is present, then neroli, benzoin and marjoram are good choices. Ylang ylang, rose otto, rose absolute, clary sage, bergamot, frankincense, lavender, violet leaf, basil, coriander and ginger can all help boost confidence.

Wearing a scent that inspires confidence can help overcome the nerves often felt before a big event, such as giving a public talk.

Fragrant courage

10 drops of lavender
10 drops of basil
8 drops of rose otto
8 drops of neroli
7 drops of bergamot
5 drops of ylang ylang
2 drops of narcissus

Indian promise

- 10 drops of jasmine
- 10 drops of neroli
- 10 drops of sandalwood
- 8 drops of ginger
- 7 drops of bergamot
- 5 drops of benzoin

Scented salvation

- 10 drops of frankincense
- 10 drops of lavender
- 10 drops of marjoram
- 10 drops of grapefruit
- 6 drops of jasmine
- 4 drops of violet leaf

Sensuous scents

Creating a mood of sensuous indulgence using essential oils is definitely one of the luxuries and pleasures of aromatherapy. The word 'sensuous' means literally 'pertaining or appealing to the senses', and this is an area where aromatherapy becomes more of a treat than a treatment.

A sensuous mood scent can either be created for yourself alone – to enjoy a relaxed evening of good food, wine, music and other sensuous arts – or it can be a prelude to passion and sexual activity. A good sensuous mood scent strikes a balance between relaxation and stimulation, so that you are neither hyped up and tense nor so relaxed that you want to fall asleep. If more than one person is involved, you should both like the perfume – otherwise the sensuous mood scent could turn into a passion-killer!

There are many sensuous essential oils, but some of the finest are rose absolute, sandalwood, jasmine, ylang ylang, patchouli and clary sage. Cardamom, black pepper, neroli, ginger, rose otto, rosewood and juniper are all sensuous and aphrodisiac, too. Creating your own sensuous mood scents also depends on what you like and including at least one of your favourite oils is a good idea.

Amorous dreams

- 10 drops of rose otto
- 8 drops of patchouli
- 8 drops of jasmine
- 6 drops of lime
- 6 drops of sandalwood
- 3 drops of juniper
- 2 drops of tuberose
- 3 drops of clary sage
- 2 drops of cardamom
- 2 drops of champaka

Sensuous scents are one of life's luxuries and are nice to use in playful, sensuous massage with your partner.

Passionate embrace

- 15 drops of rose absolute
- 15 drops of neroli
- 10 drops of lemon
- 6 drops of rosewood
- 5 drops of ylang ylang
- 3 drops of black pepper
- 2 drops of linden blossom
- 2 drops of jonquil
- 2 drops of oak moss

Magic moments

- 12 drops of rose otto
- 12 drops of rosewood
- 8 drops of sandalwood
- 8 drops of rose absolute
- 5 drops of mandarin
- 3 drops of ambrette seed
- 2 drops of cardamom

Techniques to relieve fear

Fear ranges from mild consternation, through dread and alarm, right up to sheer terror and panic. The physical symptoms include a racing heart; short, quick, shallow breaths and sometimes a feeling of paralysis, of being rooted to the spot; and faintness or dizziness. The syndrome known as 'fight or flight' may occur, when you either become aggressive or feel like running away.

All these physical manifestations of fear develop quickly, and are unpleasant and debilitating. They need to be dealt with swiftly.

Neroli, frankincense and lavender are amongst the best essential oils to use in a scent to allay fear.

Useful remedies

• As an emergency measure, sniff essential oils straight from the bottle. If there is time and availability, sprinkle a few drops on a tissue and sniff that. Try to sit down as soon as possible.

• The best essential oils to treat fear are neroli and frankincense. Neroli is one of the most calming oils and frankincense helps balance and deepen the breathing. Lavender is calming too and gentle enough to use neat on the skin on occasions like this. Apply a couple of drops to each temple, and gently and slowly rub in a circular motion. Repeat this procedure on the inside of the wrists.

• If fear is a recurring problem, with a known cause – for example, a fear of public speaking – book a course of aromatherapy massages. The aromatherapist will probably focus on the chest area, neck and shoulders, to reduce tension caused by fear. She or he may also focus on the abdomen to encourage deep breathing and to bring your attention to your centre. You can massage these areas yourself too.

• Choose a blend that includes some of the following oils: lavender, rose absolute, melissa, benzoin, ylang ylang, jasmine and clary sage. In addition to massage, use some of the above oils in the bath, both before and after the fear-provoking event. If it is possible, diffuse essential oils in the room or alternatively sniff a tissue sprinkled with appropriate oils.

Techniques to relieve worry

There is an old saying that there is no point in worrying, because if you can do something about the issue, then do it instead of worrying about it; and if you can't do anything about the issue, then there is no point in worrying. But despite these words of wisdom, worrying about different things remains a preoccupation for many.

Worry is characterized by endlessly turning over some issue in your mind, constantly thinking about it and an inability to let it go. Worrying is

Useful remedies

• Bright, sharp cephalic oils can help you cut through the worry to reconnect with the central concern, so that you are able to see things clearly and deal with them. Rosemary, basil, peppermint, pine, lemongrass and juniper can all be sniffed on a tissue or, for a longer-lasting, more pervasive effect, diffused into your room.

• Some of the calming essential oils are useful in counteracting worry. Frankincense has a reputation for breaking links with the past and letting go of persistent unwanted thoughts. In ancient times, frankincense was used literally to drive out evil spirits, and we can see worry as an evil spirit in this context. Roman chamomile and german chamomile are helpful, as are marjoram, neroli, verbena and melissa. Bathing with a selection of these essential oils can be an effective method of banishing your worries.

counter-productive because often you become so close to the issue that you can no longer 'see the wood for the trees'. In other words, you lose the ability to make logical judgements on the best way to deal with the troublesome issue or problem.

Although worry manifests originally in the mental sphere, over a long time it can lead to loss of appetite and loss of interest in anything other than the subject being worried about. This apathy can lead to depression if you are not careful, so dealing with worry before physical symptoms appear is a sensible thing to do. Essential oils can help in several ways.

The draining effects of persistent worrying can be counteracted by using a mood scent that includes appropriate essential oils.

Techniques to relieve impatience

Impatience and irritability are closely linked and influence each other, so dealing with both of these negative mental states simultaneously is a good idea. They stem from frustrated desire, from not getting your own way or not getting what you want quickly enough. In our contemporary, fast-moving, 'instant-fix' society these negative emotions are more prevalent than ever. Living in such a constant state of tension is unhealthy and can lead to heart and blood-pressure problems.

Using essential oils in methods that encourage you to slow down, take your time and reflect on the absurdity of wanting everything your own way – and instantly – is an effective way to relieve impatience. Learning how to slow down in a society that encourages activity at top speed is not easy. However, you can carve some time out of your busy day to spend by yourself quietly, trying to transform your impatience into a calm acceptance of things as they are.

Useful remedies

• Regular aromatic baths are of great benefit in relieving impatience. Choose essential oils that are calming generally, and those that are soothing to the mental turmoil caused by impatience. Roman chamomile is one of the best essential oils for impatience. It gently but powerfully soothes the grumpiness born of impatience, as well as feelings of over-sensitivity, continual dissatisfaction and self-obsession.

• Frankincense is another useful oil, as it helps you slow down, breathe deeply and calm the mind and emotions. Marjoram and lavender are traditional classics to use for calming irritability and impatience. Cypress is a strengthening, calming oil, and a symbol of eternity and inner wisdom that helps you realize the foolishness of being impatient.

• Have a long, relaxing bath and make the occasion special, rather than functional. Light candles, play soft music and place flowers and crystals close by. Choose some essential oils from the suggestions given above, and include something sweet and gentle, like geranium with its balancing quality, and something light and cheery, like orange, bergamot or mandarin.

Taking regular aromatic baths with roman chamomile and frankincense has a deeply calming effect that helps relieve impatience.

Techniques to relieve grief

The devastating feelings of grief can be overwhelming, but you can use the powerful comforting effects of rose absolute to help.

Of all the negative emotions listed in this section, grief can be the most devastating, especially in cases of bereavement. When confronted with someone else's grief, it is difficult to know what to say or do, and the encounter can leave you feeling awkward and uncomfortable. With your own grief, there is often little consolation from anything anyone else can say or do.

There is much more to dealing with grief than simply recommending some essential oils. More than anything else, it is the silent, loving care and attention of an aromatherapist giving a full body massage that can be of great benefit to someone grieving.

Useful remedies

• The first choice of all remedies and techniques to deal with grief is to book an aromatherapy treatment. The therapist will select oils to treat you holistically, dealing with the whole person rather than just the symptoms of grief. He or she will probably include rose absolute or rose otto in the blend, because rose has a special affinity with grief. It gently opens the heart to release pent-up emotions, and comforts the sorrow and heartache. Rose allows for the possibility of new feelings of love and affection to eventually arise and helps you move on.

• As a supplement to aromatherapy massage, rose otto and rose absolute are gentle enough to wear as a perfume, and a drop or two rubbed on the inside of the wrists envelops you in their comforting fragrance. Any of the uplifting mood scents described earlier (see pages 98–99) can also be applied. Bathing with and diffusing essential oils is of benefit.

• Other essential oils for grief include benzoin and marjoram, which have a warming, comforting effect on the emotions. Melissa is an excellent tonic of the heart, both physically and emotionally, and in times of grief its uplifting, anti-depressant properties help release trauma and pain. Hyssop can help when grief leaves you wide open emotionally; it helps define boundaries with others and psychically cleanses the emotional detritus of grief.

Techniques to relieve depression

The term depression covers a wide range of emotions with differing psychological states, feelings and physical behaviour traits. One depressed person may be lethargic and apathetic, feel numb and fatigued all the time, and do very little, maybe sleeping a lot. Another may have a lot of nervous tension, have difficulty sleeping, feel anxious a lot of the time and have bursts of feverish activity. Obviously these two cases require different techniques and remedies with different essential oils.

Useful remedies

- When apathy and lethargy characterize depression, then enlivening, uplifting essential oils are called for. In this case, taking baths with suitable essential oils is a good idea, not least because it makes you do something positive for yourself, rather than relying on someone giving you a massage, which might increase your passivity. Self-massage, however, can be helpful – again because it makes you do something actively to help yourself.

- The most suitable essential oils for depression characterized by apathy and lethargy are both stimulating and anti-depressant. They include bergamot – perhaps the most sunny, elevating and cheering essential oil – geranium, rosemary, juniper and jasmine. Peppermint can clear the head and blow away emotional and mental cobwebs. Melissa can help you find a renewed interest in life.

Try using stimulating, anti-depressant essential oils to lift your spirits.

• When depression is characterized by anxiety and nervous tension, then calming, soporific essential oils are called for. Receiving a full body massage from an aromatherapist is probably the best remedy here, but diffusing suitable essential oils in your room and using them regularly in the bath are good supplements.

• The most suitable essential oils in this instance are both sedative and anti-depressant. They include roman and german chamomile, neroli, sandalwood, ylang ylang, frankincense and clary sage. Including no more than one drop of narcissus, jonquil, linden blossom or violet leaf in a blend adds a deeply calming and slightly hypnotic influence, which helps you ground yourself and find your centre.

Techniques to relieve anger

Anger is the most destructive of the negative emotions, and even a moment's anger can have a devastating effect on you and other people. Anger can be described as hot, red, overwhelming, sudden and violent; it is often characterized by being overwhelming and difficult to control. It affects mind, body, feelings and spirit, and operates interdependently among these. For example, anger can be provoked by a congested liver, and can in turn provoke high blood pressure. Lack of confidence, feeling hurt and insecure can cause anger to arise as a self-defence strategy.

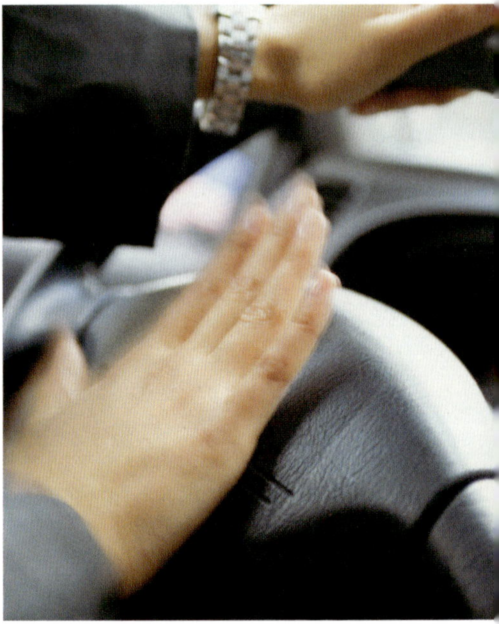

Sniffing german chamomile can help you to calm down – so keep some in your car.

Some schools of thought suggest that it is best to release anger (for instance, by shouting at other people), but this only aggravates the problem, usually inciting others to anger. It is much better to contain your anger, calm it down and – by being tolerant, compassionate and kind to yourself – transform the anger and restore harmony. Letting your anger go, rather than dumping it on someone else, is a skilful approach to dealing with it.

Useful remedies

• There are several effective essential oils to help you cope with anger. German chamomile (often called 'blue chamomile' because of its startlingly deep-blue colour) is especially calming. The cooling influence of the blue azulene (one of the components of german chamomile) calms the red heat of anger. The soothing sweetness of ylang ylang helps dispel the fury of anger, while rose absolute and rose otto open and soften the angry heart.

• Because anger is so quick to manifest, sniffing a suitable essential oil straight from the bottle is a useful technique for an immediate effect. A long, tepid bath that includes calming essential oils, with sufficient time to be alone, reflect and calm down, is ideal to counteract anger. If you know that a certain event is likely to trigger anger, apply a calming mood scent beforehand (see pages 102–103).

• The precursor to full-blown anger – irritability – can be soothed and calmed before it accelerates out of control. Take some time out and diffuse calming essential oils in your room. Irritability is particularly helped by lavender, marjoram, benzoin, cypress and sandalwood.

Techniques to relieve stress

A little stress and tension are useful to help you achieve your goals and can be inspirational for creative work. If you are too relaxed, it feels as if you are resting or on holiday, and this can make it difficult to accomplish your tasks. However, too much stress is a common complaint these days, and when stress and tension become overwhelming you need to have some techniques to help you relax.

Stress starts in the mind and the emotions, but swiftly moves into the physical body, causing tight muscles, shallow breathing, headaches, insomnia and loss of appetite. Once embedded in the body, the stress must be released physically as well as emotionally and mentally. Try to avoid too much alcohol and caffeine. Even though they seem to help in the short term, they stress the body further and are therefore counter-productive.

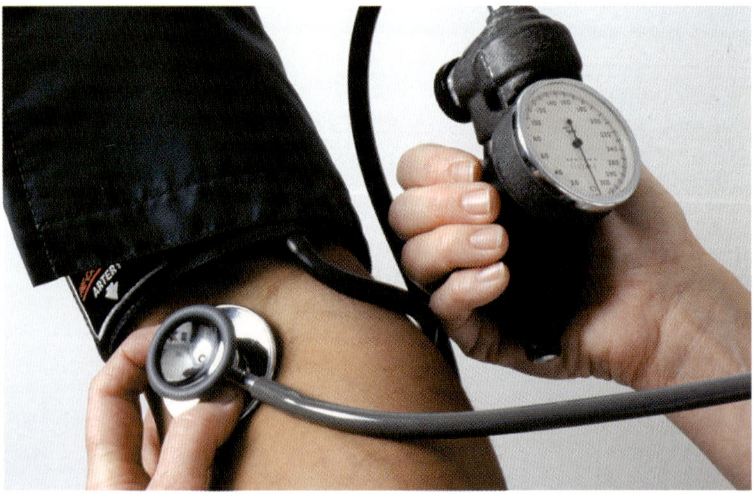

Useful remedies

• Massage is the best way to release physical tension. Try to visit an aromatherapist regularly if you find yourself feeling stressed out a lot of the time. A full body massage with appropriate essential oils releases physical stress, calms the mind and emotions, and in this way helps prevent stress arising again too quickly.

• Self-massage can also be very beneficial in releasing physical stress. Focus on the neck, shoulders and chest, and if stress gives you a headache, massage your scalp as well. Choose essential oils that are good for tense muscles, such as lavender, rosemary, marjoram and roman chamomile. Include emotionally calming oils that are also sedative to help calm the mind, such as bergamot, neroli, rose otto, benzoin, clary sage, jasmine, melissa and sandalwood.

• Bathing with calming essential oils also releases stress from mind, emotions and body. Include frankincense to help deepen your breathing, which promotes calm and relaxation. Geranium is primarily balancing, so if you need to be active after the bath, you will still have some energy. Thyme is good for fatigue and exhaustion; it helps revive and strengthen mind and body, and also stimulates the appetite.

Having your blood pressure checked is a sensible precaution for monitoring your health if you suffer from a lot of stress.

Techniques to relieve sadness

Whereas grief is usually an acute condition with a specific cause, sadness and melancholy are often all-pervasive and chronic feelings, sometimes with no readily discernible cause. Of course you can feel sad at hearing some bad news or misfortune, but if this is not so severe as to cause grief, then such sadness is usually short-lived and not really a problem.

People can feel sad sometimes and yet not know why; they simply feel low, dark, heavy and dispirited. When this mood occurs, the joy and light in life seem to disappear and it is difficult to shake off this melancholic, despondent feeling. We can recognize that some people do have a melancholic disposition, a tendency to feel unhappy and dejected for no obvious reason, but almost everyone can feel sad for no reason from time to time.

Useful remedies

• If you feel sad, diffusing uplifting essential oils is one of the best remedies. The nebulous nature of the feelings is counteracted by creating a general atmosphere of uplifting fragrance. The clarifying, uplifting effect of basil helps dispel mental fatigue and melancholy. Bergamot brings light and inspires good cheer, while patchouli comforts sadness on a deep level, and jasmine lifts the spirits.

• Another useful technique to combat sadness is to wear an uplifting mood perfume, reapplied several times during the day and before going to bed at night. Surrounding yourself with an uplifting fragrance over a period of time will gently and naturally shift the melancholic mood. Choose mood perfumes that include neroli, rose absolute, lavender, geranium or ylang ylang; these lovely floral essential oils have a subtle uplifting effect over time.

• Sometimes a sharp, fresh, clearing aroma can help shift sadness, and if the more subtle approaches outlined above are not working, then it's worth trying something a little different. Peppermint and thyme are invigorating and refreshing nerve tonics, and are very stimulating. They can lift your sadness by clearing the mind and emotions.

An effective technique to relieve sadness is diffusing uplifting essential oils in a burner to surround you with a cheerful fragrance.

Techniques to relieve low energy

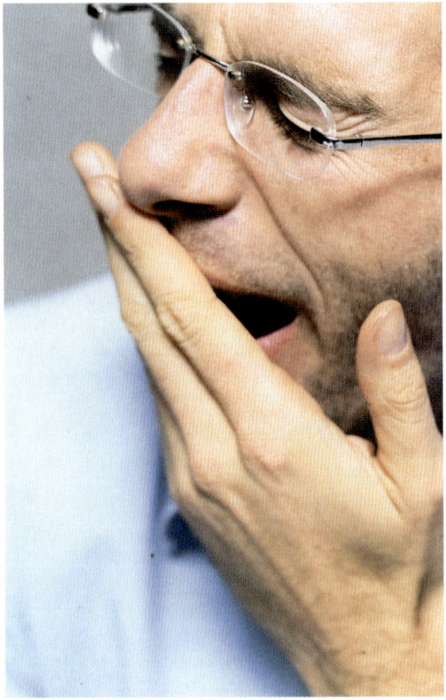

Low energy can be the body's way of telling you that you need a holiday, but stimulating essential oils can help boost energy levels.

There is a subtle difference between being tired and having low energy levels, although these two states do sometimes get confused. Whereas tiredness is caused by long and perhaps strenuous activity – whether mental or physical – low energy can affect you even first thing in the morning, before you start your day.

Low energy affects you mentally, emotionally and spiritually, as well as on the more physical level with symptoms of reluctance and sluggish activity. It can have a simple physical cause, such as not eating proper nourishment or not eating enough, but there are often underlying causes as well. It is in this sphere that essential oils can help. Low energy may be the body's way of telling you that you are chronically tired and need a proper rest. Although in this instance a vacation will help restore normal energy levels, you need to find ways to prevent tiredness affecting you so badly in the first place.

Useful remedies

- Checking your sleep routine is helpful. Perhaps you go to bed late and over-tired, so that you have difficulty sleeping or perhaps you suffer from insomnia and wake up feeling tired and lacking in energy. If so, you need to use calming, sedative oils in the evening to assist sleep and stimulating oils in the morning to boost your energy levels.

- Lavender is excellent to help you sleep easily and well, and marjoram, roman chamomile and german chamomile, neroli, clary sage and sandalwood are all useful. Take an aromatic bath (not too hot) before going to bed, and put a drop or two of lavender on your pillow.

- In the morning use stimulating essential oils to start your day with good energy, which may well sustain you throughout the day. If you start off with low energy, this will only deteriorate. Sprinkling essential oils on the floor of your morning shower just before you get in is a good technique. Rosemary and basil are stimulating and refreshing, and smell invigorating in combination with citrus oils.

Techniques to relieve nervous energy

Nervous energy, tension and stress are the body's reactions to external stress factors. These range from the physical stress of being involved in a car accident, through the stress caused by a neighbour's music, to worries about work and anxieties about relationships.

If the stress factor is prolonged for any length of time, the body reacts by overcoming the initial stress reaction and adapting to the situation. The body appears to function reasonably well on the surface, but the adrenal glands and immune system become strained, and nervous energy is the result. In the long term your body cannot cope, and you may become ill with anything from a nervous skin rash to a heart attack.

Nervous tension is characterized by a general sense of unease: you become restless, tense and edgy, and develop behavioural tendencies such as fidgeting and nervous tics or twitches. If you recognize symptoms like these, it is sensible to address the situation swiftly before you become ill, and aromatherapy is of enormous benefit to anyone suffering from nervous tension.

Useful remedies

• The best remedy is to have regular aromatherapy full body massages, where the body enters a state of deep relaxation for a while. Self-massage is of benefit between treatments. Massage your neck and shoulders, chest and abdomen, and your feet as frequently as you feel able to.

• There are many sedative, anti depressant essential oils to choose from to deal with nervous energy. These include roman chamomile, rose absolute and rose otto, neroli, clary sage, jasmine, vetiver, lavender, rosewood and marjoram. Essential oils that have a tonic and strengthening effect on the adrenal glands are also of benefit, and rosemary and geranium are especially useful.

• Bathing with calming essential oils at night promotes relaxation, and if the body relaxes properly before sleep, then its own self-healing powers can come into effect. Wearing a mood scent – calming, uplifting or confidence-inspiring – during the day is supportive, as is diffusing calming essentials oils in your room.

Fiddling can be a symptom of nervous energy. Try using your favourite sedative anti-depressant essential oils to soothe your nerves.

Aromatherapy and personality

There are several different ways to choose essential oils. When there is a physical ailment to be treated, you focus mainly on the physical properties of essential oils. For example, if you have a sore throat then you would choose an essential oil that can fight the bacterial infection that is causing the problem, such as lavender, benzoin, thyme or rosewood.

On other occasions, essential oils are selected more for their cosmetic skin-care properties, their anti-depressant and uplifting qualities, or their sedative or stimulating properties. A brief holistic consideration is always given to the way the essential oil affects you as a whole person, but this is not always the prime consideration.

Your maturing personality

Once you have some experience of using essential oils, then an interesting way to choose them is according to your own personality. This is not a static blueprint of who you are; subtle transformations in your personality occur as you move through life and are affected by your experiences. Your personality matures and grows, just as your mind and body do.

This changing nature of personality is reflected in your appreciation of essential oils. When you first encounter them, you quickly decide on those that you like, the oils that make you feel good, and those that you dislike and can't stand the smell of. However, your perception often changes over time. A once-loved essential oil may lose its attraction for you, and one that never inspired you may suddenly become your favourite. Occasionally you will notice that an essential oil you disliked at first is now appealing to you.

This observation suggests that essential oils can reflect different aspects of your personality. Choosing individual essential oils and blends that have an

Choosing essential oils that reflect your personality is an interesting approach to using aromatherapy.

affinity with who you are at this moment in time is a wonderful way to use the subtle power of essential oils. Each of us is a unique personality, shifting and transforming over time. Selecting essential oils that echo your strengths and positive emotions, and that help redress your weaknesses and negativities deepens your understanding of yourself.

Creating your own personality blend

Your personality blend represents your fragrant identity. Your unique blend is composed of essential oils with which you feel a strong affinity, which resonate with your personal rhythm and reflect the way you face the world. As you mature, this blend may alter slightly to reflect your personality changes. Occasionally you will need to replace an essential oil with another one, thereby delicately shifting the blend.

Take some quiet time to reflect upon yourself, your character and disposition, your beliefs and values, your habits and tendencies, your strengths and weaknesses.

Your fragrant identity reflects the essence of who you are. Try making up your own personality blend into a perfume.

Making your personality blend into a perfume

YOU WILL NEED

A 10 ml (2 tsp) rollette bottle with a roller-ball insert • 10 ml (2 tsp) sweet almond or jojoba oil • Essential oils of your choice (up to 50 drops)

WHAT TO DO

1 Half-fill the bottle with the sweet almond or jojoba oil, then add your chosen essential oils.

2 Shake well, top up the bottle with the remaining base oil and shake again. Leave the blend to mature – ideally for a week or two, but at least for a few days.

Simultaneously think about the essential oils. Whenever an essential oil springs to mind, put it to one side.

Take a cotton wool bud for each essential oil, and put a couple of drops on one end. Label each bud so that you don't get confused. Sniff each one in turn: if it feels right, keep it; if not, discard it. Hold two or three cotton wool buds under your nose and wave them around. Is the blend harmonious? Does it reflect your personality? Keep experimenting until you find the right combination for your personality blend.

When you first create your own personality blend, limit yourself to five essential oils. This gives you enough scope to explore all aspects of your personality, without becoming over-complicated. Once you have experience of the process, you can gradually increase the number of essential oils you use – keep going until you have eight or ten.

Aromatherapy massage for relaxation

Aromatherapy massage

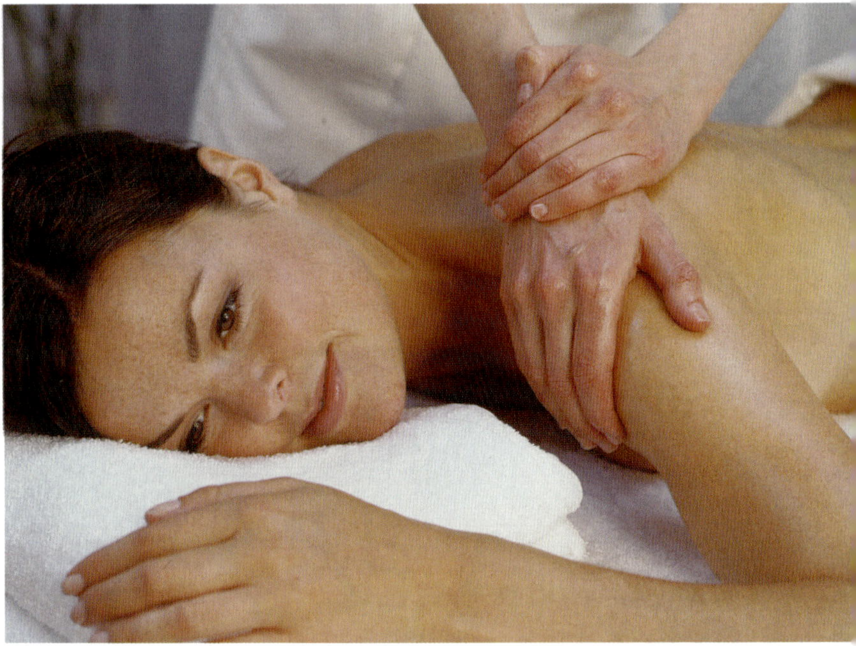

An aromatherapy full body massage from an experienced aromatherapist is a most enjoyable experience.

An aromatherapy full body massage from a qualified and experienced therapist is the pinnacle of aromatherapy treatments. The potent combination of healing touch, soft stroking, deeper massage on tight muscles and energetic work, together with the therapeutic power of essential oils, is unsurpassable.

Nevertheless, the massage techniques introduced in this section can be of immense benefit. Self-massage (see pages 164–167) and giving a simple massage to friends and family are rewarding, and clear, detailed instructions for easy massage strokes and techniques are given on the following pages.

There are many benefits of aromatherapy massage, both physical and emotional, as well as spiritual and energetic. On a physical level, the different massage strokes relieve pain, increase circulation of the blood and lymph, help to eliminate toxins and ease fatigued, tense muscles. On an emotional level, the mind and feelings are calmed, and deep relaxation is felt. An accompanying – and not strictly explicable – feeling of wellbeing and connectedness represents the spiritual and energetic benefits.

Learning about the body

Before learning how to massage it is important to know something about the body and the way the different body components and functions operate. Although massage is performed on the surface of the body, it works on the superficial muscles directly underneath and affects the deep underlying muscles, organs and other body systems.

Occasionally massage is contraindicated (advised against), and you must never massage anyone with a serious medical condition. Learning about the body helps you understand when massage is beneficial and when it is not. The following brief descriptions of the major body systems (see pages 136–153) should provide you with enough information to do simple massage on yourself and others, with knowledge, understanding and confidence.

There are several basic massage strokes to learn (see pages 160–163), which you can use to perform the different types of massage described in this section. Step-by-step instructions and pictures give you a clear idea of how each massage stroke should be performed. There is also information on the different vegetable oils used as base oils for massage (see pages 154–157), and some classic massage blends of essential oils (see pages 174–181).

The muscles

The muscles of the arm are made up of striated and skeletal muscles.

Muscles enable the body to move through interaction with the bones and joints. Whereas the skeleton is a scaffold of bones that gives the body sufficient rigidity to stay upright, the muscles connected to the bones allow movement. These muscles are known as voluntary muscles, because we control them consciously; they are the muscles that come into play whenever we decide to move.

Voluntary muscles are also known as striated (meaning striped) muscles, because under a microscope they have a stripy appearance, and as skeletal muscles, because they are attached to the skeleton. Voluntary muscles are directly affected by massage and are therefore of primary concern to the aromatherapist. However, there are two other types of muscles that are indirectly affected by massage.

Involuntary muscles – as the name suggests – are not under our conscious control. Also known as visceral muscles, they make up the body's internal organs, and are also called smooth muscles because under a

How massage can help

- As we age or if we take insufficient exercise, muscle tone is gradually lost, and the muscles appear and feel flabby. Massage can help to improve muscle tone a little, but exercise is of more benefit in this respect. Before you start to massage, feel your muscles at different times to learn the difference between normal muscle tone and tense and flabby muscles.

- When you massage, you work the voluntary muscles underneath the skin and connective tissues. There is always a slight tension in the muscles (called muscle tone), which holds the skeletal bones in place. After prolonged or vigorous exercise or bad posture, the muscles become tense, fatigued and painful. Massage releases the pain and tension and increases circulation, helping to dispel the waste products produced in the muscles from strenuous exertion.

microscope they appear smooth and sheetlike. Cardiac muscle is highly specialized muscle that makes up the heart.

These muscles are indirectly affected by massage through the relaxation of the whole body. Aromatherapy massage using anti-spasmodic essential oils relaxes involuntary muscle, and essential oils with cardiac tonic properties strengthen the heart.

The skeletal system

The skeletal system comprises all the bones of the skeleton. The skeleton provides an upright structure for the body, and the hard bones protect the soft, vital organs within the body. Although massage does not directly affect the bones, there is an indirect effect on the skeletal system because it releases tension in the muscles that hold the skeleton together.

There are several important reasons to learn where the major bones and muscles are located. For example, you do not want to confuse a very tense muscle in spasm (which can feel almost as hard as bone) with a bone itself. Deep massage is not done directly over bones, because this can feel painful and unpleasant. Therefore some familiarity with where the major bones are situated helps to prevent confusing muscles and bones.

Wherever two different bones in the body meet, a joint occurs. The muscles, tendons and ligaments that hold the bones in position allow movement at the joints. This means, for example, that we can bend down by using the hip and knee joints. These joints (called synovial joints) are the

How massage can help

- Massage around the joints is valuable, because the muscles holding the bones together there do a lot of work. However, care must be taken not to press down on the bones themselves – only on the muscle connections. This is best demonstrated by the way we massage the spine: the massage strokes are all done on the surrounding muscles up the sides of the spine, and not on the vertebrae themselves.

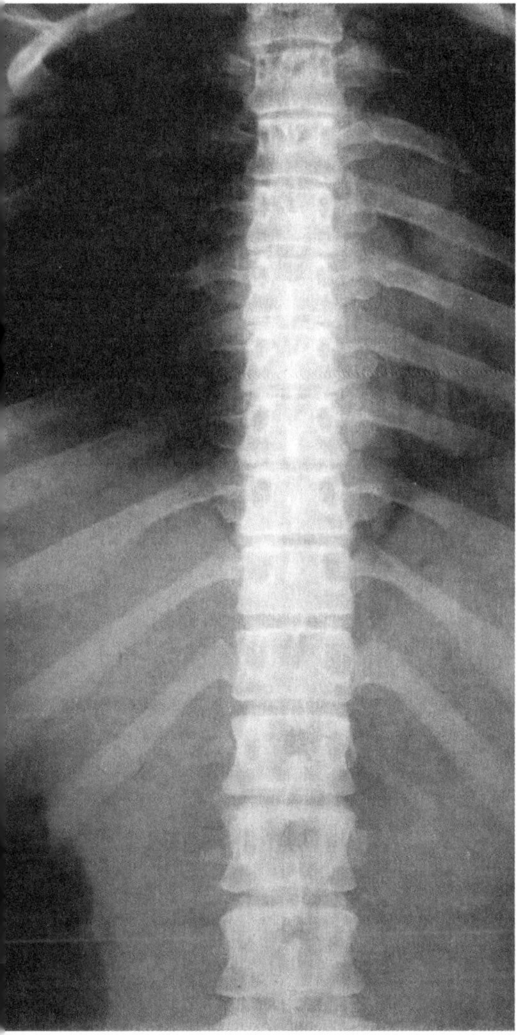

most mobile in the body and include the elbow and ankle joints. Synovial joints secrete synovial fluid, a lubricant that permits easy movement of the joint, preventing excessive wear and tear.

The discs of cartilage that lie between the individual spinal vertebrae allow limited flexible movement and are known as cartilaginous joints. The cartilage is tough and gristly, and acts to protect the spinal column inside the vertebrae (and the vertebrae themselves) from the shock of movements such as running and jumping.

The spine is made up of three sections of differing sized vertebrae, which allows sufficient flexibility for movement.

The cardiovascular system

The cardiovascular system comprises the heart, veins and arteries, and its basic function is to ensure adequate circulation of blood around the body. As fresh blood reaches every cell in the body, sugars, iron, salts, oxygen – and particles of essential oils – are exchanged for waste products such as carbon dioxide, urea and lactic acid. These are then circulated to the lungs, kidneys and skin and are excreted through breathing, urination and sweating.

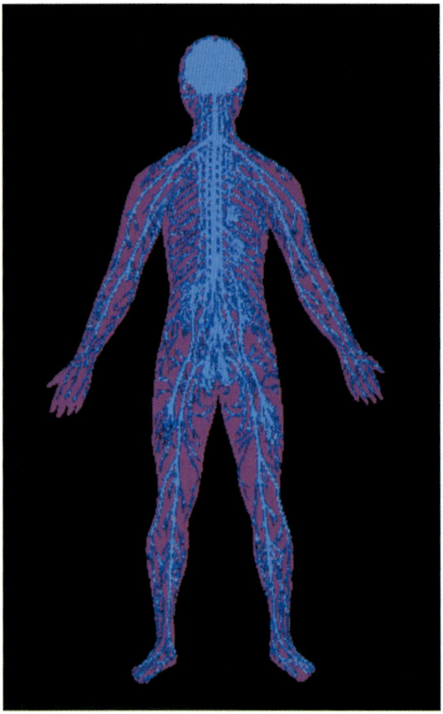

The heart is the most vital of the body's organs and is central to our existence. It is also the strongest muscle of the body, and works continuously – night and day – from the moment we are born till the moment we die. The heart pumps blood around the body, taking freshly oxygenated blood from the lungs to all parts of the body, and de-oxygenated blood from the body to the lungs for oxygenation.

The large number of arteries and veins in our bodies supply oxygenated blood and carry away de-oxygenated blood.

How massage can help

- The heart benefits from aromatherapy massage because regular treatments relax the whole body and reduces stress and tension, which can contribute to high blood pressure, strokes, angina and heart attacks. Essential oils that are cardiac tonics include rosemary, lavender, rose, peppermint, garlic and marjoram.

- Blood pressure fluctuates according to activity, eating, caffeine intake, emotional stress and so on, but normal blood pressure ranges between 100/60 and 140/90. Unnaturally high blood pressure is called hypertension. Aromatherapy massage with relaxing, calming essential oils that can gently lower blood pressure, such as marjoram, ylang ylang and lavender, is beneficial. Garlic capsules can also be taken.

- Unnaturally low blood pressure, called hypotension, also benefits from aromatherapy massage with stimulating essential oils that can gently increase blood pressure, such as rosemary and thyme.

Any problem of the cardiovascular system requires medical attention. However, aromatherapy massage, alongside lifestyle changes, can help to prevent cardiovascular problems arising in the first place, and can stimulate the circulation. Varicose veins are a minor cardiovascular problem and massage of any kind is contraindicated over varicose veins.

The respiratory system

All parts of the respiratory system are used to enjoy the wonderfully aromatic scent of fresh lavender.

The respiratory system includes the nose, pharynx (throat), larynx, trachea (windpipe), bronchi, lungs, alveoli and diaphragm. The order of these components follows the path of inhaled air through the nose, down the windpipe into the lungs, plus the rising of the diaphragm. With exhalation, the order is reversed and the diaphragm sinks. The actual respiration process is the exchange of oxygen and carbon dioxide between the atmosphere and the cells in the body.

The nose is where the olfaction process takes place. This means that when we inhale an aromatic particle such as an essential oil it is first dissolved in the mucus in the top of the nose, and then comes into contact

How massage can help

- Aromatherapy massage on the chest, abdomen, diaphragm and upper back is of direct benefit to the respiratory system, especially when there is a cold, cough or other respiratory problem. Repeated coughing can cause tension in the whole chest area and massage relaxes these tense muscles. Certain essential oils such as cedarwood, cypress, clary sage and eucalyptus have anti-spasmodic properties, which means that they relax the bronchioles in the lungs.

- Essential oils such as sandalwood, which have demulcent properties, soothe and relieve irritated or inflamed mucous membranes. When you have a cold or cough, the mucous membranes become inflamed and irritated, so aromatherapy massage and inhalations with demulcent essential oils can relieve the symptoms.

with the olfactory cells, also located there. Long nerve fibres attached to the olfactory cells (called axons) then carry the aromatic message to the olfactory bulb, which is situated in the cerebral cortex of the brain.

The nose is an important part of the respiratory process. As well as being the organ of smell, it filters out pollen and dust, and warms and moistens the air before it reaches our lungs. During aromatherapy massage, essential oils are inhaled, smelled and then travel to the lungs, from where they are distributed around the body. At the same time, essential oils enter the body through their application to the skin.

The reproductive system

Strictly speaking, this section is concerned with the female reproductive system, because aromatherapy massage and other applications of essential oils have much to offer in this area. Aromatherapy can be of benefit to the menstrual cycle, conception and pregnancy, childbirth and the menopause.

The male reproductive system is much less complex and aromatherapy has less to offer it.

The female reproductive system includes the ovaries that produce ova (eggs), the fallopian tubes that carry the eggs to the uterus, the vagina, vulva and mammary glands (breasts). The female reproductive system produces eggs, secretes sex hormones, provides a safe place for sperm to fertilize the ova and develop a baby, delivers the baby, and produces breast milk to nourish the baby.

Regular aromatherapy treatments from a qualified aromatherapist during pregnancy are of great benefit to the wellbeing of expectant mothers.

How massage can help

- Aromatherapy massage can be helpful for pregnant women (see pages 214–215 for gentle aromatherapy during pregnancy).

- Aromatherapy is also of use with both menstrual and menopausal problems. The menstrual cycle consists of the oestrogenic phase (which occurs from menstruation till ovulation) and the progesteronic phase (from ovulation to the onset of menstruation). During the first phase, certain essential oils that contain plant hormones similar to oestrogens are of benefit and can help to normalize irregular periods. These essential oils include clary sage, cypress, fennel and geranium. It is best to minimize their use during the progesteronic phase.

- Cypress can relieve painful periods and reduce excessive blood flow. Marjoram, lavender, roman chamomile, german chamomile and clary sage can relieve painful periods. Gentle abdominal massage and hot compresses over the abdomen are the best methods of application.

- The menopause occurs for most women in their late forties or early fifties. Some women are relatively symptom-free, but many suffer from excessively heavy periods, hot flushes, depression and insomnia. Geranium is a hormonal balancer, while rose tones and cleanses the uterus, and cypress helps to relieve excessive menstrual flow. These essential oils can be used in massage, as well as in baths and as hot compresses over the abdomen.

The digestive system

The digestive system consists of the digestive tract and ancillary organs. The digestive tract begins with the mouth, followed by the oesophagus (gullet), stomach, large intestine, small intestine, rectum and anus. The ancillary organs are the salivary glands, liver, gall bladder and pancreas. The functions of the digestive system are the ingestion of foods, peristalsis (waves of involuntary muscular contraction which move the food along), digestion and absorption, where the food is broken down and assimilated into the body, and the defecation of waste products.

The saying 'You are what you eat' refers to how healthy your diet is, but equally important is the way your food is eaten and digested. No matter how healthy your food, if you eat too quickly, over-eat or have a digestive malfunction, then nutrients will not be absorbed properly into your body.

Aromatherapy can aid the digestive process, but remember not to ingest essential oils orally. There are a few exceptions, such as throat,

How massage can help

• Common digestive complaints include diarrhoea, constipation and a build-up of gas. Essential oils with anti-spasmodic properties help to relax the smooth muscle that lines the intestine and facilitate the release of gas. The best anti-spasmodic essential oils in this instance are sweet fennel, ginger, aniseed, sweet orange and peppermint, massaged gently over the abdomen.

• Diarrhoea is usually caused by a too-rapid passage of food through the intestine. Fear, viral infections, bacteria, poisons, bad food and allergic reactions are all underlying causes. If fear has provoked diarrhoea, then neroli used in gentle abdominal massage, baths or sniffed from a tissue is effective. Eucalyptus is good for viral infections, and roman chamomile for allergic reactions. Constipation, which is caused by a too-slow passage of food, can be treated with firm massage over the abdomen in a clockwise direction using marjoram, rosemary, black pepper or sweet fennel.

cough and cold lozenges that contain small amounts of aniseed, hyssop, eucalyptus and peppermint. Peppermint pastilles containing peppermint essential oil are a useful aid to digestion, and may help with irritable bowel syndrome. However, aromatherapy massage and hot compresses over the abdomen are often more effective.

Eating a healthy diet, including lots of fresh fruit, helps maintain good health and a lovely complexion.

The nervous system

The nervous system is highly complex, and functions as the body's communication network and control centre. It is divided into two principal parts – the central nervous system (CNS) and the peripheral nervous system (PNS) – though there are several subdivisions as well. The nervous system operates by means of electro-chemical energy. Its main functions are to sense changes in the environment and body, assess these changes and then initiate action, either by means of muscular contractions or glandular secretions.

The CNS consists of the brain and spinal cord. The PNS comprises the nerve processes linking the CNS with muscles and glands. The PNS subdivides into the afferent and efferent systems, and the latter subdivides into the somatic nervous system and the autonomic nervous system (ANS). The ANS is divided into sympathetic and parasympathetic systems.

The sympathetic system is concerned with the body's response to danger. These nerves cause a dry mouth, dilated pupils, stimulate sweating and increase breathing and heartbeat rates in preparation for dealing with the danger. The parasympathetic system monitors the body's processes on a normal, daily basis, and so these nerves regulate breathing, heartbeat, digestion and so on.

How massage can help

• Aromatherapy has a powerful affect on the nervous system. Massage with appropriate essential oils can reduce or eliminate pain, reduce anxiety levels, alleviate muscle spasm and tension, and promote general feelings of calm, relaxation and overall wellbeing.

• Certain essential oils are nervine, meaning that they have a tonic and strengthening effect on the nervous system. Stimulant nerve tonics are strengthening and good for stress, debility and shock. They include angelica root, vetiver, peppermint, basil and lemongrass. Sedative nervines calm stress and tension, and include neroli, sandalwood, bergamot, lavender and roman chamomile.

• Analgesic essential oils alleviate muscular pain, headaches and so on. Analgesics lessen pain by reducing the activity of the sensory nerve endings. Massage and hot and cold compresses are the usual applications, but for burns neat lavender (perhaps the best analgesic) is applied to the affected area. Other analgesics include eucalyptus, marjoram, rosemary and peppermint.

Essential oils with stimulating nerve tonic properties should be sniffed immediately after suffering shock, to help relieve the symptoms.

The immune system

The immune system is our self-defence against literally millions of micro-organisms that continuously try to invade and occupy our bodies. Specialized blood cells together with the lymphatic system (see pages 152–153) make up our immune system. Some of the body's defences are non-specific and protect us against harmful microbes, while other defences target specific invading agents.

The micro-organisms or microbes that try to invade us may be viruses, parasites, bacteria or fungi. Not all of these are threatening; many are of benefit to the outer environment, and others live in happy coexistence inside our bodies. For example, the many different flora in our digestive system play an active role in keeping the digestion functioning well. When these are destroyed – for instance, by taking antibiotics – it is recommended that we eat live yogurt to replace them.

How massage can help

- Aromatherapy helps the immune system, because essential oils support and strengthen the body's immune response with a dual action. Some essential oils with anti-microbial properties fight the microbes, while other essential oils with immuno-stimulant properties boost the body's natural defences. Some essential oils have both properties, including ti-tree, lavender, manuka, ravensara, eucalyptus and bergamot. Massage, inhalations and compresses are all useful, depending on individual circumstances.

Using essential oils with anti-microbial and immuno-stimulant properties in massage boosts your immune system.

Once a threatening micro-organism enters the body, the immune system responds with a chain of action. Large white cells called phagocytes detect the foreign body, wrap themselves around it and kill it, though the cell itself often dies in the process. We can see this activity at an infected wound, where the pus is partly formed of dead bacteria and dead white blood cells.

Lymphocytes manufacture antibodies in response to invading microbes. These antibodies stay in the blood, and when the same microbe attempts to invade again, the antibody already present acts as a deterrent. When you have sufficient antibodies to prevent any symptoms arising, you are said to be immune to that organism. T-cells and adrenal glands also play a role in the body's defence.

The lymphatic system

The lymphatic system is the body's cleaning system, and it runs – by and large – parallel to the blood's circulation system. However, unlike the heart, which pumps the blood around the body, the lymph system uses pressure from the normal activity of the surrounding muscles to circulate the lymph. Lack of exercise and insufficient muscle movement can, therefore, affect the way the lymph system functions. For example, cellulite is caused by the retention of toxins due to poor lymphatic circulation.

The lymph system is a network of small capillaries, larger vessels and ducts, which all transport the lymph fluid; and lymph nodes, which act as filters. Lymph fluid is similar to plasma, but contains less protein and more lymphocytes, which help provide immunological protection against infection.

Your lymphatic system functions as the body's cleaning system by using the pressure of muscle activity.

How massage can help

- Aromatherapy massage of a brisk, stimulating nature, which manually encourages lymphatic circulation, is of great benefit. This is especially true for those with a sluggish lymphatic system, usually caused by insufficient exercise, sitting at a desk or standing all day. The massage works from the extremities (for example, from the hands up the arms, and from the feet up the legs), ultimately in the direction of the clavicle (collarbone). Here the lymph system drains into the blood at the subclavian vein, directly under the clavicle. The abdomen is also massaged, because there are many lymphatic glands and vessels situated here.

- Essential oils that have a depurative (or blood-cleansing) property are of benefit, because they encourage the elimination of toxins, thereby easing strain on the lymph system. Depurative essential oils include angelica root, carrot seed, cypress, grapefruit, fennel and juniper berry.

- Circulatory stimulant and diuretic essential oils are also recommended. The circulatory stimulants increase the flow of lymph, and include many spice essential oils, such as black pepper, clove bud, cardamom, ginger and cinnamon leaf, as well as rosemary. Diuretics increase the flow of urine by stimulating the kidneys and accelerating the elimination of toxins. Diuretic essential oils include grapefruit, lemon, sweet orange, geranium, juniper berry and fennel.

Base oils

Base oils are the carrier oils in which the essential oils are diluted before massage. Largely composed of fatty acids, the base oils used in aromatherapy massage are all of vegetable origin.

Most of these oils are extracted from nuts and seeds. They are easily absorbed into the skin, and many base oils have therapeutic properties. The best quality base oils are cold-pressed and unrefined, and you should try to purchase these ones.

Keeping a small selection of base oils means you can choose your base oil according to your skin condition.

Sweet almond oil

Sweet almond oil is pale yellow, almost odourless and has excellent emollient (soothing) properties. It is rich in minerals, vitamins and proteins, and is used extensively in cosmetics for its therapeutic properties. Sweet almond oil is especially suited to dry, sensitive and irritated skin. It is softening, revitalizing and nourishing to the skin and an excellent lubricant. It is probably the best multipurpose base oil for massage.

Apricot kernel oil

Apricot kernel oil is a slightly darker yellow than sweet almond, and has a light, silky feel and texture. It is absorbed very easily and quickly into the skin, making apricot kernel oil suitable for facial massage, as well as for body massage. Apricot oil is especially suited to mature, dry, sensitive and inflamed skins.

Avocado oil

Avocado oil is a deep vibrant green and has a slightly nutty aroma. It is viscous, but deeply penetrating, and for massage up to 25 per cent is usually mixed with a lighter base oil such as sweet almond. Avocado oil is very rich and nutritious and is suited to under-nourished, dry, dehydrated and mature skins and it can help to treat eczema.

Calendula oil

Calendula oil is an infused oil, meaning that the relevant plant parts are infused in a base oil, transferring their active properties to the base oil. Calendula oil has excellent healing qualities, aids tissue regeneration and is used on skin rashes, chapped and cracked skin, bruises and sunburn, and very gently on varicose veins.

Carrot oil

Carrot oil is also an infused oil, made from the root of the carrot. It is not to be confused with the similarly named carrot seed, which is an essential oil. Carrot oil is a beautiful bright orange and is rich in beta-carotene and vitamins. It is excellent for slowing signs of ageing, and for dry, itchy and inflamed skins. It is normally used in a 10 per cent dilution with a lighter base oil.

Coconut oil

Coconut oil is solid at room temperature in its natural, unfractionated state, and is used to make skin creams and to add gloss and shine to lacklustre hair. Fractionated refined coconut oil can be used as a very light, quickly absorbed massage oil.

Evening primrose oil

Evening primrose oil may be more familiar as a gamma linoleic acid oral supplement. However, it is also a useful base oil because it has excellent moisturizing qualities. Golden-yellow and viscous, it is best used in a 20 per cent dilution in a lighter base oil for dry, ageing skin and to treat psoriasis, pre-menstrual tension and eczema.

The various base oils have broad ranges of colours and viscosity – some are almost clear while others may be quite strongly coloured.

Grapeseed oil

Grapeseed oil is only available as a refined oil, but it is a popular massage oil because it has a fine texture that is easily absorbed by the skin. It is pale green and can be mixed with a heavier, more nutritious base oil for greater effect on the skin.

Hazelnut oil

Hazelnut oil is pale yellow with a strong nutty aroma. It is light, easily absorbed and mildly astringent, which makes it a good choice for oily skins. Hazelnut oil is also good for inflamed skin, and can be mixed with another base oil to reduce its nutty aroma.

Jojoba oil

Jojoba oil is actually a liquid wax, not an oil, although it acts like the other base oils. It is light-textured and deeply penetrating, making it a valuable base oil for all skin types. The chemical composition of jojoba closely resembles sebum, the skin's natural lubricant. This gives jojoba oil excellent moisturizing and emollient properties, making it a popular choice as a base oil for aromatherapy purposes.

Rosehip-seed oil

Rosehip-seed oil varies from pale yellow to rich orange and is an increasingly popular base oil due to its tissue-regenerating properties which can help slow the signs of ageing. Especially suited to dry, mature, sunburned and lacklustre skins, it is best used in a 20 per cent dilution with a lighter base oil.

Preparation for massage

Make sure you have all your base oils, essential oils, a dish to mix them in, towels and anything else you need before you start your massage.

Massage requires proper preparation in order to be effective and comfortable for you or for another person if you are giving a massage to someone else. On a practical level, if you have not prepared properly and halfway through your massage discover that you have run out of towels, then you must stop and wash your hands before you can touch anything.

How to prepare

1 Find a private room that is quiet, clean and spacious enough to do the massage in. It must be warm – at least a few degrees above normal room temperature – because you will remove clothing to do the massage, and you (or the other person) do not want to feel chilly. Oiled skin chills quickly, so a warm room is really important.

2 Make sure the lighting is soft, but bright enough to see what you are doing. Uplighters and side lights are better than overhead lights if you are massaging someone else, so that the light does not shine directly in their eyes when they are lying on their back.

3 Ensure that you have enough of everything you will need, including sufficient time so that you are not rushed. You require plenty of different-sized towels to cover up parts of the body after they have been massaged. A large towel can be used to cover a futon or mat on the floor where you will be doing the massage. Have several cushions available to sit on, and to support your knees if you are massaging another person.

4 Select your essential oils and blend them into sufficient base oil for your needs. A full body massage takes 15–25 ml (3–5 tsp), depending on the size of the person and how dry the skin is. Use a small, shallow dish that you can easily dip your fingers into.

5 Prepare yourself mentally to do the massage. Make sure that you have your book open at the right page, if you need to check the massage sequence.

6 Remember to cut your fingernails short, tie your hair back and remove any rings or bracelets before you start.

Massage techniques

Effleurage

Effleurage is the basic massage stroke that you use first on the body, and which you repeat throughout the massage. It comprises long, slow stroking movements, which gradually progress from light to firm. These initial strokes cover the body with aromatic oil and promote a relaxed, soothing feeling.

The technique of effleurage brings blood to the body's surface. This assists in the assimilation of nutrients, stimulates lymphatic movement and aids elimination of toxins. Effleurage introduces the massage: it is gentle, non-invasive and warms the muscles before the deeper strokes are undertaken. It is the linking stroke between different areas of the body and between deeper strokes.

How to perform effleurage

1 Use your whole hand to do effleurage, held flat, relaxed and with the fingers loosely together.

2 Use both hands alongside each other to make calm, rhythmic strokes up and down the whole part of the body you are working on – for example, up and down the back and on each side of the spine.

Petrissage

Petrissage is the kneading movement that works the muscles. The technique involves the repeated gentle and rhythmic lifting of the muscle with your hands or fingertips, squeezing or twisting slightly, and then relaxing.

The petrissage technique pumps the muscles, which increases circulation and improves lymphatic activity. Muscle tension is eased and relaxed. Always spend several minutes doing effleurage before doing petrissage, because it is a deeper stroke.

Petrissage is only done on fleshy and muscular areas of the body – never directly over bone. The shoulders, sides of the back, back and front of the thighs, back of the calves and upper arms all benefit from petrissage.

How to perform petrissage

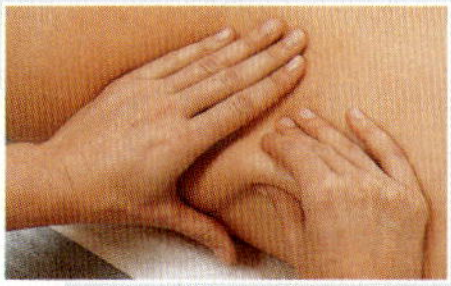

1 Hold your hands closely together on either side of the muscle and lift, stretch, squeeze and relax. Petrissage is like kneading bread dough – a gentle, rhythmic working of the flesh and muscle beneath your hands.

Friction

Friction strokes are firm, rubbing, circular movements. They are deeper than petrissage and are only ever done after effleurage (and perhaps some petrissage) has warmed the area.

Friction is often done with the fingertips or thumbs, although on tough areas, such as the soles of the feet, the knuckles can be used. It penetrates deeply into tight, tense and knotted muscles. Start gently and increase the pressure gradually, otherwise pain and resistance may occur.

Friction strokes stretch the muscle and body tissues away from the bone, increasing blood and lymphatic circulation, and releasing tension and congestion.

How to perform friction

1 Make large, circular strokes, done with the whole hands placed flat on the upper back and moving in opposite directions, to bring a warm glow and a release of tension. When done slowly, this is comforting; when done briskly, it is stimulating.

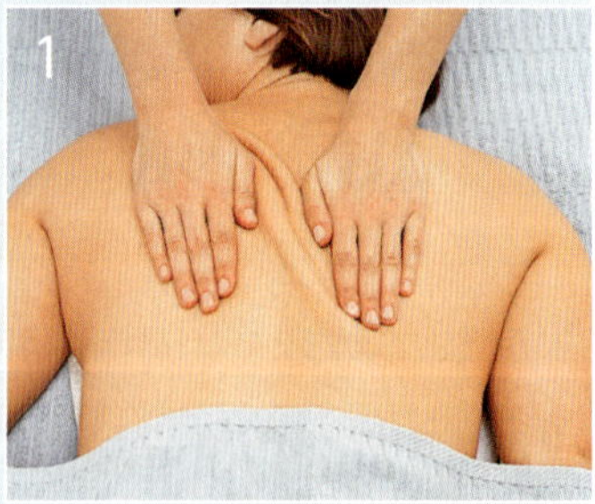

2 Using the fingertips or thumbs, make small, firm circular strokes up the sides of the spine to release tightness and tension in the back and help eliminate toxins.

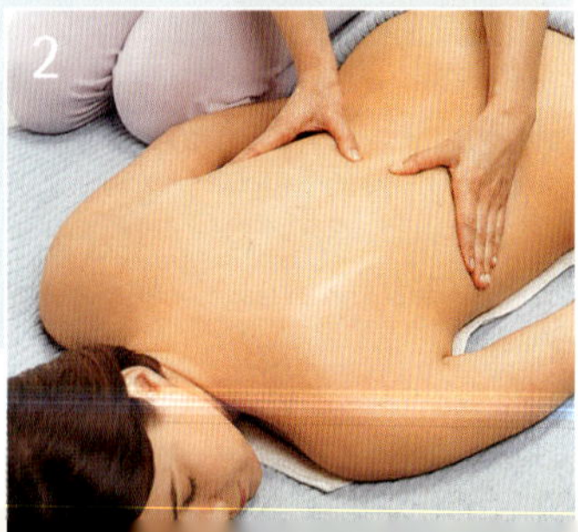

Special techniques

Drainage, feathering and auric massage

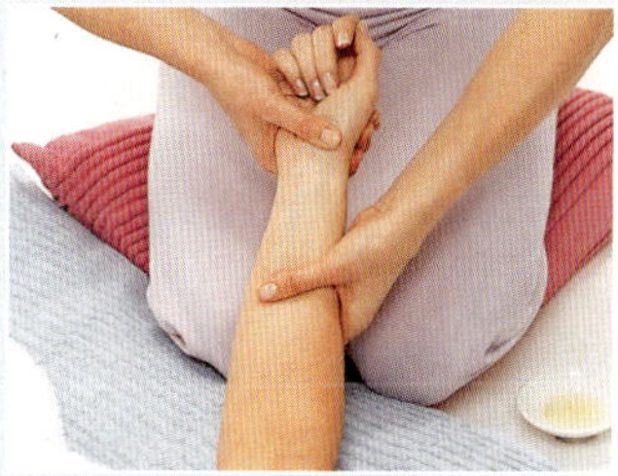

• **Drainage** This assists the flow of lymph, thereby aiding the elimination of toxins. Simple drainage goes as follows: gently lift a leg or arm, and hold and support the limb. Using firm effleurage strokes, massage in one direction only, away from the ankle or wrist towards the centre of the body.

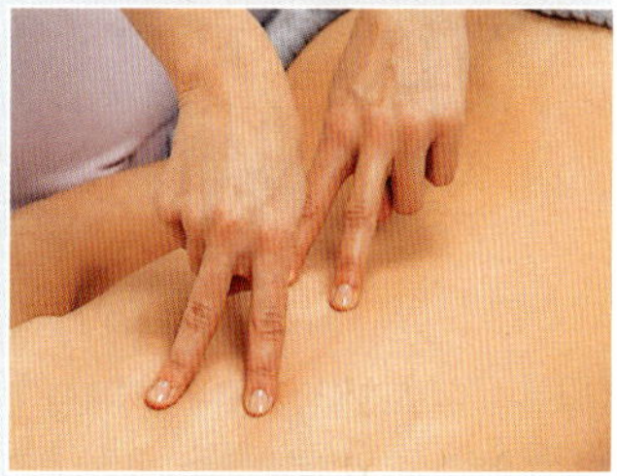

• **Feathering** This is a good way to finish a massage session, leaving the recipient feeling calm and with a sense of completion. To feather, use a very light stroke done with the gentlest pressure of the fingertips in a slow rhythmic fashion. For example, use long flowing strokes down the side of the spine.

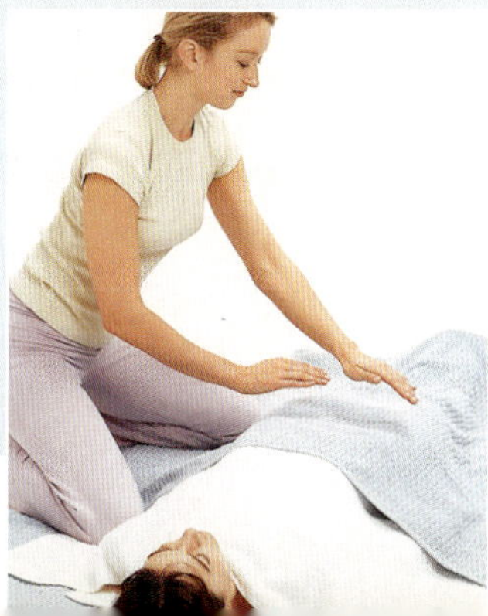

• **Auric massage** This is another good way to end a session. It works on the aura (see page 92) and is done without any physical contact. After feathering, do auric massage strokes 2.5–5 cm (1–2 in) away from the body, covering the whole body from head to toes.

Self-massage

Before massaging anyone else, it is a good idea to practise some self-massage. You will then develop good sensitivity, learn how much pressure to apply and how to touch and massage a body with confidence and conviction.

Self-massage never feels quite as relaxing as receiving a massage from someone else. Nonetheless, it is good for releasing muscle tension and general stress, and for promoting a feeling of calm and wellbeing. Self-massage also has the benefit that you can do it without another person being present, so you can massage yourself wherever and whenever you require. For example, if you develop a headache while seated at your computer, get up and stretch, then massage your shoulders and neck (see page 167).

The best self-massage is done at home using a blend of essential oils mixed into a base oil. Unfortunately you cannot massage your own back, but you can reach most other parts of your body. Do at least six effleurage strokes, up and down each part of your body, although you can continue for as long as you like. Afterwards do petrissage and friction strokes to release deep muscle tension.

You will need

A mat or futon • Towels • Essential oils of your choice, mixed into a base oil in a small dish

Feet and legs

Foot massage is relaxing, and reflexology is a specialist foot massage that benefits the whole body. Tired legs can also benefit from massage.

WHAT TO DO

1 Sit comfortably on a mat or futon on the floor, covered with a towel. Have your dish of massage oil close by. Remove trousers and any other clothing on both legs and feet. Cover your legs and one foot with a towel.

2

2 Put a little oil on your hands and do effleurage all over the first foot, gradually increasing the pressure. Move into petrissage, and do friction on the soles. Working firmly on the feet feels good. Finish with effleurage and repeat on the other foot.

3

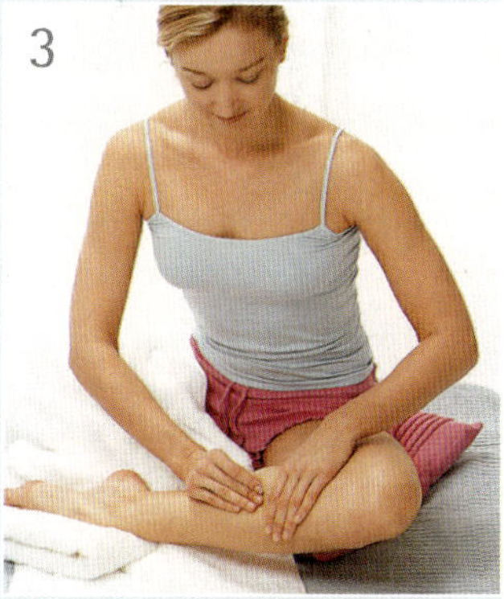

3 Uncover one leg and generously oil your hands. Do long effleurage strokes all up the leg (back and front) on as much of your leg as you can reach. Move into petrissage, but avoid the front of the lower leg. Do some friction strokes on the thigh if you have cellulite or congestion, and finish with effleurage. Repeat on the other leg.

Hands, arms and abdomen

Our hands work hard all day so they will welcome a relaxing massage. The abdomen also benefits from massage, which aids digestion.

WHAT TO DO

1 Sit comfortably on a mat or futon on the floor, covered with a towel. Have your dish of massage oil close by. Remove all clothing from your arms.

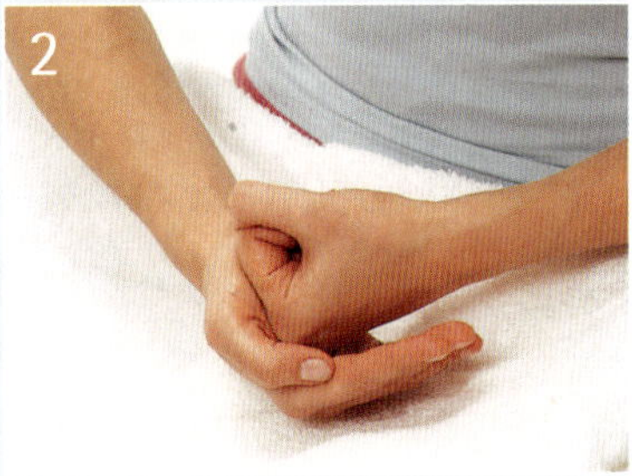

2

2 Put a little oil on your hands and effleurage over both hands, gradually increasing the pressure. Move into petrissage and do firm friction strokes on the palms. Finish with effleurage.

4

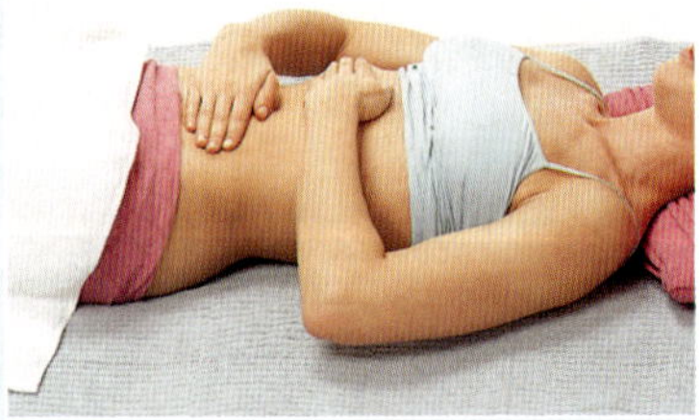

3 Oil one hand and effleurage the other arm all over, from top to bottom, followed by one-handed petrissage all over the upper arm. Finish with effleurage. Repeat on the other arm.

4 Uncover the abdomen and oil your hands. Make circular effleurage strokes all over the abdomen and diaphragm in a clockwise direction, following the direction of digestion. Petrissage the sides of the abdomen, and finish with effleurage.

Neck and shoulders

The neck and shoulders easily become stressed and tense, and benefit more from massage than any other part of the body.

WHAT TO DO

1 Sit comfortably on a mat or futon on the floor, covered with a towel. Have your dish of massage oil close by. Remove all clothing from your upper body and wrap a towel over your breasts and abdomen. Pin your hair up, if necessary, so that your whole neck is exposed.

2 Put a little oil on your hands and effleurage all over your neck and shoulders, gradually increasing the pressure.

3 Move into petrissage on one shoulder, and work the muscles firmly. Make small friction circles into the shoulder muscles wherever you feel deep-seated tension. Repeat on the other shoulder. Finish with effleurage.

4 Place your fingertips behind your head, on either side of your neck, and make friction circles up and down the neck muscles. Avoid pressing on the vertebrae. Finish with effleurage.

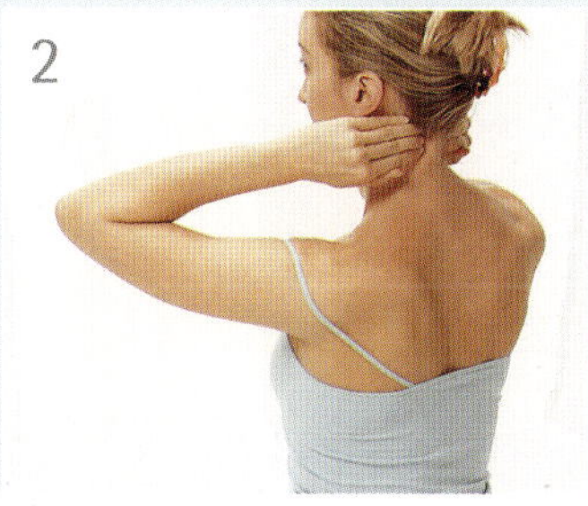

2

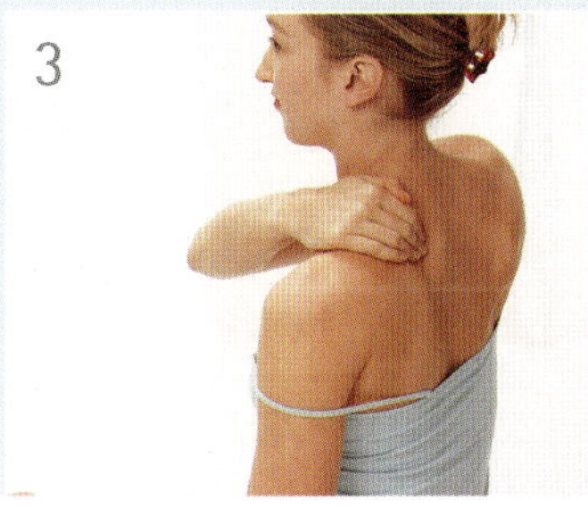

3

Giving a simple aromatherapy massage

Don't be too ambitious with your first massage on someone else – perhaps start with a back massage. To remain comfortable, experiment with your posture and keep your back straight. Make sure that all parts of your friend's body, except for the part being massaged, are covered with towels.

How to perform the massage

YOU WILL NEED

A mat or futon • Towels • Essential oils of your choice, mixed into a base oil in a small dish

---

WHAT TO DO

1 Ask your friend to undress to his or her underpants, holding a towel for modesty, and to lie on his or her front on a towel-covered futon or mat. Cover the whole body with towels, then cover the back and kneel beside them.

2 Put a little oil on your hands and do gentle effleurage down and up the back, using one hand on either side of the spine and gently increasing the pressure each time.

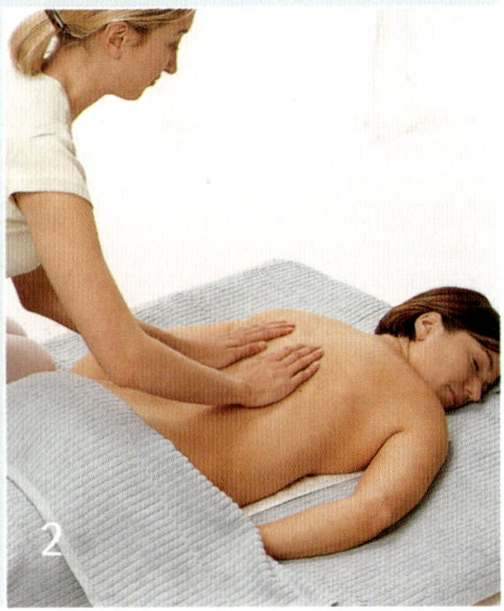
2

3 Move to one side and petrissage up and down one side of the back. Move round and repeat on the other side.

4 Make small friction circles up both sides of the spine. Move behind the head and make large friction circles, moving your hands in opposite directions, over the upper back. Effleurage the whole back and then cover it with towels.

5 Uncover one leg. Effleurage up and down the leg. Do petrissage first on the thigh and then on the calf. Effleurage the whole leg. Repeat on the other leg.

6 Ask your friend to turn over, holding the towels away from his or her body.

7 Uncover one leg. Effleurage up and down the leg, being careful not to press on the shin bone or knee. Petrissage the thigh and make small friction circles round the knee. Effleurage the whole leg. Repeat on the other leg.

8 Effleurage and petrissage one foot and make friction circles into the sole. Repeat on the other foot.

9 Uncover and effleurage up and down one arm and hand, then petrissage the upper arm and hand, and make friction circles into the palm. Effleurage the whole arm, then repeat on the other arm.

10 Uncover the abdomen and effleurage gently in a clockwise direction. Petrissage each side of the abdomen. Effleurage the abdomen.

11 Uncover the shoulders and effleurage the upper chest, shoulders and neck – working with your hands underneath – petrissage the shoulders, then effleurage as before.

12 Finish by doing sweeping auric massage over the whole body.

An intimate massage for lovers

Aromatherapy massage is healing, soothing and nurturing, but can also be sensual and erotic. This kind of sensual massage makes a wonderful form of intimate, non-verbal communication between lovers.

When sexual feelings between lovers are not urgent, then slow, sensuous and erotic foreplay can heighten each person's enjoyment of the other. Intimate massage can play a valuable role for lovers and can be enjoyed for its own sake, and not just as a prelude to sex.

How to perform the massage

YOU WILL NEED

Candles, flowers, music and beautiful objects • Towels • Sensuous and aphrodisiac essential oils of your choice (see pages 180–181), mixed into a base oil in a small dish

WHAT TO DO

1 Prepare a private room and make it an intimate space with candles, flowers, low music and beautiful objects. Make sure you have somewhere that is relaxing and comfortable, as well as towels to cover bed linen or whatever surface you will be using. Have your dish of massage oil close to hand.

2 Both of you can be naked or wearing underwear only, but use towels as you would for other massage. Start with your partner lying on his or her front and uncover your partner's back.

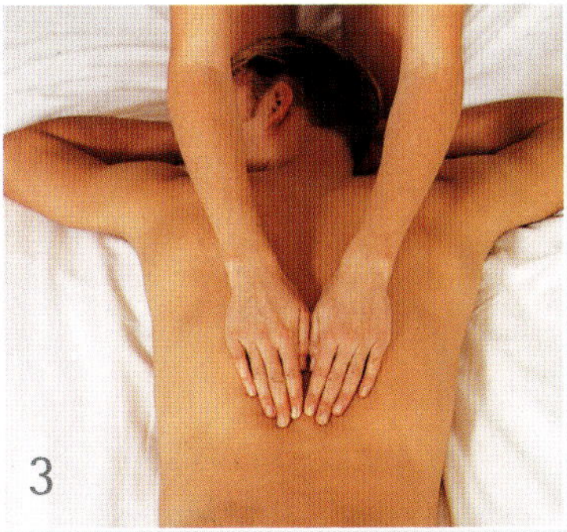

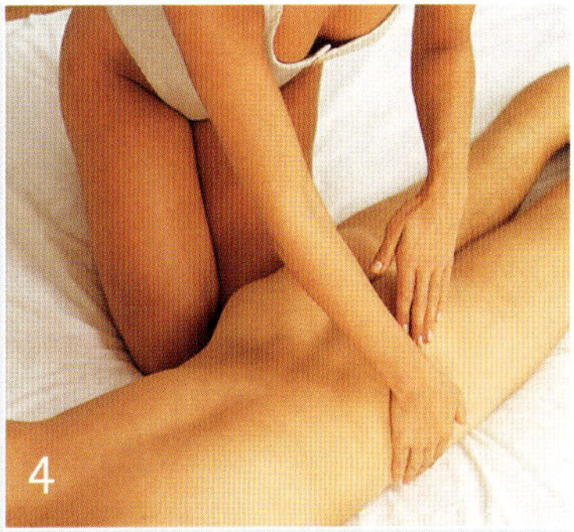

3 Oil your hands and kneel to one side of your partner, or at your partner's head or sit on your partner's buttocks, if he or she can take your weight easily. Use both hands to effleurage slowly up and down your partner's back in a rhythmic flow.

4 When you feel like moving on, ask your partner what part of their body he or she would like massaged next. Many parts of the body can feel erotic, so don't just focus on the obvious erogenous zones. Be creative and be mindful of giving a loving, sensual massage.

5 Allow sexual excitement and desire to arise naturally – don't force anything or have preconceived expectations. Sometimes intimate massage between lovers is not sexual; it can be comforting, loving and sensual without necessarily being erotic.

6 Try swapping over and encouraging your partner to massage you as well. Tell your partner what you like, what feels good and simply participate in enjoying each other's bodies.

A stimulating massage for sports

A stimulating aromatherapy massage is beneficial before and after sports and it also assists the body's detoxification process by galvinizing the lymphatic system. Stimulating the lymphatic system is also beneficial for convalescence, helping to strengthen the immune system once an illness has passed.

Sports massage is vigorous and stimulating and, unlike most other forms of massage, does not aim to relax and calm. It either helps to prepare for sporting activity by toning and warming the muscles, or to recover from sporting activity by loosening tight, tense and hard-worked muscles. The technique of sports massage is also somewhat different to normal aromatherapy massage, being brisker, deeper and more vigorous. However, it is still aromatherapy massage because you use essential oils to stimulate, tone and cleanse the body.

How to perform the massage

YOU WILL NEED

A mat or futon • Towels • Essential oils of your choice (see pages 176–177), mixed into a base oil in a small dish

WHAT TO DO

1 Prepare your friend as normal. This simple sports massage works on the legs only, as the lower limbs do a lot of the work during sport. Uncover one leg, oil your hands and effleurage up and down, as for normal massage. Then increase the pressure and speed of the effleurage strokes, making them brisk, vigorous and a

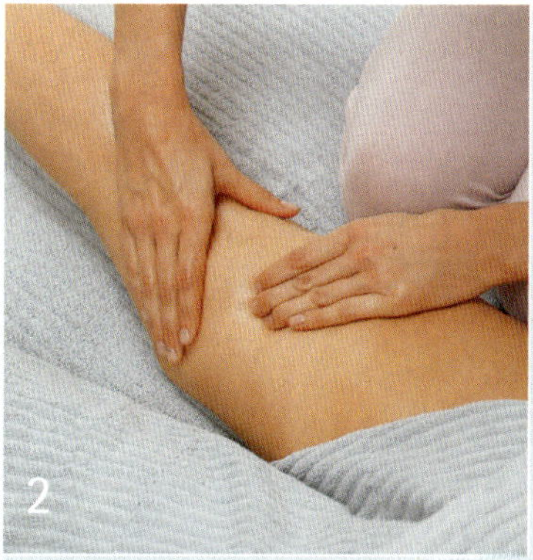

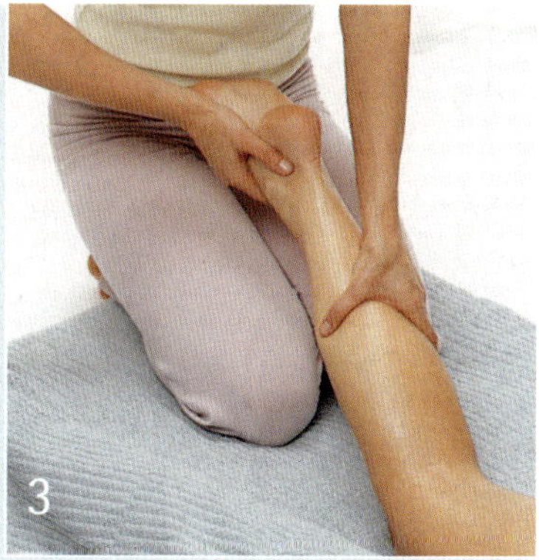

little deeper. Do not apply much pressure over the back of the knee, as this could hurt the knee.

2 Petrissage the thigh, using a deep, brisk technique, and do some friction strokes afterwards.

3 Move to the calf, avoiding the back of the knee, and continue brisk petrissage. Gently lift the leg and do some drainage strokes.

4 Now effleurage the whole leg, then cover it with a towel and repeat on the other leg.

5 Turn your friend over, and uncover one leg. Effleurage the whole leg, increasingly briskly and a little deeper. Do not apply pressure over the knee. Petrissage and friction the thigh, then effleurage the whole leg, cover and repeat on the other leg.

Calming and relaxing massage blends

These ten classic massage blends are tried-and-trusted combinations of essential oils that promote calm and relaxation. You will probably discover one or two favourite blends that you will return to many times, because these are the ones that are particularly effective for you.

However, it is a good idea to try out as many blends as possible and to create your own, perhaps drawing inspiration from these suggestions. These blends should be mixed into 20 ml (4 tsp) of base oil, or adapted proportionately.

Try creating your own personalized calming and relaxing massage blend using some of your or your friend's favourite essential oils.

Suggested combinations

3 drops of german chamomile
5 drops of lavender
4 drops of bergamot

5 drops of neroli
5 drops of lavender
2 drops of geranium

4 drops of lavender
4 drops of clary sage
4 drops of melissa

5 drops of rose
4 drops of frankincense
3 drops of german chamomile

6 drops of neroli
3 drops of geranium
3 drops of ylang ylang

5 drops of bergamot
4 drops of marjoram
3 drops of roman chamomile

4 drops of frankincense
4 drops of myrrh
4 drops of sandalwood

4 drops of clary sage
5 drops of verbena
3 drops of patchouli

5 drops of petitgrain
4 drops of jasmine
3 drops of sweet orange

5 drops of myrrh
5 drops of rose
2 drops of rosewood

Massage blends for sports and tight muscles

These classic blends combine essential oils that can help tone and warm muscles in preparation for sport or other strenuous activity, and which also release tight knotted tension after sport. These massage blends are particularly effective when used immediately before or after a sporting activity.

The following ten blends smell more herbal and robust than sweetly floral and delicate, so many of them will appeal to men as much as women. These blends should be mixed into 20 ml (4 tsp) of base oil or adapted proportionately.

A brisk, deep aromatherapy massage with one of these blends after strenuous exercise releases tight and knotted muscles.

Suggested combinations

4 drops of rosemary
4 drops of lavender
4 drops of marjoram

4 drops of pine
4 drops of cajeput
4 drops of lemon

5 drops of thyme
4 drops of lemon
3 drops of black pepper

5 drops of marjoram
4 drops of lavender
3 drops of german chamomile

5 drops of marjoram
4 drops of cedarwood
3 drops of nutmeg

5 drops of clary sage
4 drops of black pepper
3 drops of lemongrass

5 drops of manuka
4 drops of juniper
3 drops of grapefruit

5 drops of lavender
4 drops of basil
3 drops of roman chamomile

5 drops of rosemary
4 drops of clary sage
3 drops of basil

6 drops of lemon
5 drops of rosemary
1 drop of peppermint

Detoxifying and stimulating massage blends

These ten classic blends are useful for deep-cleansing the body and can also help to reduce cellulite, congestion and other toxic conditions. They can be massaged in briskly before taking a sauna, which is a particularly effective method of eliminating toxins.

Used regularly, these massage blends support the lymphatic system as well as the kidneys and liver. Make sure that you drink lots of spring water when using detoxifying essential oils. These blends should be mixed into 20 ml (4 tsp) of base oil or adapted proportionately.

Remember to drink lots of spring or mineral water when using detoxifying essential oils to deep cleanse the body.

Suggested combinations

5 drops of grapefruit
5 drops of sweet fennel
2 drops of carrot seed

4 drops of juniper
4 drops of rock rose
4 drops of lemon

4 drops of juniper
4 drops of rosemary
4 drops of lemon

4 drops of rosemary
4 drops of geranium
4 drops of sweet fennel

5 drops of geranium
4 drops of sweet fennel
3 drops of angelica root

5 drops of helichrysum
4 drops of black pepper
3 drops of carrot seed

5 drops of juniper
5 drops of lime
2 drops of helichrysum

4 drops of lemon
4 drops of grapefruit
4 drops of angelica root

6 drops of geranium
4 drops of sweet fennel
2 drops of angelica root

5 drops of juniper
5 drops of rock rose
2 drops of peppermint

Uplifting and aphrodisiac massage blends

These classic massage blends are both generally uplifting and aphrodisiac when used in an appropriate situation. They combine some of the most beautiful-smelling essential oils and are real treat to use.

The ten massage blends also incorporate anti-depressant essential oils that help release nervous tension, anxiety and depression. They are classic uplifting blends, but you can experiment with different combinations and proportions of these essential oils. These blends should be mixed into 20 ml (4 tsp) of base oil or adapted proportionately.

These uplifting and aphrodisiac blends contain some of the most beautiful-smelling essential oils.

Suggested combinations

4 drops of bergamot 4 drops of rose otto 4 drops of neroli	5 drops of rose absolute 5 drops of melissa 2 drops of cardamom
5 drops of rose absolute 4 drops of sandalwood 3 drops of patchouli	5 drops of neroli 5 drops of sandalwood 2 drops of clary sage
6 drops of jasmine 3 drops of melissa 3 drops of ylang ylang	5 drops of neroli 4 drops of rose otto 3 drops of jasmine
6 drops of rosewood 4 drops of rose otto 2 drops of ylang ylang	5 drops of rose absolute 5 drops of bergamot 2 drops of frankincense
4 drops of sandalwood 4 drops of jasmine 4 drops of bergamot	4 drops of sandalwood 4 drops of patchouli 4 drops of melissa

Aromatherapy for healing

The healing power of essential oils

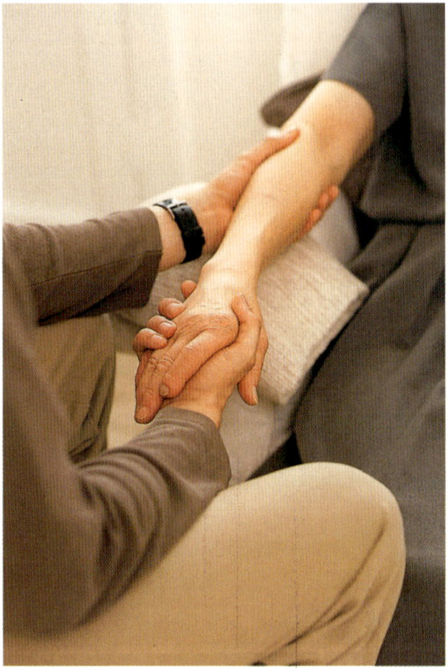

The healing power of aromatherapy can be of benefit to everyone, including the elderly.

This section looks at the healing properties of essential oils, and how they can help us regain – and maintain – health and wellbeing. A large part of this section comprises a list of common ailments and minor injuries, together with advice on how to treat them using essential oils (see pages 194–209). This aspect of aromatherapy, which focuses on physical wellbeing, is of great benefit in daily life.

As well as helping to heal on a physical level, a corresponding feeling of satisfaction and empowerment arises from treating yourself, your friends and family with aromatherapy. Working within an holistic framework, aromatherapy helps you take responsibility for everyday health care. This harks back a few generations, to a time when it was commonplace for the mother or grandmother of the family to keep a store of herbal remedies at home and look after the family's health.

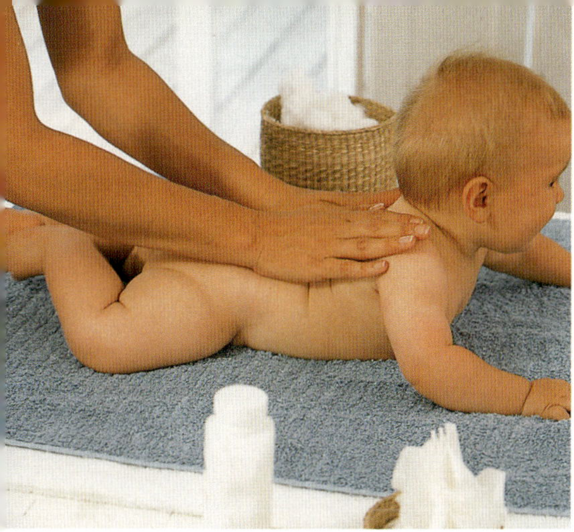

Baby massage is fun for you and the baby, and a wonderful way to connect and create a bond with your baby.

Medical aromatherapy

The healing power of essential oils is utilized in a medical context in France where some doctors undertake postgraduate specialization in aromatherapy. They practise medical aromatherapy, which is quite different from the way aromatherapy is practised in the more common therapeutic context.

Medical aromatherapy largely uses prescriptions of essential oils for internal use. The oils are measured and encapsulated in a gelatine capsule and taken orally, according to the prescription. Although this is clearly not within the remit of therapeutic aromatherapy, which *never* prescribes the internal use of essential oils (except garlic capsules), medical aromatherapy nonetheless demonstrates the extensive range and power of essential oils to aid the healing process.

In this section you will also learn how to use aromatherapy for babies, children, pregnant women and the elderly (see pages 210–217). All these groups of people are slightly vulnerable, and require gentler and sometimes slightly different treatment from healthy adults. The essential oils used on them are often considerably more diluted. However, once you have learned the guidelines for working with these groups of people, aromatherapy can be of great benefit to them.

Simple first-aid techniques

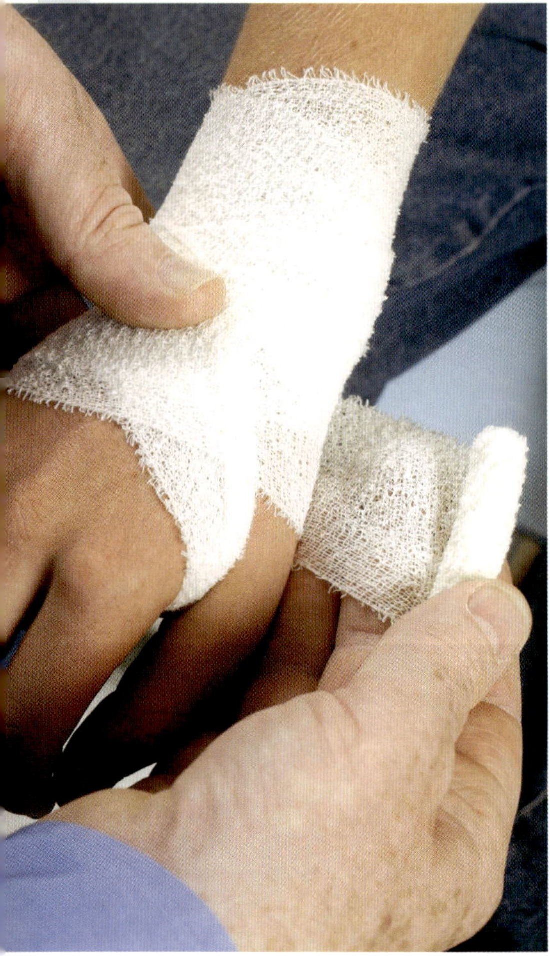

Essential oils can be used to treat a wide range of minor common complaints, discomforts, illnesses and injuries. You have already learned earlier in the book about some of the techniques for first-aid application, such as massage, bathing and vaporization. Details of how to make hot and cold compresses, antiseptic washes and steam inhalations follow on the next few pages. Some general advice on using essential oils safely to treat minor ailments, accidents and illnesses is given opposite.

Crepe bandages are useful to hold hot and cold compresses in place.

Safety guidelines

• If you are already taking medication from your doctor for a specific complaint, you need to check both with your doctor and with a qualified aromatherapist whether it is safe to use essential oils alongside allopathic remedies. For example, if you have a chest infection and have been prescribed antibiotics, it is helpful to use essential oils in steam inhalations, local chest rubs and in the bath, alongside the antibiotics. However, if you are taking other, less familiar medication and do not fully understand its purpose, you must check with your medical practitioner to ensure it is safe to use essential oils alongside your prescription.

• We have already emphasized that you must never take essential oils orally. Another area to avoid is the inner ear, and you should never attempt to pour essential oils (either neat or diluted) into the ear itself. However, essential oils can be used to great effect in compresses and local massage on the outer ear, for pain relief and to help prevent any infection spreading.

• If you have a minor accident, such as cutting your finger with a knife, it is important not to panic. There is always an element of shock or panic present – however mild – with accidents and this needs to be taken into account. However, if you act calmly and do not panic, you can apply the appropriate aromatherapy remedy safely and well.

Compresses

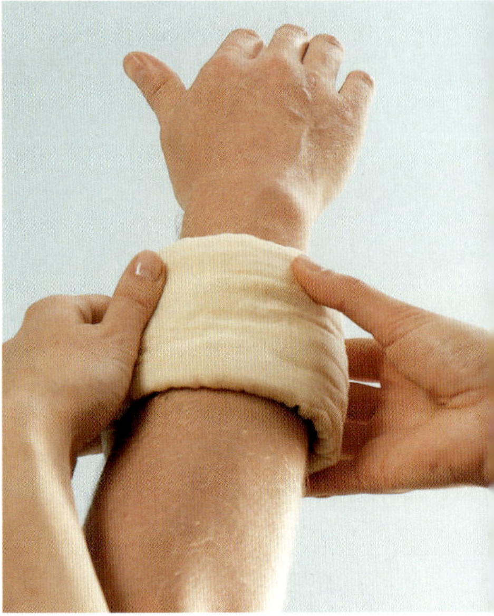

A folded face cloth dipped in either cold or hot water with the addition of a few drops of essential oil makes an efficient compress.

Using essential oils to make aromatherapy compresses is easy. Both hot and cold compresses are effective at relieving pain and swelling, and at reducing inflammation. Hot compresses are used to treat painful joints (from both arthritis and rheumatism), chronic backache, abscesses, toothache and earache. Cold compresses are used to treat headaches, reduce fever and as first aid for sprains, strains, insect bites, bruises and bumps.

Alternating hot and cold compresses is a naturopathic technique which stimulates the body into healing itself. This is especially effective for severe sprains, bringing pain relief and speeding up healing. When the incident first occurs, use cold compresses for first aid. The next day use alternate hot and cold compresses, remembering to start with a hot compress and finish with a cold one.

Making a hot compress is similar to making a cold compress, except that the water should be as hot as you can stand. Following the same technique, replace the hot compress with a fresh one when the first compress has cooled.

How to make a cold compress

YOU WILL NEED

A bowl • Ice cubes or cold water • 5–6 drops of an appropriate essential oil • A clean flannel or other absorbent piece of cloth • Plastic wrap or a towel

---

WHAT TO DO

1 Fill a bowl with cold water. Either add ice cubes or let the tap run until the water is really cold.

2 Sprinkle your chosen essential oil on the surface of the water – it will spread out on the surface, making a fine film on top.

3 Dip a face cloth slightly into the water so that it picks up as much of the essential oil as possible, along with some water.

4 Wring out the cloth to remove any excess water, then place it on the area to be treated. Cover the cloth with plastic wrap and bandage it, or wrap a towel around it, to hold the compress in place.

5 After five minutes or so, the compress will have reached blood heat and should be replaced with a new cold compress. Keep renewing the cold compresses until the pain has subsided.

Antiseptic washes

All essential oils are antiseptic, although this quality is more pronounced in some oils than in others. This means that essential oils make excellent antiseptic washes for cleaning out wounds, foot baths, douches and gargles. Each of these categories uses different essential oils in different ways and in varying amounts, according to the condition to be treated. Therefore you need to make sure that you do not confuse the different types of antiseptic washes.

Types of antiseptic wash

- To clean wounds, make an antiseptic wash as follows: take a bowl of warm to hot water, sprinkle in 5–6 drops of essential oil and mix thoroughly. Use cotton wool pads dipped in the wash to gently clean the wound and carefully remove dirt particles and blood.
- To treat chilblains, athlete's foot and verrucas, and to help improve circulation in the feet and lower legs, make a foot bath. You can purchase specialized foot spas that whirl the water around or use a bowl large enough to take both feet comfortably. Fill with sufficient water to cover the feet and then add 6–7 drops of essential oil, mixing thoroughly before immersing the feet in the water.
- To treat vaginal thrush and cystitis, make up an antiseptic douche and local wash. The delicate membrane lining the vagina means that you must use only a small amount of essential oils. Mix 6 drops of essential oil in 5 ml (1 tsp) of vodka and add this to 500 ml (17 fl oz) of boiled and cooled water. Shake well each time before use.
- Never use essential oils near or in the eyes. Rose and cornflower waters may be used to make eye compresses, and chamomile infusions as a wash to

A warming footbath in winter is a wonderful way to improve circulation in the feet and lower legs.

treat eye infections such as conjunctivitis. Place a chamomile teabag in boiling water and allow the chamomile tea to cool. Remove the teabag and then use the infusion to wash out the eyes.

- To treat sore throats, use gargles. To make a gargle, put 1–2 drops of essential oil in a cup of warm water and mix thoroughly. Gargle with this mixture for a few minutes, then spit it out.

Steam inhalation

Steam inhalations have been used for a long time to treat colds, coughs, sore throats, sinusitis, chest infections and any other respiratory problems. Before the widespread availability of essential oils, raw plant material containing traces of essential oils were used. The ready availability of essential oils in the modern world has, however, made aromatherapy steam inhalations much easier and more effective.

We have already looked at facial steaming (see pages 70–71) and steam inhalations use a similar technique. However, a major difference lies in

How to make a steam inhalation

YOU WILL NEED

A large bowl • Boiling water • 4–5 drops of an appropriate essential oil • A towel

WHAT TO DO

1 Half-fill a bowl with the boiling water, then sprinkle in your chosen essential oil.

2 Bend over the bowl, cover your head with a towel and breathe in deeply through your nose for a few minutes, remembering to keep your eyes closed.

3 Alternatively, you can use a specialist facial sauna to do a steam inhalation, but make sure that you adjust the amount of essential oil if the container of water in the sauna is quite small.

Steam inhalations with essential oils help relieve the unpleasant symptoms of colds, sore throats and coughs.

remembering to breathe in deeply through the nose, especially if you have a cold and blocked sinuses, to make sure that you target the affected area. You also choose specific essential oils to counteract the symptoms you are treating.

It is appropriate to give steam inhalations to older children, but they must be closely monitored the whole time, to make sure they do not scald themselves. Aromatherapy steam inhalations can sometimes be contraindicated for people with severe asthma, hay fever or debilitating respiratory disease. If in doubt, do the inhalation for half a minute only, and wait to see if any adverse reaction occurs. If not, then you can gradually increase the time spent inhaling.

Some essential oils can be quite harsh and might provoke a fit of coughing. If this happens, lift your face away from the steam and take a few deep breaths of air, then return to the steam inhalation.

Treatments for specific ailments

The suggestions given on the following pages are for first-aid treatments and for treating mild conditions only. If the symptoms do not improve or the condition is (or becomes) serious, seek medical advice immediately, because it would be irresponsible – and could be dangerous – to continue self-treatment or treatment on friends and family members. However, the aromatherapy treatments suggested here can certainly help you deal with minor ailments and accidents.

Headaches and migraines

- Make a cold compress using lavender and peppermint. Apply the cold compress to your forehead and lie down in a darkened room until the pain eases. Replace the compress with a new one once it reaches body temperature.
- Drink a calming herbal tea, such as lime flower, vervain, lemon balm or chamomile.
- Massage your neck with 3 drops of marjoram mixed into 5 ml (1 tsp) of base oil. Migraine and headaches are often caused by stress and tension, and a neck massage with a warming essential oil like marjoram may well reduce this.

Dandruff

There are two types of dandruff: simple dry dandruff, where small particles of dry skin flake off the scalp and get trapped in the hair; and what is known as seborrheic dermatitis, where over-production of sebum causes excess sebum to get trapped in patches of skin on the scalp, which can then become infected, causing itching, scabbing and inflammation.

- For dry dandruff, mix 3 drops each of ti-tree and lavender in 10 ml (2 tsp) of base oil, and give yourself a thorough scalp massage several times a week. Try also adding 4–5 drops of ti-tree or lavender to 5 ml (1 tsp) of a mild, unfragranced shampoo and using this to wash your hair.
- For seborrheic dermatitis, follow the same methods as above, but use bergamot, sandalwood and lemongrass instead of lavender and ti-tree. These essential oils help to balance sebum production and lemongrass is an effective treatment for dermatitis.

Acne

Refer to the advice on oily skin care (see pages 62–63), and in addition try the following treatments.

- Dab individual spots several times a day with a drop of neat ti-tree oil on a cotton wool bud, applying it carefully so that you do not touch the surrounding skin.
- If scarring occurs as the spots heal, apply a little of the following mixture twice a day: 2 drops of neroli and 1 drop of lavender mixed in 5 ml (1 tsp) of calendula oil.

The debilitating effects of headaches and migraines can be alleviated by using cold compresses and neck massage.

Earache

• Apply hot compresses of lavender and german chamomile to the outside of the ear and its immediate surrounding area. Lie down somewhere quiet and replace the hot compresses when they cool, until the pain eases.

• If the condition worsens, it is important to seek a doctor's advice. Do not stick anything in the ear, because this could aggravate a possible infection. Drinking chamomile tea is soothing and calming, and harmonizes with the chamomile essential oil.

Sinusitis

• The best remedy is regular steam inhalations, up to five times a day, using one or more of the following essential oils: lavender, ti-tree, benzoin (in the form of Friar's Balsam – a proprietary preparation, which is much easier to use for inhalations than the essential oil), thyme, eucalyptus, peppermint or pine. These essential oils all help clear the head and sinuses, thereby relieving congestion, headaches and pain around the eyes and face. They also have powerful antiseptic properties to help prevent infection occurring.

Toothache

There are two useful aromatherapy remedies you can use to treat toothache as first aid before you visit the dentist.

• Put a drop of clove oil on a cotton wool bud and apply it to the affected tooth. Clove is analgesic, helping to relieve pain, and is also a powerful disinfectant that can help prevent infection. If there is a large hole where a filling has fallen out, pour a drop or two of clove essential oil onto a small wad of cotton wool and insert it into the cavity.

• Apply hot compresses to the outside of the face near the affected area. Use german chamomile or roman chamomile as they relieve pain and inflammation.

A soothing cup of herbal tea can be drunk to help a sore throat after doing a steam inhalation and a gargle.

Laryngitis and sore throats

Laryngitis is an acute inflammation of the larynx, and often occurs after a cold, cough or sore throat. Sore throats can occur as part of a cold or because of a throat infection.

• The best treatment for both conditions is regular steam inhalations, up to five times day, with benzoin (in the form of Friar's Balsam), thyme, rosewood, sandalwood or lavender.

• Additionally, make a gargle using 1 or 2 drops of thyme in a cup of warm water, and gargle between inhalations to ease the pain.

Colds

If you get a cold, steam inhalations can help relieve the symptoms.

- To try and prevent a cold before it starts, do steam inhalations with lavender, eucalyptus and ti-tree several times a day. Use these essential oils in the bath as well.
- If the cold develops, using a burner of lavender at night and rosemary during the day will help fight the infection and prevent other people catching the cold.
- Put a few drops of eucalyptus or lemon-scented eucalyptus on a tissue and sniff it frequently to help clear a stuffy nose.
- Take one garlic capsule twice a day and drink lots of fluids, especially chamomile, elderflower or peppermint tea.

Cold sores

Cold sores are caused by the *Herpes simplex 1* virus, and tend to appear when you are run down or have a cold or other infection. You may be able to prevent a cold sore developing if you act quickly.

- At the first sign of a cold sore, use a mixture of 2 drops each of bergamot and lavender and 1 drop each of eucalyptus and ti-tree, diluted in 5 ml (1 tsp) of vodka. Dab this on the cold sore frequently until it disappears.
- If the blister develops and becomes painful, alternate neat lavender (applied on a cotton wool bud) with the alcohol mixture given above.

Influenza

• Prevention is better than cure and if you feel you are going down with influenza, take a hot bath with 3 drops each of lavender and ti-tree and go to bed immediately afterwards.

• If you succumb to the virus, bed rest is needed for the duration of the influenza. Vaporize lavender, ti-tree, rosemary or eucalyptus in a burner in your bedroom and drink lots of fluids, especially herbal teas.

Coughs

Coughs can be either dry and irritable or 'productive' (where the coughing gets rid of excess mucus).

• Benzoin, bergamot, sandalwood, myrtle and thyme all have expectorant qualities (helping to expel mucus from the respiratory system), so use one or more of these essential oils in regular steam inhalations, up to five times a day.

• You can also use these essential oils in the bath, and in local massage of the upper back, throat and chest. Sandalwood is especially good for persistent dry coughs, and lavender, frankincense, myrrh and marjoram are also beneficial.

Bronchitis

This is an inflammation of the bronchial tubes and may be either an acute condition caused by a viral infection or a chronic condition usually caused by smoking or environmental factors.

• Use steam inhalations with the essential oils suggested above for coughs.

• Moisture is helpful for coughs and bronchitis, and you could try resting in a warm room with a frequently boiled kettle to humidify the atmosphere until the symptoms ease. If bronchitis worsens or a fever develops, you should see a doctor as soon as possible.

Asthma

- If you suffer an asthma attack, sit down somewhere quiet and sniff lavender, frankincense, bergamot or roman chamomile directly from the bottle or from a tissue with a few drops sprinkled on it; or use these essential oils in a room spray.
- Do not do steam inhalations because the heat could aggravate your condition, but moisture is beneficial and repeated boiling of a kettle in your room may be helpful.
- Use regular massage on your upper back and chest with any of the essential oils mentioned above, using 6 drops mixed into 10 ml (2 tsp) of base oil, to try and lessen the severity and frequency of attacks.

Hay fever

Hay fever is an allergy to pollen and causes a runny nose, streaming eyes and constant sneezing. Try to watch a daily local weather report that includes the pollen count and avoid, as much as possible, going outside or opening windows when the pollen count is high.

- At the first sign of symptoms, sprinkle a few drops of roman chamomile or melissa on a tissue and sniff it frequently. If this does not clear the symptoms, try a steam inhalation with lavender or eucalyptus, but revert to sniffing the essential oils on a tissue if this is too powerful.
- Use ice-cold rosewater or witch hazel on a cold compress over your eyes and nose.
- Drink herbal teas of chamomile and lemon balm to soothe the symptoms of hay fever.

Enjoying a meadow full of wild flowers and grasses can unfortunately bring on symptoms of hay fever.

Eczema

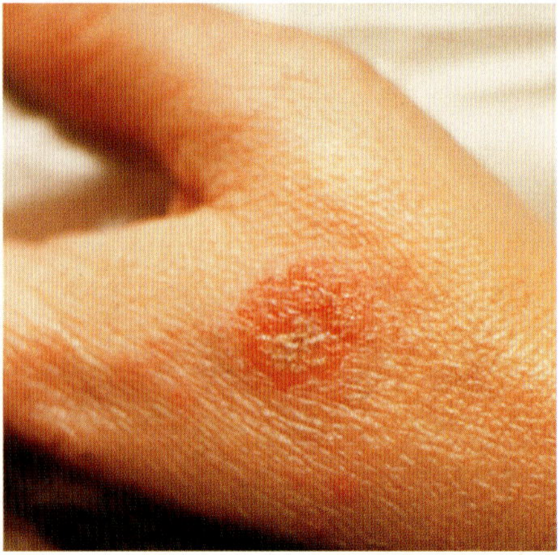

Eczema can be a debilitating condition for some sufferers.

Eczema is usually aggravated by underlying stress and nervous tension which must also be treated. The symptoms of red, itchy, flaky skin are similar to allergic reactions and dermatitis, and the following aromatherapy treatments are suitable for all these conditions.

- Aromatherapy massage helps relieve stress and tension, so visit an aromatherapist and do self-massage as often as possible.
- Take regular aromatic baths with roman chamomile or german chamomile, geranium, melissa or lavender, using a maximum of 5 drops mixed into a little evening primrose oil.
- Drink chamomile tea and use the chilled teabags as a cold compress on patches of affected skin.
- Use a body lotion with a 1 per cent dilution – 1 drop per 5 ml (1 tsp) – of german chamomile and melissa on the affected skin.

Burns

The most important action to take is to immediately cool the skin by plunging the affected body part into ice-cold water and leaving it there for at least five minutes.

• Treating burns is one of the few occasions when an essential oil – in this instance, lavender – is applied neat to the skin. Lavender reduces the pain, promotes rapid healing and can prevent blisters appearing. Gently dry the skin after cooling it in water, cover the burn with lavender and repeat if necessary after half an hour.

Bruises

• An effective first-aid remedy is to use a cold comprcss of witch hazcl to reduce the pain and swelling. Follow this with further cold compresses using fennel, hyssop or lavender.

• If the bruise is still painful at bedtime, add 3 drops of lavender to 5 ml (1 tsp) of calendula oil and massage gently into the bruise.

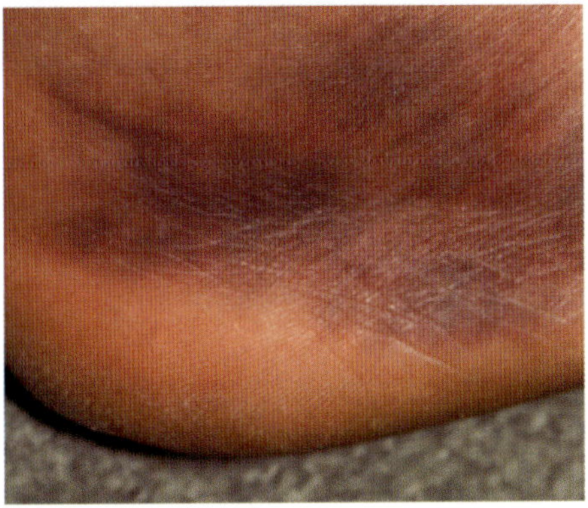

With severe and widespread bruising it is best to seek medical attention before attempting self treatment.

Abscesses and boils

• For abscesses and boils, the most effective aromatherapy treatment is repeated hot compresses of roman chamomile, lavender or ti-tree.

• To treat boils, keep the whole area hygienic by frequently using a local antiseptic wash made of lavender or ti-tree.

• Boils are a toxic condition that benefits from detoxifying massage and essential oils such as rosemary and juniper, which can also be used in the bath.

• Take one garlic capsule twice a day.

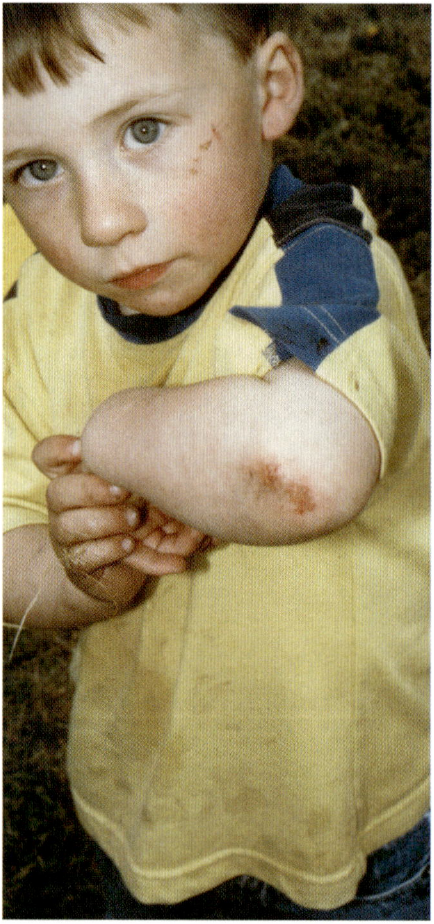

Children's minor cuts and grazes heal quite quickly, especially with the aid of simple aromatherapy remedies.

Cuts, wounds and grazes

- First wash the affected area with an antiseptic wash to remove all dirt. Add 5–6 drops of ti-tree or lemon to a bowl of warm water, and swab the area gently with cotton wool soaked in the antiseptic wash.
- You may need a few cotton wool balls soaked in antiseptic wash to cleanse the wound thoroughly.
- Once the wound is clean, dab neat lavender directly onto the affected area. If it requires a plaster or bandage, put a couple of drops of lavender on the plaster or bandage before applying it.
- If the wound becomes weepy after a few days and has not healed, change the dressing and use myrrh or ti-tree instead of lavender.

Sprains and strains

- Make cold compresses of lavender or german chamomile and keep replacing them with fresh ones until the swelling subsides and the initial level of pain has receded. Strap the joint lightly and gently to give some support overnight.
- The following day, use the naturopathic technique of applying alternate hot and cold compresses of lavender, german chamomile or roman chamomile to aid the healing process.
- Over the next few days, monitor the healing process and apply compresses and strapping for support as required.

Minor sprains and strains can be quite painful and distressing, but applying aromatherapy compresses speeds up the healing process.

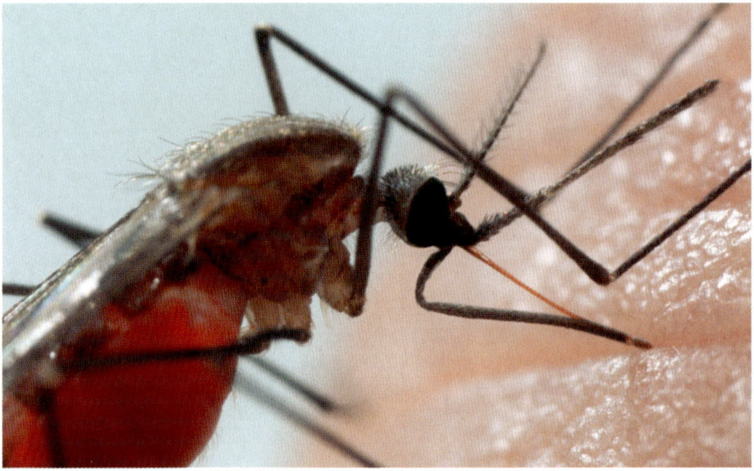

Insect stings and bites

Ensure that you remove the insect sting from the wound using tweezers before applying the aromatherapy remedy.

Before treating an insect sting, make sure that you get the sting out if at all possible, using tweezers.

• For wasp and bee stings, apply repeated cold compresses of witch hazel and lavender, until the immediate pain has eased. Then apply a couple of drops of lavender or ti-tree directly to the sting, repeating as necessary.

• For mosquito bites, apply neat lavender or ti-tree as required. If the bite becomes swollen and painful, apply cold compresses of lavender and german chamomile.

Digestive problems

Mild digestive problems include flatulence, nausea and indigestion.

• To treat flatulence, try drinking a cupful of fennel tea after meals. Also massage your abdomen gently in a clockwise direction with any of the following essential oils, using 6 drops in 10 ml (2 tsp) of base oil: basil, black pepper, cardamom, fennel, hyssop, marjoram, peppermint and rosemary.

• To relieve nausea, sniff peppermint, lavender or ginger straight from the bottle or from a tissue with a few drops of essential oil sprinkled on it. Additionally, drink peppermint, chamomile, lemon balm or ginger tea to help prevent vomiting.

• To relieve indigestion, gently massage your stomach and solar plexus in a clockwise direction with 1 drop each of marjoram, lavender and roman chamomile mixed in 5 ml (1 tsp) of base oil. If the indigestion is painful, try a hot compress with the same essential oils and slowly sip a herbal tea such as ginger, peppermint, fennel or chamomile.

PMS/PMT

Pre-menstrual syndrome (also known as pre-menstrual tension) affects many women to varying degrees. PMS most usually occurs a few days or even a week before your period is due, but occasionally the symptoms only appear once menstruation has started. Those who are affected tend to become over-emotional and either irritable, weepy or both.

• When you are affected by PMS, wear an uplifting perfume that contains rose and includes petitgrain, neroli or roman chamomile.

• Visit an aromatherapist for a full body massage or do some self-massage and take aromatic baths.

• If you are prone to irritability, use rose otto, roman chamomile, cypress and frankincense.

• If you are inclined to be weepy, use rose absolute, jasmine, roman chamomile and melissa.

• Drink chamomile, lemon balm and vervain herbal teas, which are relaxing, calming and mildly sedative and help to relieve PMS.

Menstrual cramps and fluid retention

• To relieve the pain and discomfort of menstrual cramps, use repeated hot compresses of marjoram and clary sage over the abdomen. As you lie back and rest, drink a cup of chamomile tea. A warm aromatic bath with lavender and rose absolute soothes and comforts before and during menstruation.

• Fluid retention produces a general bloated feeling and may include specific symptoms of tender breasts and a swollen abdomen. To ease fluid retention, take warm aromatic baths with the following mixture: 3 drops each of lavender and clary sage mixed into a little evening primrose oil. You can also mix 2 drops each of lavender, roman chamomile and clary sage into 5 ml (1 tsp) each of evening primrose oil and jojoba oil, and gently massage your abdomen in a clockwise direction.

• To help prevent fluid retention and other menstrual problems, visit an aromatherapist for a course of lymphatic drainage massage. Then try to have a monthly lymphatic drainage massage a few days before your period is due.

The pain and discomfort of menstrual cramps can be relieved by using hot compresses of marjoram and clary sage over the abdomen.

Cystitis

- Drink lots of water and chamomile tea at the first signs of cystitis.
- Use one garlic capsule as a suppository placed up the rectum.
- Make an aromatic wash with 3 drops each of bergamot and ti-tree in 500 ml (17 fl oz) of boiled, cooled water. Use this frequently as a local wash, making sure that you swab the opening of the urethra.
- Make a hot compress using bergamot, chamomile and sandalwood and place it over the abdomen, repeating as the compress cools.
- If the discomfort of cystitis increases or there is blood or pus when you urinate, see a doctor immediately.
- To help prevent cystitis, take regular baths with ti-tree, lavender, bergamot and roman chamomile.

Athlete's foot

This irritating fungal infection between the toes responds well to ti-tree, myrrh and lavender.

- Mix 3 drops of any of these essential oils into 5 ml (1 tsp) of vodka, then use this solution to swab the affected area. After a few days, when the skin has dried out, use calendula oil instead of vodka with the same essential oils.
- Use an antiseptic wash made with myrrh and ti-tree in a foot bath to keep the feet scrupulously clean, which will discourage the infection.

Insomnia

- To combat insomnia, take a warm, not hot, bath and add up to six drops in total of roman chamomile, neroli, frankincense and clary sage shortly before going to bed.
- Sprinkle a couple of drops of lavender on your pillow.
- Drink chamomile tea.

Gentle aromatherapy for babies

If you follow the safety guidelines given opposite, alongside the adult safety guidelines (see page 187), not only is it quite safe to use aromatherapy on babies, but it is also of benefit to the baby and the parents. This is especially so when a baby is having difficulty sleeping or is agitated and restless, because calming essential oils can help the baby calm down and sleep, thereby giving the parents some rest too.

Baby massage is a lovely way to bond with your baby, and studies show that babies who receive regular massage are healthier, sleep better and have less anxiety than babies who are not massaged at all.

Baby massage is a lovely way for a parent and child to really connect with each other.

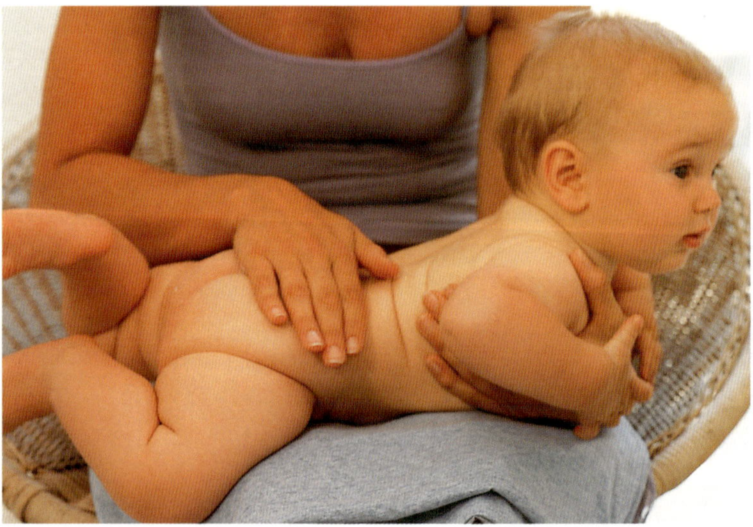

Safety guidelines

- You can start baby massage at around two months, but avoid it for a week or two before and after a baby is vaccinated.

- For babies under a year old, use just 1/2 per cent dilution or less, and not more than 1 drop of essential oil in total at any one time. Only use roman chamomile, neroli, lavender, mandarin or rose with young babies – avoid all other essential oils.

- For baby massage, mix 1 drop of essential oil in 10 ml (2 tsp) of base oil, then gently massage the arms, hands, legs, feet, back, chest and stomach. If the baby shows signs of wanting you to stop, then do so, but most babies enjoy being massaged. It is unlikely that you will use up the full massage mixture, so keep what is left over in a dark glass bottle. You can use this the following day for another massage or in the baby's bath.

- Use only diluted essential oils in the bath. Baby skin is very sensitive, and babies have a habit of putting their fingers in their mouths and rubbing their eyes.

- If a baby is restless and agitated, use roman chamomile or neroli for massage or in the bath. To help a baby sleep, use lavender in the bath or for massage, or alternatively put one drop on the baby's sheet or pyjamas.

Gentle aromatherapy for children

For the purposes of aromatherapy, it is best to categorize children into infants of between one and five years old and older children. After 14 years, the child can be treated with aromatherapy as you would treat an adult. Children catch all manner of childhood ailments, and aromatherapy is a safe and effective way of treating them, as long as you follow the guidelines given below, in addition to the adult safety guidelines (see pages 186–187).

Make sure you mix the essential oil in a little base oil before adding it to a child's bath.

Safety guidelines

- For infants over a year old, use $\frac{1}{2}$ or 1 per cent of essential oil and not more than a total of 3 drops at any one time. In addition to the essential oils used for young babies (see pages 210–211), you can include myrtle and benzoin because both of these essential oils are gentle and effective.

• As with young babies, chamomile is one of the best essential oils to use with infants. The calming, soothing properties of chamomile have earned it the nickname of the 'children's essential oil'. For sleeplessness, irritability, tummy upsets and teething, use chamomile in local massage and baths. Dilute essential oils in base oil before using them in the bath.

• For children between six and 14 years old, you can use 1–1½ per cent of all the essential oils that have no skin sensitization or other warnings (see the directory of essential oils on pages 268–385).

• For both infants and older children with coughs and chest complaints, use myrtle for chest massage in the appropriate dilution in a base oil. Myrtle is gentle yet effective and slightly sedative, and most children like its clean, fresh smell. You can also use myrtle, perhaps mixed with lavender, in the bath, and in a burner in a child's room. However, you must ensure that the burner is situated somewhere the child is unable to reach it.

• Lavender and benzoin (in the form of Friar's Balsam) are good to use with older children in inhalations, for colds, sinus problems and sore throats. Supervise children at all times to make sure they do not burn themselves and use only 4 drops of essential oil in the inhalation.

Gentle aromatherapy for pregnant women

Aromatherapy is nurturing and comforting and promotes a sense of happy wellbeing in pregnant women; it can also help ease some of the discomforts of pregnancy. One of the interesting links between aromatherapy and pregnancy is that pregnant women have a heightened sense of smell. This needs to be taken into consideration when choosing which essential oils to use, because it is important for the woman to enjoy the smell of the blend.

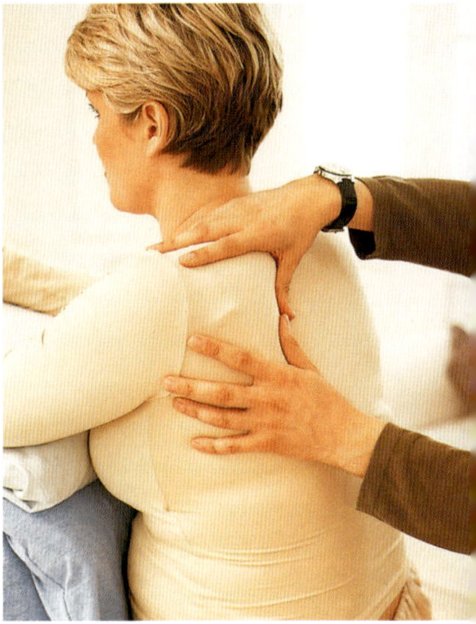

Aromatherapy massage, particularly on the lower back, brings great comfort and pain relief to pregnant women.

Safety guidelines

- Refer to the directory of essential oils (see pages 268–385) for full information on which essential oils must be avoided. The following essential oils are tried-and-trusted favourites for use in pregnancy and can be used with confidence and safety: neroli, mandarin, petitgrain, vetiver, frankincense, ginger, myrtle and sandalwood.

• Certain essential oils that have a property described as emmenagogue (promoting menstruation) are contraindicated for use in pregnancy. These oils must in general be avoided throughout pregnancy, although a few (such as lavender, chamomile and rose) can be used in a low dilution after the first four months. Throughout pregnancy use only half of the usual amount of essential oils – for example, 1–1½ percent in massage, and 3–4 drops in a bath.

• Backache (especially of the lower back during later pregnancy) is a common complaint for pregnant women. As it is uncomfortable for them to lie on their front for back massage, a good alternative is for pregnant women to sit astride a chair and lean forward onto a cushion. The back can then be massaged easily.

• Tired and slightly swollen legs and ankles are another common complaint which can be relieved by leg massage. Use firm pressure up the legs and just very light strokes down the legs. Making circles around the ankle joints also feels good.

• Morning sickness is best relieved with herbal teas such as ginger, peppermint and chamomile. Sniffing ginger essential oil from the bottle or on a tissue can also help, but avoid using peppermint essential oil.

Gentle aromatherapy for the elderly

Giving gentle aromatherapy massage to an elderly person helps prevent loneliness.

Caring for the elderly can be rewarding and increasing numbers of aromatherapists are working in care and respite homes for the elderly and in associated hospital departments. If you have an elderly relative or friend you can offer them some simple aromatherapy treatments.

Loving care and touch are particularly important to the elderly and this aspect of aromatherapy should be your main concern. Although aromatherapy treatments help the aches and pains of the elderly and are valuable and worthwhile in themselves, old age and the decline of the body are often accompanied by fear and loneliness. This means that your company, a sympathetic ear and caring attention will be most welcome.

Safety guidelines

• When working with the elderly, use only half the normal percentage of essential oils used for adults. As we age, our metabolism slows down and our skin becomes fragile, so it is prudent to use small amounts of essential oils. Massage strokes also need to be softer, lighter and more gentle.

• It is important to choose essential oils that the elderly person likes. Some elderly people – especially men – do not like flowery smells and will feel safer with eucalyptus and other familiar, medicinal-smelling essential oils. However, for those who are receptive, the rich, exotic and floral essential oils can bring back memories and reawaken the senses.

• Elderly people should not be asked to undress fully. Feet, lower leg, hand and arm massage are all beneficial for aching joints and improving circulation. The neck and shoulders can be massaged with a slight adjustment of clothing. Foot baths with stimulating essential oils are often welcome, especially in winter.

• Elderly people often have problems sleeping and generally need to sleep less, but more frequently. To help insomnia, use calming, sedative essential oils in the bath before bedtime, in a burner or room spray or a couple of drops on a tissue or pillow. Lavender and bergamot are often enjoyed by elderly people, and ylang ylang, sandalwood, neroli, cedarwood, jasmine, rose absolute and rose otto may all be welcome.

Aromatherapy for mind and spirit

Aromatherapy and meditation

Since ancient times aromatic plants have been used for religious and spiritual purposes. Regarded as sacred because of their magical healing properties and divine scents, they were 'sacrificed' by being burned and the fragrant smoke was offered to the gods. These ceremonies also benefited the priests, because inhaling the aromatic smoke often brought about mystical and spiritual states.

Incense and other aromatic compounds are still offered on altars in temples throughout Asia, parts of Africa and South America in a similar fashion to the days of old. All types of incense contain a significant proportion of aromatic plant material, traditionally including sandalwood, cedarwood, juniper, frankincense, myrrh, pine, sage and cypress. These are combined with other aromatic substances and with locally grown aromatic – and, for special rituals, hallucinogenic or psychotropic – plants.

The sweet aromatic smoke from burning incense can still help to create a suitable environment for meditation, introspection, contemplation and prayer. However, in a modern and more secular context, using individual essential oils (or mixing specific blends) allows you to create more precisely the atmosphere and mood you would like to achieve to complement and assist your meditation.

Using essential oils

The most effective method of practising meditation with essential oils is to use a burner – not dissimilar from the ancient sacrificial method. Burners vaporize the essential oils effectively, but gradually, thereby allowing meditation to calm the mind for a few minutes before you are affected by the essential oils vaporized into the atmosphere. However, you can also use a

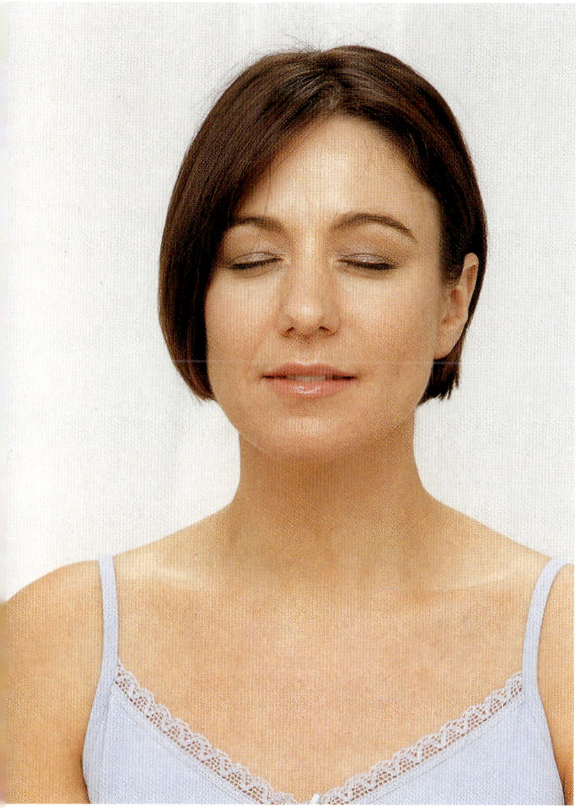

Meditation is a wonderful method of creating peace and calm, and vaporizing essential oils can enhance the experience.

room spray, practise informal meditation in an aromatic bath, or wear a mood perfume created from suitably meditative essential oils. You could try sprinkling essential oils onto a tissue and keep it in a top pocket.

You can also meditate to ground and centre your energies and to focus your mind before you undertake an aromatherapy massage. Meditating for ten minutes or so is a wonderful way to prepare yourself for giving massage, either to yourself or another person. It helps you to connect with your inner self, deepens your concentration and lengthens your attention span, all of which can improve your massage technique.

Using essential oils for meditation

Before you meditate with essential oils, you need to decide whether to use a burner, a room spray or a meditative mood perfume. Using a burner or electric vaporizer of some kind is generally best, because the effect of the essential oils is more powerful than it is with mood perfumes or room sprays. However, meditative perfumes are useful if you wish to meditate outside, or practise the walking meditation (see pages 230–231). If you want a very subtle effect, then a room spray is a good choice.

Using room sprays and mood perfumes

You can achieve a more subtle effect from essential oils as you meditate by using a room spray. Choose your essential oils as described above, add them to the water in your spray bottle and shake well. Spray the area you will be meditating in just before you start.

To use a meditative mood perfume, choose your essential oils as described above. Blend them into base oil, then apply behind your ears, at the base of your throat and on the inside of your wrists.

How to use a burner

YOU WILL NEED

A blend of essential oils of your choice • Cotton wool buds • A burner or electric vaporizer • Matches or a lighter

---

WHAT TO DO

1 First, decide which essential oils you are going to use. Analyse how you are feeling and what you wish to gain from the meditation. For example, you may feel tired and want to feel refreshed after your meditation and not fall asleep. In this instance you would choose a mentally stimulating essential oil, such as rosemary, cardamom or basil, and would blend it with something uplifting, such as bergamot, orange or rosewood, and with a balancing essential oil like geranium.

2 Choose three or four essential oils according to your feelings. Then do a sniff test, using cotton wool buds, to make sure the blend is pleasing.

3 Fill the burner's bowl three-quarters full of cold water and float the essential oils on top. (This method allows you to begin your meditation as the water slowly heats, so that the essential oils diffuse gradually. If you would like a more instant effect, start with hot water.)

4 Light the candle once you are ready to begin meditating.

It is important to be able to sit comfortably with a straight back for the duration of your meditation session.

Basic meditation technique

Many different spiritual traditions use meditation, and within each tradition there are several techniques. For instance, in Christianity there is a tradition of solitary contemplation and also the silent, mental repetition of a mantra: the Aramaic word *maranatha*, which means 'Come, lord; come, Lord Jesus'.

You may find it more comfortable to sit in a chair, but you still need to keep a straight back.

Calm meditation

This basic meditation technique is drawn from a Buddhist meditation called 'tranquil abiding', or 'calm meditation'. It is suitable for beginners and more experienced meditators.

YOU WILL NEED

A cushion or hard-backed chair • An alarm clock

WHAT TO DO

1 Find a quiet room and sit on a cushion or hard-backed chair. Either cross your legs and sit on the cushion on the floor, or sit upright on the chair. It is important to keep your back straight and to be able to sit comfortably for the duration of the meditation.

2 Set an alarm clock for 15 minutes and then forget about the time. Relax into your posture, but remember to keep your back straight. Close or half-shut your eyes and place your hands in your lap.

3 Bring your attention to your breathing by becoming aware of the sensation at the tip of your nostrils as you inhale and exhale. Be conscious of watching your breath without judging the process. Don't try to change the way you breathe, just watch your breath.

4 This simple focus on your breathing puts you in touch with what it means to be alive. Becoming aware of the natural rhythm of your breathing is calming and inspires tranquillity. Because breathing does not require conscious effort, your body breathes without you noticing much of the time.

5 When your mind wanders off into your usual thoughts and feelings, gently bring your attention back to your breath, without judging or being hard on yourself. It is the nature of the mind for thoughts to arise and you are used to letting your mind think freely.

6 When the alarm rings, gently open your eyes and shift your position, but take a few minutes to reflect on your meditation before getting up.

Mindfulness meditation

This meditation is similar to the basic calm meditation. Once the mind has quietened down a little from practising calm meditation, you can begin to deepen the meditation process by being mindful of what is going on inside you and being aware of your immediate environment.

Preparing your burner with essential oils before your meditation is a mindful ritual that mentally prepares you to meditate.

How to do the meditation

YOU WILL NEED

A cushion or hard-backed chair • An alarm clock

WHAT TO DO

1 Start off as you would for practising calm meditation (see pages 224–225), sitting comfortably with a straight back and a relaxed posture in a quiet room. Set the alarm for 20 minutes,

close or half-close your eyes and place your hands in your lap.

2 Now bring your attention to your breathing by becoming aware of the sensation at the tip of your nostrils as you inhale and exhale. Be conscious of watching the breath without judging the process, and don't try to change the way you breathe. Just watch your breath for a few minutes.

3 Now let your attention gently expand into your whole body, becoming mindful of any tension or pain anywhere. Really be in your body and be aware of how it feels. Be mindful of your immediate environment, the sensation of the air on your skin, and any little sounds that arise and pass.

4 The point of this meditation is to be in the present moment as fully and authentically as possible. This means being mindful of all your physical, emotional and mental processes as they happen, but not being drawn into them. If a sound arises, simply be aware of it – don't think about it at all. Simply observe sounds, thoughts, feelings and sensations as they arise and then let them pass.

5 When your mind wanders off into your usual thoughts and feelings, or you become distracted by a noise, gently bring your attention back to your breath for a few minutes. Then practise mindfulness meditation, as described above.

6 When the alarm rings, gently open your eyes and shift your position, but take a few minutes to reflect on your meditation before getting up.

Insight meditation

By practising calm meditation, then deepening the practice with mindfulness meditation, you will eventually achieve some calm and clarity. However, although this tranquillity brings inner peace, you can take the meditation still further with insight meditation and observe more clearly what is taking place within your mind.

Insight meditation involves looking closely at your thoughts and feelings, analysing them and noticing habitual patterns and tendencies. We usually identify with our thoughts and feelings without questioning them. Practising insight meditation helps you let go and see thoughts and feelings as transient contents of the mind, rather than the mind itself.

Insight meditation is a natural development from calm meditation and deepens the whole meditation process.

How to do the meditation

YOU WILL NEED

A cushion or hard-backed chair • An alarm clock

WHAT TO DO

1 Sit comfortably in your usual meditation posture, set your alarm for 20 minutes, and then watch your breath in calm meditation (see pages 224–225) for a few minutes.

2 When you feel ready, become aware of your thoughts, feelings and sensations as they arise and pass. Notice how they are fleeting and insubstantial, and how following them without questioning does not bring inner freedom or happiness.

3 Now bring your attention to whatever arises in your mind. Concentrate strongly on the thought or feeling, going beyond your usual casual, superficial attention. Try to analyse the thought, investigate it thoroughly and gain some insight into it.

4 When you become distracted and are following random thoughts, stop. Watch your breath for a few minutes to calm the mind and deepen your concentration. Then start the insight meditation again.

5 When you practise insight meditation, old repressed feelings might surface and these can be painful. If this happens, remind yourself that old memories are as insubstantial as your thoughts. Don't dwell on it – let it go, watch your breath until you feel calm, then return to the meditation.

6 When the alarm rings, spend a few minutes watching your breath in calm meditation. Open your eyes gently, reflect upon your meditation and take your time getting up and moving on.

Walking meditation

Practising walking meditation in beautiful surroundings allows you to feel an interconnection with all life.

Walking meditation is often alternated with sitting meditation, and can be regarded as an alternative posture rather than a different activity. If you have a bad back or painful joints, walking meditation allows you to do as much meditation as you like. It is easy to use essential oils for walking meditation: either a few drops on a tissue or wearing a meditative mood perfume.

Walking meditation isn't about going anywhere; the point is simply the walking. It is generally done in a short straight line, with a pause at the end when you turn around and retrace your steps. Although you can do walking meditation indoors, practising it in Nature – in a quiet and beautiful spot – allows you to feel an interconnectedness with all life.

How to do the meditation

YOU WILL NEED

A walking path of 5–10 m (16–32 ft), either outside in Nature or in a large room (however, if space is a problem, walk in a circle and use the point where you began to turn around) • Essential oils of your choice on a tissue or in a mood perfume

WHAT TO DO

1 Stand at the beginning of the line and spend a couple of minutes watching your breath. Then slowly and mindfully lift one foot and move it forward, feeling all the muscles involved. Place it down, feeling heel and toes separately as they contact the ground.

2 Repeat this slow stepping forward until you reach the end of your line. Then pause, turn, pause and retrace your steps. Keep your arms hanging loosely at your sides, and your eyes focused downwards a few steps ahead of you.

3 As you walk, be mindful of all the sensations in your body: feel your muscles moving, the sensation of the ground beneath your feet, the feel of the wind in your face. Be completely present to the whole experience.

4 If you become distracted by thoughts, or by gazing at something nearby, pause. Watch your breath and practise mindfulness meditation (see pages 226–227) before walking on.

5 After 20 minutes or so, stop at the end of the line and spend a few minutes watching your breath, before moving on.

Purification meditation

If you have done something you know is wrong – even a long time ago – feelings of guilt may lurk somewhere in your unconscious, causing discomfort and suffering from time to time. When you acknowledge that you have done something wrong, it is easy to fall into the trap of low self-esteem. So, if you feel depressed about a negative action, recall positive actions you have also done, alongside practising purification meditation.

The essence of purification meditation is to let go of your mistakes by seeing them as temporary blips on your stream of consciousness, not as an intrinsic part of your nature. It is not just your negative actions that you purify, but the state of mind underlying the action. In other words, you purify your negative thinking.

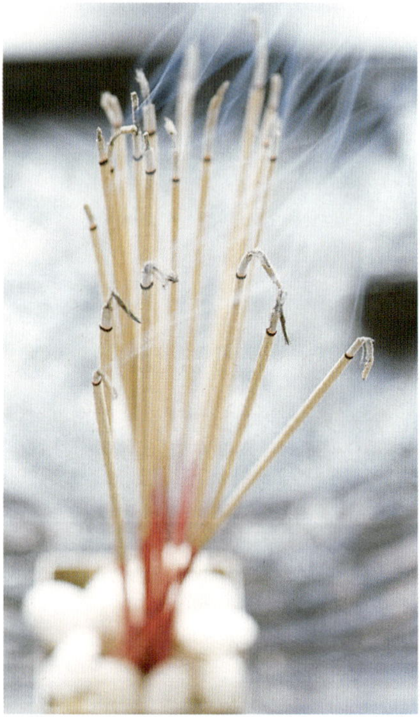

The ancient tradition of burning lots of aromatic incense for purification is still useful in modern times.

How to do the meditation

YOU WILL NEED

A blend of essential oils to assist purification meditation: try juniper berry, lemon, violet leaf, grapefruit, myrrh, cypress, mimosa, hyssop, basil and frankincense • A burner or electric vaporizer • Matches or a lighter • A cushion or hard-backed chair

---

WHAT TO DO

1 Float your chosen blend of essential oils on the water of your burner (see pages 222–223) and light the candle.

2 Sit comfortably in your usual meditation posture, watch your breath in calm meditation (see pages 224–225) for a few minutes, and become aware of the essential oils you are vaporizing.

3 Bring to mind one or more negative actions you have committed in the past that you would like to purify.

4 Generate sincere repentance and regret for having done these negative actions and resolve not to repeat them. Then request to whichever god or spiritual source is appropriate to you for help in keeping your resolution.

5 Return to watching your breath. On the next exhalation visualize any negative energy from your bad action as black smoke dissipating on your out-breath. Then visualize spiritual strength in the form of pure white light entering your body during the next in-breath.

6 Repeat for a few breaths, enjoying the vaporized essential oils, until you feel that the purification is completed.

7 Finish with a few minutes of watching your breath, and take your time getting up and moving on.

Letting go of anger

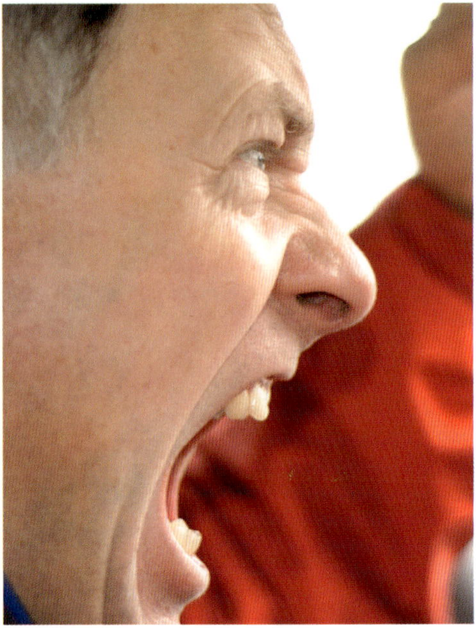

Anger is a frightening, sudden and violent emotion, but meditating with essential oils is calming and helps you let go of anger.

Anger cannot be overcome by expressing it. It can only be transformed by tolerance, compassion and patience. Meditation with appropriate essential oils is an excellent way to calm down and deal with anger, which is a complex emotion and may have different, subtly interrelated causes.

For example, if you tend to feel angry when asked to do something that you find challenging or difficult, then your anger is fuelled by insecurity and lack of self-confidence. In this instance, choose an essential oil such as jasmine to help build confidence alongside essential oils that help counteract anger. So the next time you feel angry, take time to meditate.

How to do the meditation

YOU WILL NEED

A blend of essential oils to assist you in letting go of anger: try roman chamomile, german chamomile, ylang ylang, benzoin, melissa, rose absolute, lavender, marjoram, sandalwood and frankincense • A burner or electric vaporizer • Matches or a lighter • A cushion or hard-backed chair

---

WHAT TO DO

1 Float your chosen blend of essential oils on the water of your burner (see pages 222–223) and light the candle.

2 Sit comfortably in your usual meditation posture, watch your breath in calm meditation (see pages 224–225) for a few minutes, and become aware of the essential oils you are vaporizing.

3 If your anger has made your breathing quicker and shallow, take a few slow, deep breaths, experiencing the smell of the essential oils.

4 Allow your angry feelings to be present, without trying to repress or judge them, but without being drawn into them. Acknowledge that you feel angry and try to let the feeling go.

5 Be aware of the vaporized essential oils entering your nose, and visualize them travelling round your body. Imagine them soothing your anger, softening your heart and deepening your breathing.

6 Don't be too hard on yourself: angry feelings arise when the causes of anger are present. Breathe into your anger and let it calm down, helped by the vaporized essential oils.

7 Finish with a few minutes of watching your breath, and take your time getting up and moving on.

Developing patience

Patience is an attitude of inner calm in the face of adverse circumstances, when things are not going your way. Being patient means keeping calm despite the difficult conditions and not reacting with irritability. If you allow impatience to manifest, you only make things worse. Patience allows you to assess the situation calmly and take rational steps to improve it.

The following meditation encourages you to engage with whatever circumstances are making you feel impatient. It helps you accept things if you cannot change them, and to act skilfully if you can. So the next time you feel impatient, resolve to meditate to let go of your irritability and develop patience instead.

Frequently checking your watch is a sign of impatience, but patience can be cultivated through meditation.

How to do the meditation

YOU WILL NEED

A blend of essential oils to assist you in calming down and being tolerant: try cypress, lavender, roman chamomile, marjoram, petitgrain, angelica root, neroli and frankincense • A burner or electric vaporizer • Matches or a lighter • A cushion or hard-backed chair

---

WHAT TO DO

1 Float your chosen blend of essential oils on the water of your burner (see pages 222–223) and light the candle.

2 Sit comfortably in your usual meditation posture, watch your breath in calm meditation (see pages 224–225) for a few minutes, and become aware of the effect of the essential oils you are vaporizing.

3 Reflect upon the circumstances that have caused you to feel impatient. Can you do anything to change things for the better? If so, resolve to act calmly and skilfully once you have finished meditating.

4 If you realize there is nothing you can do to improve the situation, then you will have to transform the impatient feelings. Be mindful of how you are feeling throughout your body, and relax any stress and tension. Breathe deeply and inhale the essential oils.

5 Consider how impatience makes you feel worse. The frustrating circumstances are bad enough, but allowing impatience to rage through your body does nothing to help. Resolve to accept the situation steadfastly, and feel the essential oils give you a calm inner strength.

6 Finish with a few minutes of watching your breath, and take your time getting up and moving on.

Strengthening your resolve

Whenever you decide to undertake a course of action, you need resolve to follow it through. It's all too easy to make resolutions – such as a New Year's resolution to go on a diet – and then revert to your old ways after a few days. Resolve requires courage, determination and dedication, and meditation with essential oils can help you cultivate these qualities.

This meditation is best practised regularly – ideally on a daily basis, for as long as it takes to see your course of action through to its conclusion. The purpose is to cultivate strength and determination, renewing your resolution each time you meditate. It then becomes much harder to abandon your resolution when you feel tired or lazy.

Meditation with essential oils helps you cultivate and strengthen your resolve, courage and determination.

How to do the meditation

YOU WILL NEED

A blend of essential oils to assist you in strengthening your resolve: try cypress, cedarwood, jasmine, angelica root, patchouli, coriander, lime, mimosa, thyme, basil, bay and pine (After a week, change the blend to generate fresh, new resolve.) • A burner or electric vaporizer • Matches or a lighter • A cushion or hard-backed chair

---

WHAT TO DO

1 Float your chosen blend of essential oils on the water of your burner (see pages 222–223) and light the candle.

2 Sit comfortably in your usual meditation posture, watch your breath in calm meditation (see pages 224–225) for a few minutes, and become aware of the effect of the essential oils you are vaporizing.

3 Bring to mind your resolution. Be clear about your reasons for making the resolution, and make a commitment to yourself to see it through. Focus your attention on your resolution.

4 As you focus on your resolve, the reality of carrying your resolution through to its conclusion will become evident. You will be faced with potential difficulties, and will see what it really means to follow the resolution through. Your mind may come up with reasons and excuses not to fulfil it.

5 Breathe deeply and be aware of the strengthening effect of the essential oils. Face up to all the reasons why you might not see your resolution through, and dispel them with strong determination.

6 Finish with a few minutes of watching your breath, and take your time getting up and moving on.

Bereavement

Losing someone you love is devastating, and it takes time to come to terms with your loss, although meditation is calming and supportive.

Death is an integral part of life; it completes the circle started at conception. Without death, life could not come into being, and we know that death is inevitable. However, we usually try to forget what we regard as an unpleasant future event, and we are only touched by death when it happens to someone we know.

There are specific meditations on death that, when practised regularly, can help you accept your own death. In this way you can make the most of life while you still have it. Aromatics have traditionally been used in bereavement rituals in many different cultures. This bereavement meditation uses essential oils to help soothe the trauma of a recent loss and to support you in letting go and moving on. Practise it as many times as you need to, until you have reached a sense of completion.

How to do the meditation

YOU WILL NEED

A blend of essential oils to assist your bereavement meditation: try rose absolute, rose otto, benzoin, melissa, frankincense, hyssop, marjoram, angelica root, cypress, rosewood, myrrh and bergamot • A burner or electric vaporizer • Matches or a lighter • A cushion or hard-backed chair

WHAT TO DO

1 Float your chosen blend of essential oils on the water of your burner (see pages 222–223) and light the candle.

2 Sit comfortably in your usual meditation posture, watch your breath in calm meditation (see pages 224–225) for a few minutes, and become aware of the effect of the essential oils you are vaporizing.

3 Bring the deceased person to mind. Visualize him or her and yourself enclosed together in a circle of gold light, spinning through the universe. Recall the times you spent together and think of the person fondly, thanking him or her for sharing time with you.

4 Honour your connection with that person and accept that it is now time to let go. Visualize the circle dividing in two, separating you into your own circles of light. Let the deceased go in peace with your blessings, as his or her golden circle spins away.

5 Breathe deeply and be aware of the effect of the essential oils strengthening and soothing you at this sad time.

6 Finish with a few minutes of watching your breath and take your time getting up and moving on.

Clearing the mind

When life becomes very stressful, it is all too easy to feel overwhelmed by the many different events happening around you. Confusion, indecision and frustration arise, and the mind seems full to bursting. Meditation alone is very helpful in creating some inner mental space, but meditation with mind-clearing essential oils is even more effective.

This meditation helps you let go of racing, confused thoughts and find some tranquillity and inner peace. Choosing essential oils that are stimulating, clarifying and cephalic will assist you in sorting out your thoughts, helping you to prioritize them according to importance and to let go of extraneous thoughts. Include a calming essential oil as well, such as lavender.

The meditation with essential oils for clearing the mind helps you calm down and let go of racing thoughts.

How to do the meditation

YOU WILL NEED

A blend of essential oils to assist in clearing your mind: try rosemary, basil, juniper, lemon, pine, cypress, cedarwood, bergamot, cardamom, peppermint, thyme, frankincense and geranium • A burner or electric vaporizer • Matches or a lighter • A cushion or hard-backed chair

---

WHAT TO DO

1 Float your chosen blend of essential oils on the water of your burner (see pages 222–223) and light the candle.

2 Sit comfortably in your usual meditation posture, watch your breath in calm meditation (see pages 224–225) for a few minutes, and become aware of the effect of the essential oils you are vaporizing.

3 As you watch your breath, also become conscious of the many different thoughts as they arise in your mind and are replaced by other thoughts. Try not to get caught up in any of them; simply observe them as transient thoughts and let them go.

4 Once your mind has calmed, but is alert and aware, start assessing each thought as it arises. Question whether it will lead towards a beneficial outcome or whether it is cluttering your mind. Let go immediately of any thought that is not of benefit to you at this time.

5 Breathe deeply and be aware of the stimulating, clarifying effect of the essential oils. Once you feel calm, alert and clear, you are ready to end the meditation.

6 Finish with a few minutes of watching your breath and take your time getting up and moving on.

Separation

It is hard to be separated from people you desire. This meditation helps you accept separation more easily.

Throughout our lives we are frequently separated from what we like and want, and we end up with what we don't want to have or experience. This can be very frustrating! Meditation can help you accept that often there is nothing you can do to prevent separation from your objects of desire. However, you can learn to change the way you feel about and deal with separation through meditation with appropriate essential oils.

Separation might occur from a dearly loved friend who moves away, or when a relationship breaks up. Separation could also mean losing or breaking a treasured object or any feeling of loss. This meditation with essential oils helps you accept the reality of your situation without feeling negative and enables you to move on and stay open to what life has to offer.

How to do the meditation

YOU WILL NEED

A blend of essential oils to assist separation: try rose otto, rose absolute, geranium, bergamot, benzoin, frankincense, hyssop, marjoram, lavender, patchouli, ylang ylang, angelica root, sandalwood and clary sage • A burner or electric vaporizer • Matches or a lighter • A cushion or hard-backed chair

---

WHAT TO DO

1 Float your chosen blend of essential oils on the water of your burner (see pages 222–223) and light the candle.

2 Sit comfortably in your usual meditation posture, watch your breath in calm meditation (see pages 224–225) for a few minutes, and become aware of the effect of the essential oils you are vaporizing.

3 Bring to mind the object or person from which or from whom you are separated. Allow the painful feelings of separation simply to exist, without judging them or trying to change them in any way. Be open, spacious and accepting of your feelings.

4 Mentally check whether there is anything you can do to change the situation at all and whether this course of action is viable. Even when there is nothing you can do to change a situation, reflecting in this manner helps you accept separation.

5 Breathe deeply and be aware of the calming, nurturing effect of the essential oils helping you to come to terms with your separation and move on in life.

6 Finish with a few minutes of watching your breath and take your time getting up and moving on.

Letting go of fear

Fear causes mental paralysis, like a rabbit trapped in front of a car's headlights, unable to move. We seek to avoid fear, but when we are engulfed by it, we have to deal with it. This meditation helps you face up to your fears and gives you courage to act despite feeling fearful.

Next time you feel afraid, take time to meditate and do not remain paralysed by fear. In meditation you become aware of your body and its sensations. Meditating when you feel fear helps lessen the powerful physical symptoms such as short, rapid breathing. Choose appropriate essential oils to inspire strength and courage and to lessen the feelings of weakness and debility.

Just like this rabbit which is trapped by its fear of fast moving traffic, we too can feel paralyzed by fear.

How to do the meditation

YOU WILL NEED

A blend of essential oils to assist you in letting go of fear: try clary sage, jasmine, roman chamomile, neroli, ylang ylang, basil, melissa, rose absolute, juniper, lavender, marjoram, angelica root and frankincense • A burner or electric vaporizer • Matches or a lighter • A cushion or hard-backed chair

---

WHAT TO DO

1 Float your chosen blend of essential oils on the water of your burner (see pages 222–223) and light the candle.

2 Sit comfortably in your usual meditation posture, watch your breath in calm meditation (see pages 224–225) for a few minutes, and become aware of the effect of the essential oils you are vaporizing.

3 Bring your attention to your body. Notice if your breathing or heart beat has become more rapid. Take a few slow, deep breaths and be aware of the essential oils.

4 Allow your fear to be present, without trying to suppress it. Acknowledge your fearful feelings and breathe into them deeply.

5 Visualize the vaporized essential oils entering your nose and travelling round your body. Feel them calming and dispelling your fear and deepening your breathing.

6 Breathe into your fear, accept it and let the feelings go, helped by the vaporized essential oils. Repeat silently to yourself a few times the phrase 'Feel the fear and do it anyway'.

7 Finish with a few minutes of watching your breath and take your time getting up and moving on.

Finding joy

This meditation on finding joy is a celebration of life and happiness.

This last aromatherapy meditation is about finding joy in your life from the simplicity of your own meditation and from the sheer enjoyment of using essential oils. As well as a burner, this meditation uses a large candle as a symbol of light and happiness. Unlike some of the other meditations, which assist you in transforming and letting go of negative emotions, this meditation is a celebration of life and of the potential you have to be joyful.

How to do the meditation

YOU WILL NEED

A blend of essential oils to inspire joy: use any essential oils that make you feel happy, including rose otto, bergamot, roman chamomile, mandarin, rosewood, linden blossom, palmarosa, neroli, basil, nutmeg, clary sage, melissa, jasmine, verbena, mimosa, narcissus and orange • A burner or electric vaporizer • Matches or a lighter • A large candle • A cushion or hard-backed chair

WHAT TO DO

1 Float your chosen blend of essential oils on the water of your burner (see pages 222–223) and light its candle as usual.

2 Then light the large candle and sit comfortably in your normal meditation posture for a few moments, enjoying the flickering light. Practise calm meditation (see pages 224–225) for a few minutes. Become aware of the effect of the essential oils you are vaporizing.

3 Bring your attention to the large candle. Notice the blue inner flame, the outer golden flame, how the candle flickers and seems alive. Take several deep breaths, experiencing the joyful fragrance of the essential oils.

4 Visualize the glowing light from the candle streaming into your heart, filling you with the simple joy of being alive. Your whole body feels light and vibrant. Visualize your body from the outside, glowing and luminous like crystal.

5 Be aware of the vaporized essential oils entering your nose and filling you with joy. As you watch your breath, rejoice that you are alive and appreciate the precious gift of life.

6 Imagine the light expanding to fill the room, then flowing out to fill the immediate environment, and then the whole world. Wherever the light goes, it brings people joy. Feel aware and joyful in the present moment.

7 Finish with a few minutes of watching your breath and take your time before getting up and moving on.

Subtle aromatherapy

Meditating with essential oils or practising meditation before giving an aromatherapy treatment is a good introduction to subtle aromatherapy. As you have seen, meditation helps you access your spiritual essence and when you use essential oils with the different meditations you also discover their subtle aspect. Working in this subtle way can have a profound healing effect on mind, body and spirit.

Subtle aromatherapy has several other manifestations such as using essential oils with crystals. You can also use essential oils to work with the chakras – or psychic energy centres – in the body, and with the aura that surrounds the physical body to cleanse blocked or negative energy. The subtle vibrational healing energy of essential oils complements the subtle energetic fields, centres and channels that exist within us all. The following pages offer clear, simple advice on how to use subtle aromatherapy in these various ways.

Subtle aromatherapy is another important aspect of holistic aromatherapy, and works harmoniously alongside aromatherapy massage, aromatic baths and all other aromatherapy treatments. In this way it is not seen in isolation as a separate discipline, but as a complement to the more tangible practices of aromatherapy. Any attempt to separate and compartmentalize the different aspects of aromatherapy works against the principle of holism.

Keeping an open mind

Working with the subtle side of yourself and with essential oils requires an open mind – but without losing sight of your common sense. You need to avoid New Age mumbo-jumbo, yet remain open to subtle, psychic

phenomena, which often cannot be empirically or scientifically demonstrated as 'real' and cannot usually offer a rational explanation for the way a healing effect is achieved.

Plants were often ascribed ruling planets by the ancient herbalists, and in modern aromatherapy we can also look at essential oils from a subtle, astrological perspective. In this way we can see how the characters or 'personalities' of essential oils are reflected in the different signs of the zodiac. This approach offers an alternative, subtle method of choosing essential oils for use in aromatherapy treatments, according to their astrological influences and dispositions.

Auric massage is a good way to end a massage session (see page 163). It is done without any physical contact.

Aromatherapy and crystals

Crystal healing is a therapy that heals weaknesses and imbalances in the subtle energy body. The crystals used are different varieties of rock crystals from the quartz family, composed of silicon dioxide. Crystal healers utilize their own innate healing powers and transmit these through the crystal into the client. The subtle healing energy of the therapist, amplified by the crystal's healing vibrations, is attracted to any areas of the client that need energy balancing or that require the release of blocked or negative energy.

Crystal healing is a sophisticated therapy, requiring thorough training in developing your own healing energy, and learning about crystals and how to use them. Nonetheless, crystals can be used in simple ways with aromatherapy, to great effect.

How to use crystals

• A simple way to connect with the healing energy of quartz crystals is to wear a crystal pendant next to your skin.

• Crystals enhance the subtle energy of essential oils when they are used in aromatherapy treatments. If you plan to give a massage, you can place a crystal in your bowl of blended essential oils. This will potentize the oils, making them more effective, so it is best to use only a 1 per cent dilution. Place the crystal in the bowl for five to ten minutes before you start. You can also use this method with bath oils.

• Different colours of quartz crystals – the most common being clear quartz, rose quartz, amethyst quartz, smoky quartz, blue quartz and green quartz – can be used with essential oils (or without) in chakra-balancing (see pages 254–262). The different crystals also have affinities with certain essential oils; for instance, rose quartz has an affinity with rose absolute and rose otto.

• If you are giving an aromatherapy massage to someone, you can place a crystal in each of the four corners of the area in which you are working (such as a futon on the floor). Alternatively, suggest that the person being massaged holds a crystal in each hand. In both of these instances try to use crystals as similar as possible in size and colour.

Using essential oils in combination with crystals and chakra healing are two of the applications of subtle aromatherapy.

Aromatherapy and the chakras

When you focus on the various sensations of the physical body in meditation, you may become aware of the presence of subtle flowing energies and energy centres. Subtle energy, called *prana* or *chi*, flows through subtle energy channels, and there are seven energy centres called chakras.

Although there is no direct physical proof of prana, channels and chakras, there are physical correlations with the chakras of nerve centres and endocrine glands. For example, the throat chakra correlates with the thyroid gland and the major nerves affecting the throat. For centuries, acupuncturists have inserted needles along subtle channels called meridians at specific points in order to effect healing. Practitioners of yoga and t'ai chi work with the prana that flows through the channels and chakras.

According to the Hindu Kundalini Yoga Chakra system, the subtle body has three main channels (like psychic nerves) called nadis and six chakras plus the thousand-petalled lotus at the crown of the head (often called the seventh chakra). The following pages describe the chakras and how you can use aromatherapy with them to effect subtle healing.

Using essential oils with the chakras

Essential oils can be used to restore balance and harmony to the chakras. Although the chakras are part of the subtle body, physical aromatherapy treatments such as massage and baths can nonetheless have a positive healing effect on them. Aromatherapy mood perfumes that include relevant essential oils can even be applied directly to some of the chakras.

If you give an aromatherapy massage and wish to do some chakra healing, ensure that you include appropriate essential oils. Ask the person – or yourself – to direct attention to the relevant chakra during the massage.

Rub a drop of essential oil between your hands to prepare yourself for doing auric massage.

Some of the chakras can be worked on directly by holding them or by auric massage (see page 163) over the relevant spot.

A more subtle method is to first select an appropriate essential oil, then put one drop on your palms and rub your hands together. Do auric massage all round the wider area of the chakra, working from the outside in, then directly over the chakra. Quartz crystals can be incorporated into the treatment, if desired.

The base chakra

The base chakra is also called the root chakra or *muladhara chakra*, and is located at the base of the spine, in the perineum (the area between the anus and the genitals). It has four petals and bears the yellow square of the earth element. The associated colour of this chakra is red.

The base chakra is concerned with how grounded you are, and how good your connection with the earth is. This can be described as how firmly you keep your feet on the ground. This means that the base chakra is about functioning well in the material world, dealing with physical needs and the basics of survival.

Base chakra.

Using essential oils

- Any essential oils that you find grounding, centring and strengthening are appropriate for the base chakra. Vetiver, myrrh, oak moss, benzoin, patchouli and violet leaf are especially effective.

- You can use essential oils associated with the base chakra to strengthen any weaknesses or to correct energy imbalances. For example, a dreamy person may become more grounded through base-chakra healing.

The sacral chakra

The sacral chakra is also called the navel chakra or *svadhisthana chakra*, and is located in the pubic region, between the navel and genitals. It has six red petals, bears a white lunar crescent and is associated with the water element.

The sacral chakra represents creative energy, sensual emotions and sexuality. It is associated with the reproductive organs, bladder, large and small intestines, appendix, sacrum and lumber vertebrae. The energy of the sacral chakra is about enjoyment of life, creation and pleasure.

Sacral chakra.

Using essential oils

• Any essential oils that you find sensual, erotic and warming are appropriate for the sacral chakra. Jasmine, rose absolute, sandalwood, clary sage, ylang ylang, cardamom and ginger are especially effective.

• You can use essential oils associated with the sacral chakra to strengthen any weaknesses or to correct energy imbalances. For example, a person who is frigid or who suffers from chronic cystitis, menstrual problems or chronic lower back pain may benefit from sacral-chakra healing.

The solar plexus chakra

The solar plexus chakra is also called the *manipura chakra*, and is located in the auric body directly over the physical solar plexus (the pit of the stomach). It has ten blue-grey petals and bears the red triangle of the fire element. The associated colour of the solar plexus chakra is yellow.

The solar plexus chakra is concerned with personal power and control, what it means to be a unique individual in this world, and how you make connections with others. It is associated with the stomach, pancreas, liver, gall bladder, spleen, adrenal glands and general digestion.

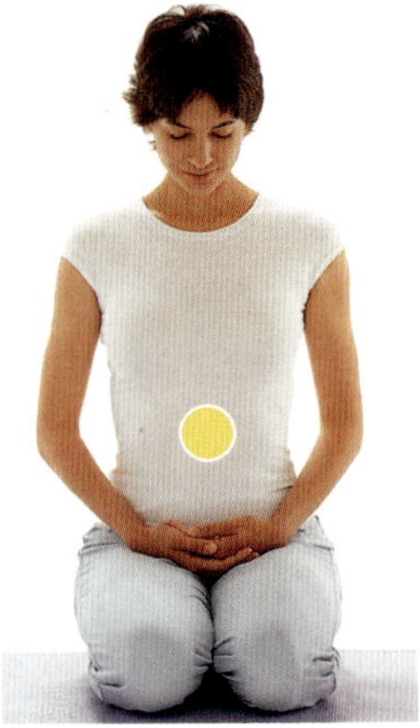

Solar plexus chakra.

Using essential oils

- Any essential oils that you find protecting, balancing and purifying are appropriate for the solar plexus chakra. Juniper, vetiver and geranium are especially effective.

- You can use essential oils associated with the solar plexus chakra to strengthen any weaknesses or to correct energy imbalances. For example, someone who lacks control over their life and who is angry, domineering or abusive may benefit from solar plexus chakra healing.

The heart chakra

The heart chakra is also called the *anahata chakra*, and is located in the auric body directly over the heart. It has 12 red petals and bears the blue-black six-pointed star of the air or wind element.

The heart chakra is concerned with the sympathetic and harmonious coexistence of body and spirit, and is associated with the heart and chest. It represents unconditional love, forgiveness, compassion and love of God or spiritual and divine love. When your heart chakra is balanced and strong, it is easy to express love to others.

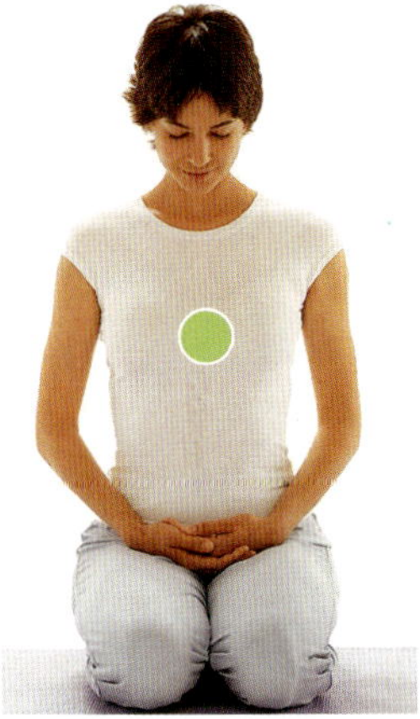

Heart chakra.

Using essential oils

- Any essential oils that you feel are associated with love are appropriate for the heart chakra. Rose otto, rose absolute, melissa, neroli, ylang ylang and bergamot are especially effective.

- You can use essential oils associated with the heart chakra to strengthen any weaknesses or to correct energy imbalances. For example, someone who is emotionally immature or a person with heart disease or breast cancer may benefit from heart-chakra healing.

The throat chakra

The throat chakra is also called the *vishuddha chakra* and is located in the auric body at the throat. It has 16 purple petals and bears a white circle representing the full moon of the space element. The colour associated with the throat chakra is blue-green.

The throat chakra is concerned with meaningful communication and self-expression. It is also the centre of the will. It is associated with the mouth, vocal cords, trachea and thyroid glands. When the throat chakra is strong and balanced, it is easy to express higher spiritual truths.

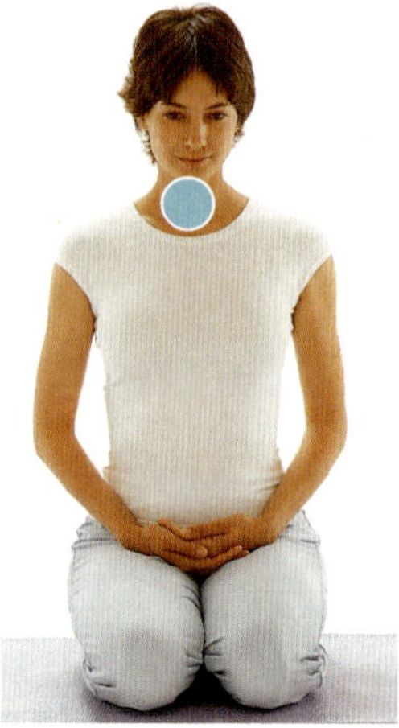

Throat chakra.

Using essential oils

- Any essential oils that you find aid your self-expression are suitable for the throat chakra. Roman chamomile, german chamomile, angelica root, rosewood and thyme are especially effective.

- You can use essential oils associated with the throat chakra to strengthen any weaknesses or to correct energy imbalances. The subtle and physical bodies can be seen operating together – for example, when someone has physical difficulty and an emotional, subtle problem at the same time, they may benefit from throat-chakra healing.

The third eye chakra

The third eye chakra is also called the *ajna chakra*, and is located in the auric body in the middle of the forehead, above and between the eyebrows. It has two grey-white petals and bears a pure-white circle symbolizing the subtle essence of consciousness.

The third eye chakra is concerned with intuition, wisdom and focusing on inner spiritual development. Regular meditation is an ideal way to 'open the third eye'. The third eye chakra is associated with the pineal and pituitary glands, the spinal cord, eyes, ears, nose and sinuses.

Third eye chakra.

Using essential oils

- Any essential oils that you find aid concentration, insight and intuition are appropriate for the third eye chakra. Helichrysum, rosemary, basil, holy basil, juniper and thyme are especially effective.

- You can use essential oils associated with the third eye chakra to strengthen any weaknesses or to correct energy imbalances. For example, a spiritually unevolved person who is only concerned with materialism may mature spiritually through third eye chakra healing.

The crown chakra

The crown chakra is also called the *sahasrana padma*, or 'thousand-petalled lotus', and is located at the crown of the head. The thousand petals are pink or white and bear the 50 Sanskrit syllables. The thousand-petalled lotus arises at the end of the central psychic channel in the pure realm where Kundalini and Shiva unite. Violet is the associated colour of the crown chakra. The crown chakra is concerned with the spiritual quest for enlightenment. Meditation and spiritual searching for the meaning of life help awaken this chakra. The cerebral cortex and nervous system are associated with the crown chakra.

Crown chakra.

Using essential oils

- Any essential oils that you find embody divine wisdom are appropriate for the crown chakra. Lavender, rosewood, frankincense, myrrh and sandalwood are especially effective.

- You can use essential oils associated with the crown chakra to strengthen any weaknesses or to correct energy imbalances. For example, someone who has lost the meaning of their life may benefit from crown-chakra healing.

Aura and psychic cleansing

In ancient times it was thought that anger, fear and arguments created negative psychic energies that adversely affected the atmosphere. Sometimes, long after the event, the atmosphere still felt desecrated and in need of psychic cleansing.

People confessed and purified their souls in churches and temples, which led to the burning of incense to psychically cleanse their atmospheres. Today you can use essential oils in a burner or vaporizer to psychically cleanse rooms with a negative atmosphere. Appropriate essential oils include juniper berry, frankincense, myrrh, cypress and pine.

The mystical and spiritual nature of the aura is represented in pictures of saints with haloes.

Because of its mystical, subtle nature, the human aura was depicted in the form of haloes around Western Christian saints, and as the wisdom flames surrounding Buddhist and Hindu deities. Ordinary mortals – less pure than saints and deities – needed spiritual purification in order for their auras to become radiant.

You can psychically cleanse your own aura by putting 2 drops of juniper berry on your hands, rubbing them together and brushing them all over your aura. This is particularly effective after being in a crowd of people.

Aromatherapy and astrology

The great 17th-century herbalist and apothecary Nicholas Culpeper wrote several books that combined herbal medicine and astrology. Of particular interest is Culpeper's method of ascribing a ruling planet to each plant. You can use this information to select essential oils according to their planetary influences.

Astrological aromatherapy is growing in popularity and utilizes a great deal of knowledge and ancient wisdom. Below is a simple guide to help you choose an emblematic essential oil according to your sun sign.

Aries

♈

Aries (the ram) runs from 21 March to 20 April. Aries is a fire sign and its ruling planet is Mars. Basil and black pepper have Mars as their ruling planet and their sharp cephalic qualities make either one a suitable emblematic essential oil for Aries.

Taurus

♉

Taurus (the bull) runs from the 21 April to 21 May. Taurus is an earth sign and its ruling planet is Venus. Palmarosa, ylang ylang and rose have Venus as their ruling planet. The sweet, grounded, balancing qualities of these florals make any one a suitable emblematic essential oil for Taurus.

Gemini

Gemini (the twins) runs from 22 May to 22 June. Gemini is an air sign and its ruling planet is Mercury. Mercury rules fennel, peppermint and thyme. These clean, bright cephalic essential oils all reflect the Gemini character.

Cancer

Cancer (the crab) runs from 23 June to 23 July. Cancer is a water sign and its ruling planet is the Moon. Chamomile is ruled by the Moon and the calm nurturing qualities of roman and german chamomile make either one a good emblematic essential oil for Cancer.

Leo

Leo (the lion) runs from 24 July to 23 August. Leo is a fire sign and its ruling planet is the Sun. Benzoin, myrrh, frankincense and helichrysum have the Sun as their ruling planet. Any one of these warm, sultry, resinous essential oils makes a good choice for Leo.

Virgo

Virgo (the young maiden) runs from 24 August to 23 September. Virgo is an earth sign and its ruling planet is Mercury. Lavender and myrtle have Mercury as their ruling planet and the calm, gentle innocence of these two essential oils makes either one a good choice for Virgo.

Libra

Libra (the pair of scales) runs from 24 September to 23 October. Libra is an air sign and its ruling planet is Venus. Venus is the ruling planet of geranium and the balanced poise of this sweet floral makes it the ideal emblematic essential oil for Libra.

Scorpio

Scorpio (the scorpion) runs from 24 October to 22 November. Scorpio is a water sign and its ruling planets are Mars and Pluto. Pluto is the ruling planet of patchouli and this musty, smoky, aphrodisiac essential oil well reflects the Scorpio character. The fiery sweetness of ginger ruled by Mars makes a good alternative emblematic essential oil for Scorpio.

Sagittarius

Sagittarius (the centaur) runs from 23 November to 21 December. Sagittarius is a fire sign and its ruling planet is Jupiter. Jupiter is the ruling planet of hyssop and this sweet, calming, spicy herbal essential oil is well suited to Sagittarius.

Capricorn

Capricorn (the goat) runs from 22 December to 20 January. Capricorn is an earth sign and its ruling planet is Saturn. Eucalyptus and vetiver are ruled by Saturn. Either clear eucalyptus or earthy, woody vetiver makes a good emblematic essential oil for Capricorn.

Aquarius

Aquarius (the water bearer) runs from 21 January to 19 February. Aquarius is an air sign and its ruling planets are Uranus and to a lesser extent Saturn. Uranus is the ruling planet of both sandalwood and violet leaf. Either one of these sensuous, deep, mysterious essential oils is ideal for Aquarius.

Pisces

Pisces (the fish) runs from 20 February to 20 March. Pisces is a water sign and its ruling planet is Neptune. Cypress is ruled by Neptune and this sacred, purifying and drying essential oil suits the Piscean character.

PART THREE

DIRECTORY OF ESSENTIAL OILS

How to use the directory

The directory of essential oils offers a concise overview of each essential oil. Throughout the book you have been reading about how to use all the different essential oils in specific circumstances and methods. This should have given you a good general picture of many of the commonly used essential oils. However, the directory gives you all the necessary information for each essential oil in an easy and accessible form.

When you first start to use essential oils, you will find the directory especially helpful, and it is a good idea to read the whole entry for each essential oil before you use it for the first time. This allows you to check whether there are any contraindications (uses that are advised against) – for example, if you have very sensitive skin, you will discover which essential oils to avoid or use only in tiny amounts. You will also gain a sense of the overall 'personality' of the essential oil in question, and learn which other essential oils it blends well with. The main therapeutic properties of each essential oil are also given – see the glossary of therapeutic terms (pages 386–389) for explanations of any terms with which you are unfamiliar.

How the essential oils are listed

Many directories use a straightforward alphabetical listing system. Although this enables you to find each entry quickly, such a system has limitations. This directory lists essential oils according to type – for instance, all the floral or flower essential oils are listed together. This is useful because many of the citrus essential oils, for example, have overlapping actions and similar qualities. Listing them together in the same section allows you to compare all the essential oils of each type, which helps you choose the most appropriate essential oil.

The directory

The directory lists the essential oils in the following order:

- Flowers
- Herbs
- Resins and roots
- Citruses
- Trees and woods
- Spices
- Grasses, seeds and shrubs
- Exotic essential oils
- Hazardous essential oils

The botanical name and family are given for each essential oil. You will notice that sometimes there are several botanical names or two families listed, because some essential oils are derived from plants that have several different cultivars, species or chemotypes. Listing the different options enables you to know all the names of the appropriate essential oils that are suitable for use in aromatherapy.

Essential oils in common use

Flowers

Lavender

(Lavandula vera, Lavandula angustifolia, Lavandula officinalis)

Family: Labiatae or Lamiaceae

Description: Lavender is a perennial, bushy shrub with silver, grey or green linear leaves and purple, violet or blue spiky flowers. The essential oil is steam-distilled from the flowering tops.

Countries of origin: France, Bulgaria, England, Morocco, Australia, Hungary, Spain, Tasmania

Characteristics: Lavender has clean, fresh, floral top notes and subtle, green, herbaceous undertones. It blends well with most other essential oils, especially other florals, citruses and herbs.

Main therapeutic properties: Analgesic, anti-depressant, antiseptic, anti-viral, cytophylactic, decongestant, deodorant, emmenagogue, hypotensive, nervine, sedative, tonic.

Lavender is by far the most popular, versatile and widely used of all essential oils. At first lavender sounds too good to be true: a cure-all with a reputation lasting for thousands of years. However, many of lavender's properties are due to its prime actions of balancing and normalizing body functions and emotions. Overall, lavender is soothing, calming and relaxing.

It is used to great effect in massage and bath oils for muscular aches and pains. A few drops in the bath or a drop or two on the pillow help to combat insomnia. Lavender is also valuable in treating colds and flu. Not only does it counteract the viruses causing the infection, but it relieves many of the symptoms. In these cases, lavender is best used in steam inhalations.

*Lavender (*Lavandula angustifolia*)*

A cold compress of lavender or a couple of drops rubbed into the temples relieves headaches. Lavender repels insects and, if you are bitten, a drop rubbed over the bite will remove the stinging. Lavender also heals minor burns with incredible and speedy effectiveness. It is also good used in an antiseptic wash to help heal minor cuts and burns. Lavender is used extensively in skin care and perfumery, where its fresh, delicate, floral fragrance is comfortingly familiar.

Psychologically, lavender is soothing, balancing and calming, helping with mood swings, depression and PMT. Its calming, relaxing effects can be used to facilitate meditation. Lavender's balancing qualities can restore harmony to the aura and help to balance the chakras.

Contraindications: Avoid in early pregnancy, especially if there is a history of miscarriage.

German chamomile

(Matricaria chamomilla, Matricaria recutita)

Family: Compositae or Asteraceae

Description: German chamomile is an annual herb with delicate feathery leaves and simple, daisylike white and yellow flowers on single stems. The viscous, inky-blue essential oil is steam-distilled from the flower heads.

Countries of origin: England, Hungary, Bulgaria, Spain

Characteristics: German chamomile has an intense odour that some people find overwhelming until it is diluted. The fragrance has strong, sweet, green herbal top notes with an almost fruity but slightly bitter undertone. It blends well with most other florals, citruses and herbs, and also with patchouli, frankincense, petitgrain and benzoin.

Main therapeutic properties: Analgesic, anti-allergenic, anti-inflammatory, antiseptic, anti-spasmodic, anti-viral, digestive, diuretic, emmenagogue, hepatic, nervine, sedative.

German chamomile is the first choice to treat inflammation. The presence of azulene – which gives german chamomile its deep-blue colour – makes this essential oil a powerful anti-inflammatory. Avoid buying it if the blue is turning to green, as this is a sign of ageing and means the essential oil is no longer fresh. Overall, german chamomile is soothing, calming and balancing.

It is especially valuable in treating cystitis. Hot compresses over the abdomen relieve the hot, burning symptoms and calm the nerves, allaying

*German chamomile (*Matricaria chamomilla*)*

the anxiety and exhaustion that often accompany cystitis. Drinking copious quantities of chamomile tea alongside the aromatherapy compresses is of great benefit, and the two forms of chamomile work in harmonious synergy.

Skin allergies, such as eczema and other rashes, respond well to german chamomile, which should be mixed into a base cream or lotion. Avoid using base oils, as these can aggravate skin allergies, worsening the symptoms of hot, red, dry flaky skin. The gentle action of german chamomile calms, heals and soothes the skin condition while simultaneously alleviating the causes of the allergy.

Psychologically, german chamomile is calming and soothing, especially for irritability and depression, and helps to cool the heat of anger. However, this essential oil does need to be blended carefully with others to make it appealing and aesthetic.

Contraindications: Avoid in early pregnancy, especially if there is a history of miscarriage.

Roman chamomile
(Anthemis nobilis, Chamaemelum nobile)

Family: Compositae or Asteraceae

Description: Roman chamomile is a perennial herb with a low-growing creeping habit, delicate feathery leaves and daisylike white flowers carried on the plant's many hairy stems. The essential oil is steam-distilled from the flowering tops.

Countries of origin: France, England, Belgium, Hungary

Roman chamomile (Anthemis nobils)

Characteristics: Roman chamomile has hints of sweet, fruity apple among bitter, herbaceous undertones and warm, flowery, grassy top notes. It blends well with most other florals and herbs, and also with bergamot, frankincense, verbena and nutmeg.
Main therapeutic properties: Analgesic, antiseptic, anti-spasmodic, carminative, digestive, diuretic, emmenagogue, febrifuge, hepatic, nervine, sedative, stomachic.

Roman chamomile overlaps somewhat with german chamomile and with lavender. A useful tip to help you know which of these essential oils might be best for treating specific aches and pains is to choose lavender for sharp, piercing, sudden pain, german chamomile for hot, red pain, and roman chamomile for dull, persistent pain. Roman chamomile is especially good to use with children and infants, helping most of their common ailments, as it is both gentle and effective and safe. Overall, roman chamomile is calming, soothing and comforting.

One of the best essential oils to choose for menstrual conditions, roman chamomile soothes PMT, helps to relieve menstrual cramps and calms the mood swings and weepiness associated with menstruation. Baths, compresses and mood perfumes are all suitable methods. Roman chamomile is often used in massage oils because it is a traditional favourite for promoting relaxation, reducing muscular tension and helping stress-related conditions, such as nervous tension and insomnia. It is also useful in skin care, having a strong affinity with people with fair complexions and blonde hair.

Psychologically, roman chamomile is calming, balancing and deeply relaxing, and has a gentle, restorative effect. It makes a good choice to use for calming meditations, and roman chamomile has an affinity with the throat chakra.

Geranium

(Pelargonium gravolens)

Family: Geraniaceae

Description: Geranium is an aromatic, perennial, hairy plant with serrated leaves and flowers varying from light pink through to deep rose, magenta or red. The essential oil is steam-distilled from the flowers, leaves and stalks.

Countries of origin: Rèunion, China, Egypt, South Africa, Morocco

Characteristics: Geranium has light, lemon-fresh, green herbal top notes and soft, rosy, sweet floral undertones. It blends well with many other essential oils, especially bergamot, lavender, basil, rosemary, black pepper, rose, neroli, sandalwood, rosewood, juniper, lemon, patchouli, jasmine and orange.

Main therapeutic properties: Anti-depressant, antiseptic, astringent, cicatrizant, deodorant, diuretic, haemostatic, tonic, vulnerary.

Geranium is the great balancer of essential oils, due to it being an adrenal cortex stimulant, and it helps to regulate hormones and moods alike. One of the most useful essential oils to detoxify the lymphatic system and help eliminate cellulite, geranium is often included in lymphatic drainage massage blends. It also helps heal wounds quickly, and makes a good deodorant, both for personal hygiene and for freshening rooms. Overall, geranium is balancing, uplifting and refreshing.

Because geranium smells a little like rose – but is much cheaper – it is used in the perfume industry to 'extend' rose. The lovely floral fragrance makes geranium a valuable skin-care essential oil, and it is helpful in balancing sebum production.

Geranium is especially good for menstrual problems as it balances the hormones. This quality, combined with its anti-depressant and uplifting qualities, means that geranium might be helpful in massage blends for those

*Geranium (*Pelargonium gravolens*)*

women who have difficulty becoming pregnant. It is also useful for those undergoing the menopause.

Psychologically, geranium creates a sense of security and comfort, and is gently uplifting and balancing. It is reputed to strengthen the flow of subtle energy, or chi, and is one of the most valuable essential oils in treating anxiety associated with nervous debility. It is useful in mood perfumes to bring about a balanced harmony and to counteract excessive mood swings.

Ylang ylang

(Cananga odorata)

Family: Amonaceae

Description: The cananga tree is a tall evergreen with branches that bend down. All year round it produces quantities of large yellow and white flowers with a powerful, fragrant scent. The essential oil is steam- and water-distilled from the flowers. There are several different grades of ylang ylang that are produced, with ylang ylang extra generally considered the best for use in aromatherapy.

Countries of origin: Madagascar, Malaysia, Indonesia, Rèunion

Characteristics: Ylang ylang has intensely sweet, almond, floral, tropical top notes and slightly cloying, exotic, woody, balsamic undertones. It blends well with most other florals and citruses, and also with verbena, nutmeg, rosewood, patchouli, clove, vetiver and sandalwood.

Main therapeutic properties: Anti-depressant, antiseptic, aphrodisiac, hypotensive, sedative.

Ylang ylang means 'flower of flowers' in Malayan, and it is much used in the perfume industry for its voluptuous, exotic fragrance. One of its most important aromatherapy uses is in helping to reduce high blood pressure, especially if this is accompanied by heart palpitations. Ylang ylang also treats anxiety, anger, shock and fear, helping to slow over-rapid breathing and reducing the 'fight-or-flight' syndrome. Overall, ylang ylang is soothing, erotic and euphoric.

In skin care, ylang ylang is valued for its pleasing fragrance and is especially suited to oily skin. Traditionally the flowers are macerated in coconut oil and used as a hair dressing, and it makes a good addition to base shampoo and conditioner. When used in a massage oil, ylang ylang can help to treat frigidity and impotence. In a mood perfume, its sweet voluptuous

Ylang ylang (Cananga odorata)

and erotic fragrance can help to release inhibitions and bring out fiery passion. Ylang ylang is particularly suited to women and helps them find their inner femininity, confidence and sensuality.

Use only small amounts of ylang ylang and not for long periods of time, otherwise the perfume can become sickly and heavy, and may cause headaches and nausea. Blending it with lemon, bergamot and other fresh-smelling essential oils lightens the fragrance, and this is strongly recommended. Ylang ylang is good in an evening bath to promote relaxation and aid sleep. It is also valuable in treating depression, especially when there is a lot of nervous tension. It is one of the best essential oils to use with meditation to counteract anger.

Psychologically, ylang ylang calms, uplifts, creates a sense of peace and aids self-expression of repressed inner feelings.

Rose absolute

(Rosa centifolia, Rosa damascena, Rosa gallica)

Family: Rosaceae

Description: Rose bushes are so familiar that they need little description. *R. centifolia* produces pink flowers, *R. gallica* dark-red flowers and *R. damascena* pink flowers. The absolute is made by solvent extraction from the rose petals.

*Rose (*Rosa gallica*)*

Countries of origin: France, Bulgaria, Turkey, Morocco, Italy, China

Characteristics: Rose absolute is viscous, varies in colour from browny-red to greeny-orange and has deep, sweet, floral top notes with dusky, honeyed, rosy undertones. It blends well with the other florals, and also with bergamot, clary sage, sandalwood, rosewood, melissa, frankincense, palmarosa, patchouli, clove, myrrh and benzoin.

Main therapeutic properties: Anti-depressant, antiseptic, anti-spasmodic, aphrodisiac, emmenagogue, hepatic, nervine, sedative, tonic, uterine.

Rose absolute is less expensive than rose otto (see below), although it is still costly. Because it is extracted with solvents, some aromatherapists consider it inferior to rose otto. However, it is quite safe to use in small quantities and, because the aroma is strong, 1 or 2 per cent dilution is quite sufficient.

It has a stronger, more passionate fragrance than the more delicate, subtle rose otto, and this information can help you decide which rose you would like to use in different circumstances. Other than the difference in fragrance, the qualities of rose absolute and rose otto overlap to a great extent, so see the entry for rose otto below for further details of rose absolute.

Rose otto

(Rosa centifolia, Rosa damascena, Rosa gallica)

Family: Rosaceae

Description: Rose bushes are so familiar that they need little description. *R. centifolia* produces pink flowers, *R. gallica* dark-red flowers and *R. damascena* pink flowers. The essential oil, also called otto or attar, is steam- or water-distilled from the rose petals.

Countries of origin: France, Bulgaria, Turkey, Morocco, Italy, China

Characteristics: Rose otto varies in colour from pale yellow to clear, and is sometimes solid at room temperature, though if you hold the bottle for a few minutes the warmth of your

*Rose (*Rosa damascena*)*

hand turns it into a viscous liquid. It has light, sweet, floral top notes with deep, almost spicy, rosy undertones. Rose otto blends well with other florals, and also with bergamot, clary sage, sandalwood, rosewood, melissa, frankincense, palmarosa, patchouli, clove, myrrh and benzoin.

Main therapeutic properties: Anti-depressant, antiseptic, anti-spasmodic, aphrodisiac, emmenagogue, hepatic, nervine, sedative, tonic, uterine.

Rose otto has often been described as the 'queen of flowers', and for many aromatherapists there is no finer essential oil. Rose comforts the heart in grief and helps the bereaved, as well as those grieving for the end of a relationship. Rose is a tonic of the physical heart and also lifts the spirits, allays anxiety and is generally nurturing. Overall, rose is quite exquisite; it is tender, uplifting and soothing.

Rose is the first choice in treating many of the female reproductive problems, helping with PMT, menopausal symptoms, regulation of periods. It may even help women who have problems conceiving, and there are several anecdotal stories and aromatherapy case histories where rose has seemed to help a woman conceive after other more traditional aids to conception have not succeeded. This is partialy explained by the fact that rose has a tonic, purifying effect on the uterus. Its aphrodisiac qualities mirror its physical action, and it helps women to express their femininity and sexuality by alleviating anxiety and nervous tension and inspiring a confident sensuality. Rose also helps those suffering from postnatal depression. It is best used in a massage oil or mood perfume for these conditions, as it is very expensive.

Its valuable skin-care qualities and delicious fragrance make rose a good choice in caring for the skin. Mixed into lotions and creams, it treats mature, dry, inflamed and sensitive skins particularly, but is useful for all skin types. Rose makes a wonderful and special addition to massage oils and bath oils, and is extensively used in mood perfumes. It is gentle enough to use in tiny quantities with children.

Psychologically, rose alleviates sorrow, sadness and disappointment, gently supporting you until the mood shifts. It also lessens anxiety and grief, and strengthens the inner spirit. It is associated with the heart chakra, and it opens and heals the heart to love oneself and others.

Contraindications: Avoid in early pregnancy, especially if there is a history of miscarriage.

Neroli

(Citrus bigardia, Citrus aurantium var. *amara)*

Family: Rutaceae

Description: The bitter orange is an evergreen tree with a smooth grey trunk, dark-green leaves, small fruit and deeply fragrant white flowers. The essential oil is steam-distilled from the flowers.

Countries of origin: France, Egypt, Tunisia, Morocco, Italy, Algeria

Characteristics: Neroli is also called orange-flower blossom or orange blossom. The pale-yellow essential oil has delicate, fresh, floral top notes and warm, heady, bitter-sweet undertones. Neroli blends well with almost all other essential oils, especially lavender, melissa, rose, jasmine, frankincense and bergamot.

Main therapeutic properties: Anti-depressant, antiseptic, anti-spasmodic, aphrodisiac, cicatrizant, sedative, tonic.

Neroli is the best choice to treat anxiety and other problems of an emotional or psychological origin. Traditionally used in wedding bouquets, it calms and soothes the nerves before major events. Neroli also helps those with long-term, chronic anxiety and can help to alleviate panic attacks, hysteria and shock. Overall, it is calming, soothing and uplifting.

Particularly valuable in skin care, neroli helps the regeneration of healthy new skin cells and has a noticeable rejuvenating effect on mature skins. It is good for all skin types, but especially valuable for mature, dry and sensitive skins. The hauntingly beautiful fragrance of this essential oil makes it a wonderful addition to all skin-care products, massage oils and bath oils, and mood perfumes. As neroli is very expensive, the methods listed above are the most effective ways to use this lovely essential oil.

Neroli is also useful for treating diarrhoea. Its anti-spasmodic properties relieve spasm in the smooth muscles of the intestines, while its calming

*Neroli (*Citrus aurantium)

effect relieves the anxiety or shock that can cause or aggravate diarrhoea. A few drops of neroli in a night-time bath can relieve insomnia. A wonderful, gentle and subtle aphrodisiac, neroli is especially useful for those who are nervous of sexual encounters.

Psychologically, neroli is calming and uplifting, especially for those who are easily agitated, emotionally unstable or insecure, and it eases the intensity of strong emotions. Neroli is often associated with the qualities of innocence and purity, and it inspires creativity. Neroli is a useful aid to meditation and facilitates spiritual healing.

Jasmine

(Jasminum grandiflorum, Jasminum officinale)

Family: Oleaceae

Description: Jasmine is a perennial climbing shrub with fine, small green or variegated leaves and delicate flowers, usually white, although they can be pink or yellow. Jasmine is a dark orange-brown, viscous absolute produced by solvent extraction from the flowers.

Countries of origin: France, India, Morocco, Italy, China, Egypt

Characteristics: Jasmine has a powerful, heady fragrance that some people find overwhelming, although once diluted it becomes more subtle. The perfume is strongest at night, hence its Indian name of 'queen of the night', so night-time is also the best occasion to harvest the flowers. Jasmine has sweet, floral, exotic top notes and heady, warm,

Jasmine (Jasminum officinale *'Affine')*

honeyed undertones. It blends well with the citruses, and also with clary sage, rose, sandalwood, rosewood, frankincense, neroli, cypress, verbena and melissa.

Main therapeutic properties: Analgesic, anti-depressant, anti-inflammatory, antiseptic, anti-spasmodic, aphrodisiac, galactagogue, nervine, sedative, tonic, uterine.

Jasmine is the best choice to inspire confidence, because it is emotionally warming and uplifting. It is a powerful anti-depressant of a stimulating nature, and all these qualities combine to help those suffering from lack of confidence, vacillation, indecision and the lethargy born of depression. Mood perfumes and massage oils are the best ways to use it, as jasmine is very costly. Overall, it is intoxicating, euphoric and aphrodisiac.

Like rose, jasmine is useful in treating the female reproductive system. It is excellent to use during childbirth in massage over the lower back and abdomen in the early stages of labour, and alleviates pain, strengthens contractions and helps to expel the placenta. Jasmine also strengthens the male sexual organs and can be used to treat enlargement of the prostrate gland. Unsurprisingly, it is one of the most powerful aphrodisiacs, and can help couples to reignite their sexual spark.

The lovely floral fragrance makes jasmine useful in skin care, especially for hot, dry, sensitive, inflamed and mature skins. It is best used in very small amounts (1 per cent dilution is ideal), as the perfume can be overwhelming if too much is added.

Psychologically, jasmine inspires euphoria, helping restore confidence and optimism. It warms and opens the emotions, helping those who are habitually repressed. Jasmine is associated with intuitive wisdom and perception, so it is a useful aid for insight meditation, releasing inhibitions and liberating the imagination.

Contraindications: Avoid in early pregnancy, especially if there is a history of miscarriage.

Violet leaf
(Viola odorata)

Family: Violaceae

Description: Violet is a small, tender perennial with heart-shaped green leaves and fragrant, violet-blue flowers. The absolute is obtained by solvent extraction from the concrete, which is in turn obtained by solvent extraction of the leaves. Occasionally an absolute from the flowers is also available.

Countries of origin: France, Egypt, Italy

Characteristics: Violet leaf is dark green and viscous with subtle, green, freshly mown-hay top notes and elusive, heady floral undertones. It blends well with most other florals, and also with lemon, bergamot, cumin, basil and clary sage.

Violet leaf (Viola odorata)

Main therapeutic properties: Analgesic, anti-depressant, anti-inflammatory, antiseptic, decongestant, diuretic, sedative.

Violet leaf is deep and mysterious, but is one of the least used of the florals, partly because of its high cost. It helps treat menstrual pain and irregularities; it is also very calming and helps to relieve insomnia. Violet leaf is useful for treating skin problems such as thread veins and eczema. The scent of violets was reputed to 'comfort and strengthen the heart', and it is good in a mood perfume or massage oil to help overcome emotional grief. Blended with rose, violet leaf has a tonic effect on the heart. Overall, it is soporific, tranquil and comforting.

Psychologically, violet leaf is strengthening and calming, helping to alleviate anxiety, insecurity, dizziness, headaches and nervous exhaustion. It has been used with great success by doctors on psychologically disturbed patients, which suggests that violet leaf is most effective in calming a troubled mind. It is good in meditations to deal with grief.

Contraindications: Use in moderation – no more than 4 drops in the bath and no more than 2 per cent in massage oils.

Herbs

Sweet marjoram

(Origanum majorana, Majorana hortensis)

Family: Labiatae or Lamiaceae

Description: Sweet marjoram is a tender, bushy perennial herb with dark-green leaves, a hairy stem and clusters of white flowers. The essential oil is steam-distilled from the leaves and flowering tops.

Countries of origin: France, Bulgaria, Turkey, Morocco, Italy, Tunisia, Hungary, Egypt, Poland

Characteristics: Marjoram has spicy, herbaceous top notes and warm, woody, camphoraceous undertones. It blends well with most other herbs and also with lavender, bergamot, cypress, chamomile, juniper and eucalyptus.

Main therapeutic properties: Analgesic, anaphrodisiac, antiseptic, anti-spasmodic, carminative, digestive, emmenagogue, hypotensor, sedative, tonic, vasodilator.

*Sweet marjoram (*Origanum majorana*)*

Marjoram is the great comforter of essential oils and helps with pain on all levels. It is warming and comforting, and is good for grief, soothing and giving solace to the heart and emotions. However, the effect of marjoram can be a little numbing, and so this essential oil must be used with care and discretion and not for too long periods of time, so that it does not end up dulling the senses. Overall, marjoram is fortifying, warming and comforting.

Useful for relaxing tight, stiff muscles and for easing rheumatic pain, marjoram is excellent in massage and gently dilates the blood vessels to produce a local warming effect. It is also good in the bath, but smells nicer when blended with lavender or other sweeter essential oils. Used in a hot compress, marjoram relieves menstrual cramps, and in a local abdominal massage it relieves flatulence and constipation.

Psychologically, marjoram acts like a second skin, calming over-sensitivity and easing stress and nervous tension. It comforts the sad and lonely, and is good for those who are celibate as it reduces sexual desire. Marjoram helps the flow of subtle energy throughout the body, and brings out hidden strength and endurance.

Contraindications: Avoid throughout pregnancy.

Rosemary

(Rosmarinus officinalis, Rosmarinus coronarium)

Family: Labiatae or Lamiaceae

Description: Rosemary is an aromatic, perennial shrubby bush with silver-green leaves and distinctive, prolific sky-blue flowers. The essential oil is steam-distilled from the flowering tops.

Countries of origin: France, Spain, Portugal, Tunisia

Characteristics: Rosemary has sharp, fresh, green top notes and herbaceous, balsamic, camphoraceous undertones. It blends well with most spices, and also with lavender, bergamot, basil, frankincense, juniper, pine, thyme, verbena, melissa, cedarwood and petitgrain.

Main therapeutic properties: Analgesic, antiseptic, anti-spasmodic, astringent, carminative, digestive, diuretic, hepatic, hypertensor, rubefacient, stimulant, tonic.

Rosemary is the strongest cephalic essential oil, and scientifically proves correct the old folk saying 'Rosemary for remembrance'. One drop of rosemary mixed with 2 drops of neroli can be dabbed on the wrists before taking an examination (neroli calms the nerves and rosemary strengthens the mind and increases creativity). Overall, rosemary is reviving, refreshing and strengthening.

Excellent in massage, rosemary is used for relaxing tight, over-worked muscles, relieving fluid retention and detoxifying the lymphatic system. It is reputed to help hair growth, makes a good tonic for the scalp and helps to prevent dandruff. As a powerful antiseptic, when used in a burner rosemary can help to prevent the spread of airborne infections. It is also a liver tonic and a few drops in a morning bath can help to relieve a hangover.

Psychologically, rosemary is stimulating, purifying and protecting. It is a traditional ingredient of incense and aids meditation, keeping the mind clear and alert.

*Rosemary (*Rosmarinus officinalis*)*

Rosemary is a psychic protector, a symbol of friendship and love and, as a reminder of love and death, it was traditionally burned at weddings and funerals. It is associated with the third eye chakra, assisting clear thought and inner vision.

Contraindications: Avoid throughout pregnancy and do not use on those who suffer from epilepsy.

Clary sage

(Salvia sclaria)

Family: Labiatae or Lamiaceae

Description: Clary sage is a tall biennial or perennial herb with big, hairy, purple-green leaves and prolific, small blue-violet or white flowers. The essential oil is steam-distilled from the flowering tops and leaves.

Countries of origin: France, Russia, Morocco, England, America

Characteristics: Clary sage has sweet, musky, herbaceous top notes and nutty, almost floral undertones. It blends well with the citruses, and also with lavender, coriander, cardamom, frankincense, jasmine, pine, geranium, cedarwood and palmarosa.

Main therapeutic properties: Anti-convulsive, anti-depressant, antiseptic, anti-spasmodic, aphrodisiac, astringent, carminative, digestive, emmenagogue, hypotensor, nervine, sedative, tonic.

Clary sage is the most euphoric of the essential oils, and it can produce an almost druglike narcotic 'high'. Combined with its pronounced anti-depressant qualities, this euphoria makes clary sage a powerful aid to easing depression, melancholia, anxiety, stress and chronic general dissatisfaction. Overall, clary sage is intoxicating, sensuous and uplifting.

One of the most valuable essential oils in treating menstrual cramps, clary sage in baths or hot compresses on the abdomen relaxes mind and body, eases pain and its oestrogenic action helps to bring on and regulate menstruation. Clary sage also helps to treat menopausal symptoms, and can be used in childbirth in a massage oil during early labour. It is an aphrodisiac, especially good for those who are so stressed that their sexuality has diminished.

Clary sage is good in a massage oil over the chest and back to help relieve asthma. Added to shampoo or massaged into the scalp, it can prevent dandruff and balances sebum levels, so it is beneficial for all skin and hair types. Clary sage can also help to reduce excessive sweating when used in a footbath or bath.

Psychologically, clary sage is deeply relaxing, euphoric and revitalizing. Used in small quantities, it is a useful aid to meditation, and facilitates dream work by encouraging powerful and vivid dreams. Clary sage helps strengthen subtle energies and divine inspiration.

Contraindications: Avoid throughout pregnancy. Do not use before or after drinking alcohol.

*Clary sage (*Salvia sclaria*)*

*Melissa (*Melissa officinalis*)*

Melissa
(Melissa officinalis)

Family: Labiatae or Lamiaceae

Description: Melissa is also called lemon balm or balm, and is a sweet-scented, perennial bushy herb with green serrated leaves and small white or pink flowers. The essential oil is steam-distilled from the flowering tops and leaves.

Countries of origin: France, Germany, Italy, Spain, England

Characteristics: Melissa has warm, fresh, lemon-sherbet top notes and sweet, radiant, delicate, balsamic, herbal undertones. It blends well with the florals and citruses, especially lavender, rose and geranium, and also with myrtle.

Main therapeutic properties: Anti-depressant, antiseptic, anti-spasmodic, anti-viral, bactericidal, carminative, febrifuge, hypotensor, nervine, sedative, tonic.

Melissa is one of the best essential oils for shock, depression, grief and anxiety; it enhances life, gladdens the spirit and chases away dark thoughts.

It helps you find inner contentment by calming a troubled mind, strengthening the emotions and surrounding you with joy. Melissa has been called the 'elixir of life', which admirably describes this lovely essential oil. Overall, melissa is revitalizing, uplifting and fortifying.

The tonic properties of melissa benefit the cardiovascular system, lowering high blood pressure, having a general tonic effect on the heart and regulating over-rapid breathing. Melissa also has a regulating effect on the digestive system, reducing cramps and helping with nausea and indigestion, especially when aggravated by stress. It relieves stress, insomnia and nervous tension. Melissa is incredibly expensive, so is best used sparingly in mood perfumes and massage oils.

Psychologically, melissa is sedative, uplifting and deeply calming, and is good for meditation, especially to counteract anger and allay grief. It strengthens the heart chakra and inspires universal love and divine joy.

Contraindications: Avoid if you have very sensitive skin and always use it in small amounts – no more than 1 per cent.

Basil, holy basil

(Ocimum basilicum, Ocimum sanctum)

Family: Labiatae or Lamiaceae

Description: Basil is a tender, aromatic annual herb with green leaves and small white or pink flowers. The essential oil is steam-distilled from the leaves and flowering tops.

Countries of origin: France, Egypt, Comoro Islands, India, Italy, Bulgaria, Hungary

Characteristics: Basil has sweet, green, herbaceous top notes and spicy, liquorice/aniseed undertones. Holy basil has a similar aroma, but with more depth. Basil blends well with most other herbs, and also with lavender, geranium, bergamot, lime, lemon, frankincense and pine.

*Basil (*Ocimum basilicum*)*

Main therapeutic properties: Antiseptic, anti-spasmodic, carminative, cephalic, digestive, emmenagogue, febrifuge, nervine, tonic.

Basil has a more subtle, less sharp cephalic effect than rosemary and is the first choice for relieving intellectual fatigue, when the mind is weak or indecisive. It is useful for nervous disorders, and for those in need of protection, and is especially suited to those suffering from debilitating illness. Overall, basil is restorative, fortifying and clearing.

Although basil's properties can help with digestive and menstrual problems and provide a useful alternative to other essential oils, it is best used for its excellent tonic effect on the nerves and mind. This is because prolonged or over-use of basil is not recommended. Basil is also better blended to avoid associations with Italian cooking – you don't want to end up smelling like a pizza!

Psychologically, basil is awakening, uplifting and strengthening. It is good in meditations to clear the mind and stimulate mental activity. It is a subtle psychic protector, and its gentle anti-depressive and tonic effects make it suitable for those with long-term psychic exhaustion.

Contraindications: Avoid throughout pregnancy and if you have very sensitive skin. Use in small amounts – no more than 2 per cent – and avoid prolonged use.

Thyme

(Thymus vulgaris)

Family: Labiatae or Lamiaceae

Description: Thyme is a perennial aromatic shrub with small green-grey leaves and violet or white flowers. The essential oil is steam- or water-distilled from the flowering tops and leaves. There are many varieties of thyme available, but try to purchase only linalol thyme, which is the most gentle and non-toxic.

Countries of origin: France, Morocco, Spain, Greece, Algeria, Germany, America

Characteristics: Thyme has intense, fresh, green, herbal top notes and sweet, spicy medicinal undertones. It blends well with most other herbs, and also with lavender, bergamot, lemon, pine, cypress and black pepper.

Main therapeutic properties: Antiseptic, anti-spasmodic, bactericide, carminative, digestive, emmenagogue, expectorant, hypertensive, stimulant, tonic.

Thyme is one of the best essential oils to use for convalescence and infection prevention. Its use in lymphatic drainage massage helps increase the production of white corpuscles, strengthening the body's defence mechanisms. Thyme is especially good against respiratory infections. Thyme increases and regulates the appetite and has a tonic effect on the digestion. It is restorative, reviving and stimulating.

*Thyme (*Thymus vulgaris*)*

Although classified as a stimulant, thyme has an overall balancing quality that makes it excellent for those suffering from chronic fatigue, as it both enlivens and calms as the body requires. It is good in baths, burners and massage, but is best blended to balance its strong herbal fragrance.

Psychologically, thyme is fortifying, protecting and energizing. It is useful for those who are prone to lethargy and melancholia, stimulating both physical vigour and emotional and spiritual strength. Thyme can help those who are 'spaced out', and it has a psychic grounding quality.

Contraindications: Avoid throughout pregnancy. Use only in small amounts on the skin and avoid prolonged use.

Peppermint

(Mentha piperita)

Family: Labiatae or Lamiaceae

Description: Peppermint is a perennial herb with green stems and leaves and white flowers. There are many other types of mint, some of which are also used in aromatherapy. The essential oil is steam-distilled from the flowering tops and leaves.

Countries of origin: America, England, Bulgaria, Morocco, Italy, China, Tasmania, Holland, Spain, Germany, Brazil

Characteristics: Peppermint has fresh, bright, penetrating, minty top notes and sharp, grassy, camphoraceous undertones. It blends well with lavender, rosemary, eucalyptus and lemon.

Main therapeutic properties: Analgesic, antiseptic, anti-spasmodic, astringent, carminative, cephalic, decongestant, digestive, expectorant, febrifuge, nervine, stimulant, stomachic.

*Peppermint (*Mentha x piperita*)*

Peppermint is one of the best essential oils for all types of digestive upsets and should be used in a massage oil, gently massaged over the abdomen in a clockwise direction. Drinking peppermint tea at the same time creates a harmonious synergy between the two forms of peppermint. Overall, peppermint is refreshing, stimulating and restorative.

Combined with lavender, peppermint helps prevent colds and flu. Use no more than 3 drops in a bath, massage oil or inhalation. Peppermint is also good in a facial steam to deeply cleanse and decongest the skin, especially if acne is present. Combined with lavender in cold compresses, peppermint relieves headaches and migraines.

Psychologically, peppermint is bold, promoting clarity and alertness. A few drops of peppermint sniffed from a tissue can alleviate the symptoms of shock. It helps alleviate feelings of inferiority and insecurity, and can deepen intuitive insight.

Contraindications: Use only in small amounts in the bath and on the skin. Avoid using peppermint alongside homeopathic remedies.

Sweet fennel

(Foeniculum vulgare, Foeniculum officinale, Anethum foeniculum)

Family: Umbelliferae or Apiaceae

Description: Sweet fennel is a biennial or perennial herb with distinctive, delicate feathery leaves and golden flowers. The essential oil is steam-distilled from the crushed seeds.

Countries of origin: France, Greece, Italy, Hungary

Characteristics: Sweet fennel has clean, sweet, aniseed top notes and earthy, spicy, peppery undertones. It blends well with geranium, lavender, black pepper, rosemary, sandalwood, verbena and lemon.

Main therapeutic properties: Antiseptic, anti-spasmodic, carminative, depurative, diuretic, emmenagogue, expectorant, galactagogue, splenic, stomachic.

Sweet fennel is one of the best detoxifying essential oils and is much used in lymphatic drainage massage. Its diuretic qualities help to rid the body of toxins, and it is a good urinary-tract antiseptic. Fennel is also excellent for alleviating flatulence and digestive problems, and local massage combined with drinking fennel tea is recommended. Overall, fennel is deeply cleansing, purifying and revitalizing.

As a galactagogue, fennel helps in the production of breast milk, and it can help to normalize and regulate the menstrual cycle and reduce the fluctuation of hormones during the menopause.

Psychologically, fennel is protecting, warming and grounding. A couple of drops rubbed between the palms and brushed over the aura can protect against psychic disturbance.

Contraindications: Avoid throughout pregnancy and do not use on those who suffer from epilepsy.

*Fennel (*Foeniculum vulgare*)*

Hyssop
(Hyssopus officinalis var. *decumbens)*

Family: Labiatae or Lamiaceae

Description: Hyssop is a perennial aromatic shrub with small lance-shaped green leaves and purple-blue flowers. The essential oil is steam-distilled from the flowering tops and leaves.

Countries of origin: France, Holland, Hungary

Characteristics: Hyssop has intense, sweet, woody, camphoraceous top notes and warm, spicy, herbal undertones. It blends well with most other herbs and citruses, and also with lavender, myrtle, bay and geranium.

Main therapeutic properties: Antiseptic, anti-spasmodic, astringent, bactericide, carminative, cephalic, digestive, diuretic, emmenagogue, expectorant, hypertensive, nervine, tonic.

*Hyssop (*Hyssopus officinale*)*

Hyssop has a special affinity with the respiratory system, and is a useful expectorant, calming persistent coughing. It can be used in a burner, inhalation or local massage. It is good in cold compresses over bruises, and has an invigorating effect on the mind, being especially good for nervous debility. Overall, hyssop is warming, purifying and rejuvenating.

Psychologically, hyssop is centring and uplifting and is a good aid to meditation, aiding inspiration and concentration. It is psychically cleansing and purifying; it stimulates creativity and protects those who lack personal boundaries.

Contraindications: Avoid throughout pregnancy and do not use on those who suffer from epilepsy. Avoid prolonged use and use only small amounts.

Verbena

(Lippia citriodora, Verbena triphylla, Aloysia triphylla)

Family: Verbenaceae

Description: Verbena is a deciduous perennial shrub with fragrant lance-shaped green leaves and small white or purple flowers. The essential oil is steam-distilled from the leaves.

Countries of origin: France, Spain, Morocco, Tunisia, Algeria, Italy

Characteristics: Verbena has sweet, lemon-fresh top notes and fruity, floral undertones. It blends well with most other herbs and citruses, and also with neroli, palmarosa, frankincense, jasmine, juniper, cedarwood, myrtle and geranium.

Main therapeutic properties: Antiseptic, anti-spasmodic, carminative, detoxifying, digestive, febrifuge, sedative, stomachic.

Verbena is indicated for digestive problems caused or aggravated by nervous tension, and it also cleanses and decongests the liver and the digestive system. Drinking verbena tea (known as vervain) alongside using the essential

Verbena (Aloysia triphylla)

oil is recommended. Overall, verbena is calming, refreshing and stabilizing. Its lemon-fresh, uplifting fragrance calms anxiety, reduces stress, promotes restful sleep, and reinvigorates those who are listless and apathetic. Use no more than 2 drops in a bath, perhaps mixed with 4 drops of lavender, and use tiny amounts in massage oils. Psychologically, verbena alleviates tiredness and apathy, and stimulates creativity and concentration. It helps you open up to cosmic energies and make the most of the present moment by dispelling dreamy procrastination.

Contraindications: Avoid throughout pregnancy. Do not use if you have sensitive skin, do not use in the sunlight and use only small amounts.

Garlic
(Allium sativum)

Family: Amaryllidaceae or Liliaceae

Description: Garlic is a strongly scented perennial herb with long, flat, green leaves, small white flowers and a bulb of compacted cloves. The essential oil is steam-distilled from the crushed bulbs.

Countries of origin: France, Bulgaria, Egypt, Germany, China, Japan

Characteristics: Garlic has an overwhelmingly powerful unmistakeable odour.

Main therapeutic properties: Antibiotic, antiseptic, anti-toxic, anti-viral, carminative, depurative, diuretic, expectorant, febrifuge, fungicidal, hypotensive, stomachic, tonic.

Garlic (Allium sativum)

Garlic is unique among essential oils in that it is never used externally, and is only ever ingested orally and anally in gelatine capsules. Garlic is Nature's antibiotic, and counteracts all infections. It helps to lower cholesterol, may protect against heart disease and helps to reduce high blood pressure.

Take one or two capsules orally daily to treat respiratory infections or as a general supplement. For urinary-tract infections, insert one capsule in the rectum after a bowel movement. Garlic has a reputation for warding off evil spirits and vampires.

Resins and roots

Angelica root

(Angelica archangelica, Angelica officinalis)

Family: Umbelliferae or Apiaceae

Description: Angelica is a biennial or perennial hairy herb with large, ferny leaves, white flowers and a large rhizome (underground stem). The essential oil is steam- or water-distilled from the roots and rhizomes.

Countries of origin: France, Hungary, Belgium, Holland, Germany

Characteristics: Angelica has spicy, peppery, herbal top notes and earthy, woody, musky undertones. It blends well with the citruses, and also with neroli, patchouli, frankincense, clary sage, cedarwood, vetiver, pine and juniper.

Main therapeutic properties: Antiseptic, anti-spasmodic, carminative, depurative, digestive, diuretic, emmenagogue, expectorant, nervine, stomachic, tonic.

Angelica is one of the best essential oils to help convalescents fully recover and to generally restore strength and stamina. It is an excellent essential oil to use for the elderly. It counteracts weakness and fatigue, stimulates the immune system, and has a pronounced tonic effect on the nervous system. Overall, angelica is healing, balancing and fortifying.

With its excellent detoxifying and diuretic properties, angelica is much used in lymphatic drainage massage, and in body massage angelica relieves painful joints. It is a powerful general tonic for stress and nervous tension. Angelica can also help with indigestion and flatulence, and is good for respiratory problems, especially chronic coughs and asthma.

Psychologically, angelica is strengthening, soothing and healing. It helps you keep going when you feel faint-hearted and increases your perseverance. Angelica also increases your

*Angelica (*Angelica archangelica*)*

awareness of the angelic realms and helps you to be receptive and open to divine forces and energies.

Contraindications: Avoid in early pregnancy. Do not use if you have sensitive skin or are diabetic, and do not use in the sunlight. Use no more than 1 per cent.

Frankincense

(Boswellia carteri, Boswellia serrata)

Family: Burseraceae

Description: Frankincense is also known as olibanum and is a small, shrubby tree with white flowers. Incisions in the bark produce a milky-white resin that hardens into orange-brown 'tears', and the essential oil is steam-distilled from these 'tears' of hardened resin.

Countries of origin: India, Somalia, Oman, Yemen, Ethiopia, Saudi Arabia

Characteristics: Frankincense has fresh, citrus, turpentine top notes and sweet, warm, balsamic, camphoraceous, wood-smoke undertones. It blends well with most florals, woods, spices and citruses, and also with patchouli, clary sage, rosemary, basil and vetiver.

Main therapeutic properties: Anti-inflammatory, antiseptic, astringent, carminative, cicatrizant, cytophylactic, digestive, diuretic, emmenagogue, expectorant, sedative, tonic.

Frankincense is the most valuable essential oil for slowing and deepening the breathing, helping to allay fear, anxiety, nervous tension and stress. It literally smells divine and was traditionally burned as an offering to the gods. Useful in massage and bath oils, frankincense is also good in inhalation, burners and mood perfumes. Overall, it is deeply calming, revitalizing and uplifting.

Recommended especially for dry, sensitive and mature skins, frankincense is one of the best essential oils in skin care, helping to rejuvenate skin tone and prevent wrinkles. It counteracts respiratory problems and is useful in treating colds, bronchitis, asthma, coughs and sore throats. In a hot compress or local wash, frankincense can also help to relieve cystitis. Psychologically, frankincense is a valuable aid to meditation and prayer, inspiring mystical, divine mind states and generally stilling the mind. It was traditionally used to drive away bad spirits, and frankincense helps to break links with the past.

*Frankincense tree (*Boswellia *sp.)*

Myrrh
(Commiphora myrrha)

Family: Burseraceae

Description: Myrrh is a shrubby bush or small tree with gnarled branches, aromatic leaves and white flowers. Incisions into the bark produce a yellow resin that hardens into red-brown 'tears' and the essential oil is steam-distilled from these 'tears' of hardened resin.

*Myrrh (*Commiphora myrrha*)*

Countries of origin: Somalia, Yemen, Ethiopia

Characteristics: The name 'myrrh' comes from the Arabic word *mur*, meaning bitter. Myrrh is dark brown and viscous, with bitter, spicy, balsamic top notes and resinous, medicinal, wood-smoke undertones. It blends well with the other resins, and also with patchouli, rose, sandalwood, mandarin, geranium, thyme, lavender, juniper, cypress and pine.

Main therapeutic properties: Anti-inflammatory, antiseptic, astringent, carminative, cicatrizant, emmenagogue, expectorant, fungicidal, sedative, stomachic, tonic, uterine.

Myrrh is the first choice to treat athlete's foot, chronic wounds, ulcers and gum infections, and can also be used as a tincture. Its healing reputation stretches back more than four thousand years, and ancient Greek soldiers carried myrrh into battle for psychic protection and first aid. Overall, myrrh is healing, soothing and restorative.

Myrrh is excellent in skin care, and is especially recommended for use in hand creams and on inflamed skin conditions. It is calming and soothing and good for all stress-related conditions and anxiety. Myrrh is also a useful expectorant and treats coughs and colds; it has a drying effect on excess mucus. It can be used to bring on menstruation and relieve painful periods.

Psychologically, myrrh inspires peace and tranquillity. Like frankincense, it is one of the most spiritual essential oils and is excellent for meditation. Myrrh heals the base chakra, and helps people who are stuck to move on in life.

Contraindications: Avoid during pregnancy.

Benzoin

(Styrax benzoin)

Family: Styracaceae

Description: Benzoin is a tropical tree with pale-green leaves and hard-shelled fruit. Incisions into the bark produce a resin that hardens into brown 'tears' with reddish streaks. The essential oil is steam-distilled from these 'tears' of hardened resin, but it is an almost solid resinous mass. This is then dissolved in ethyl glycol (or similar) to render it suitable for aromatherapeutic purposes.

Countries of origin: Sumatra, Java, Laos, Vietnam, Thailand, Cambodia

Characteristics: Benzoin has vanilla ice-cream top notes and sweet-molasses, balsamic undertones. It blends well with other resins and most spices, and also with rose, sandalwood, jasmine, cypress, juniper, lemon and pine.

Main therapeutic properties: Anti-inflammatory, antiseptic, astringent, carminative, deodorant, expectorant, sedative, styptic.

Benzoin is the 'cuddly' essential oil, and its sweet fragrance comforts people who are sad, lonely, alienated, depressed and bereaved. Most commonly used in the form of Friar's Balsam, it is a valuable cold remedy, gentle enough for children, and is used in steam inhalations, for treating asthma, bronchitis and coughs. Overall, benzoin is warming, soothing and mothering.

Benzoin (Styrax benzoin)

Like myrrh, benzoin is useful in skin care, especially when the skin is cut, chapped, cracked or inflamed.

Psychologically, benzoin acts like a shield or comfort blanket, protecting you from the harshness of life. Bezoin comforts, elevates and protects; it was traditionally used in incense to drive away evil spirits.

Citruses

Bergamot
(Citrus bergamia)

Family: Rutaceae

Description: The bergamot tree was originally grown only in Italy. It produces small citrus fruits that ripen from green to yellow, but the fruit is inedible because it is so sour. Bergamot is the finest of the citrus essential oils and is expressed from the peel of the nearly ripe fruit.

Countries of origin: Corsica, Morocco, Italy

Characteristics: Bergamot has sweet, lemon-fresh top notes and warm, floral, balsamic undertones. It blends well with other citruses and florals, and also with cypress, sandalwood, juniper, coriander, black pepper, ginger, clary sage, rosemary and frankincense.

Main therapeutic properties: Analgesic, antiseptic, anti-depressant, anti-spasmodic, carminative, cicatrizant, deodorant, digestive, febrifuge, sedative, stomachic, tonic.

Bergamot is the sunny essential oil. As well as being an excellent treatment for depression and anxiety, it is first choice for urinary-tract infections and cystitis, because it is a powerful disinfectant of the urinary system. Chronic

Bergamot (Citrus bergamia)

sufferers of cystitis become tense and anxious with the onset of symptoms, and in a local wash bergamot calms the nerves and relieves the symptoms. Overall, bergamot is cheering, uplifting and calming.

The lovely fragrance and powerful antiseptic qualities of bergamot make it a valuable addition to skin-care creams and lotions, and it is especially suited to oily skins and acne. Bergamot has a regulating effect on the appetite, and is useful both in convalescence and for those who are dieting, in a mood perfume or massage oil. Bergamot used in the bath is cooling for feverish conditions.

Psychologically, bergamot is reviving, soothing and balancing. Its sunny, anti-depressant qualities make it useful in treating Seasonal Affective Disorder, and it is cheering generally on cold, grey, winter days. Bergamot is heart-warming and has an affinity with the heart chakra, gently relieving sadness, depression and grief.

Contraindications: Do not use if you have very sensitive skin or before exposure to sunlight. Use no more than 3 drops in the bath.

Sweet orange

(Citrus sinensis, Citrus aurantium var. *dulcis)*

Family: Rutaceae

Description: The sweet-orange tree is smaller than the bitter orange and has dark-green, shiny leaves, fragrant white flowers and abundant fruit. The essential oil is expressed from the peel of the nearly ripe fruit.

Countries of origin: Israel, Brazil, America, Italy, Australia

Characteristics: Orange has sweet, fresh, fruity top notes and radiant, sensuous undertones. It blends well with other citruses and spices, and also with sandalwood, neroli, clary sage, myrrh, geranium, palmarosa and frankincense.

Main therapeutic properties: Anti-depressant, anti-inflammatory, antiseptic, anti-spasmodic, carminative, digestive, sedative, stomachic, tonic.

Orange is known as the 'smiley oil' and is familiar, joyful and warming. It is gentle enough to use on children who enjoy its fruity fragrance. Orange is very good in local massage and compresses for settling digestive upsets, and has a normalizing, regulating effect that is beneficial for constipation, cramps, diarrhoea and flatulence. Overall, orange is tonic, soothing and refreshing.

Orange has a similar (though considerably lesser) effect to neroli on the nervous system, and is good in massage and baths for anxiety, stress and insomnia. It is good in massage oils and it is used in the bath to help relieve anxiety, stress and insomnia.

Psychologically, orange is cheering and uplifting, helping you to find laughter and joy in life. Orange is reputed to reduce an irrational fear of the unknown and it can lessen self-doubt. It can help you to find an inner radiance and optimism. Orange also helps to stimulate and refresh stagnant subtle energies.

Orange (Citrus sinensis)

Mandarin, tangerine

(Citrus reticulata, Citrus nobilis, Citrus madurensis)

Family: Rutaceae

Description: Mandarin and tangerine are considered the same botanical species, although there is a slight difference in fragrance between them. Mandarin is generally preferred for aromatherapeutic purposes. It is a small evergreen tree with glossy leaves, fragrant flowers, and fruit varying from yellow to orangey-red. The essential oil is expressed from the peel of the nearly ripe fruit.

Countries of origin: Italy, Spain, Algeria, Cyprus, Greece, Brazil

Characteristics: Mandarin has delicate, sweet, citrus top notes and deep, warm, almost floral undertones. It blends well with other citruses and spices, and also with neroli, lavender, sandalwood, petitgrain, melissa, ylang ylang, juniper, geranium, rosewood and cypress.

Main therapeutic properties: Antiseptic, anti-spasmodic, carminative, depurative, digestive, diuretic, sedative, tonic.

Mandarin is one of the safest essential oils and is particularly recommended for children and for use during pregnancy. Blended with lavender and neroli in apricot-kernel oil, mandarin helps to reduce stretch marks during pregnancy when massaged daily into the abdomen from the fifth month until childbirth. Overall, it is uplifting, cheering and soothing.

Mandarin has a tonic effect on the digestion, and is good for all digestive upsets. It makes a pleasant addition to massage blends and mood perfumes, bringing a light, gentle, calming note.

Psychologically, mandarin is strengthening and has a slight hypnotic quality, helping to switch off an over-active mind and promoting restful sleep. It has a soft, delicate quality that helps people to connect with their inner child.

Mandarin (Citrus madurensis)

Lemon
(Citrus limon)

Family: Rutaceae

Description: Lemon is a small evergreen tree with oval leaves, fragrant flowers and green fruits turning to yellow. It fruits all year round. The essential oil is expressed from the peel of the nearly ripe and ripe fruit.

Countries of origin: Italy, Sicily, Cyprus, Israel, America

Characteristics: Lemon has clean, fresh, light, sharp top notes with slightly sweet, citrousy undertones. It blends well with other citruses and florals, and with most other essential oils. A useful tip is that if a blend smells wrong or confused, adding a few drops of lemon often improves the fragrance.

Lemon (Citrus limon*)*

Main therapeutic properties: Anti-microbial, anti-rheumatic, antiseptic, anti-spasmodic, astringent, bactericide, carminative, diuretic, depurative, febrifuge, haemostatic, tonic.

Lemon is a useful essential oil in many ways. Its haemostatic properties help to stop bleeding and, combined with its bactericidal properties, this means that lemon is excellent in a wash for cuts and grazes. It is also detoxifying and good in lymphatic drainage massage. Lemon is a tonic of the circulatory system and cleanses the blood, and it is helpful for varicose veins. Overall, lemon is refreshing, purifying and cleansing.

Its ability to counteract acidity makes lemon useful for rheumatic conditions, gout, arthritis and digestive acidity. Lemon is also useful in skin care to brighten the complexion, and is indicated for oily skin and acne. It helps the body to fight infection and is useful in sprays and burners to prevent the spread of infection.

Psychologically, lemon is radiant, reviving and stimulating. It helps to prevent emotional outbursts and assists in making decisions. Lemon helps spring-clean the mind, bringing clarity and shedding light when the mind has become foggy or confused. Useful in meditation for clearing the mind, lemon also opens the heart.

Contraindications: Do not use if you have very sensitive skin or before exposure to sunlight. Use no more than 3 drops in the bath.

Grapefruit

(Citrus x *paradisi)*

Family: Rutaceae

Description: Grapefruit is a big tree with glossy leaves and large fruits. The essential oil is expressed from the peel of the ripe fruit.

Countries of origin: America, Brazil, Israel

Characteristics: Grapefruit has clean, fresh, light, sharp top notes with slightly sweet, citrousy undertones. It blends well with other citruses and spices, and also with palmarosa, neroli, rosemary, cypress, juniper, lavender, jasmine and ylang ylang.

Main therapeutic properties: Anti-depressant, antiseptic, anti-spasmodic, astringent, depurative, diuretic, stimulant, tonic.

*Grapefruit (*Citrus x paradisi*)*

Grapefruit is useful in lymphatic drainage massage, helping to treat water retention and cellulite. It is good for a congested or over-heated liver and, in a morning bath blended together with rosemary and fennel, grapefruit can help to relieve a hangover. It has a tonic effect on the scalp and is useful in skin care for oily skin and acne. Overall, grapefruit is uplifting, cleansing and stimulating.

Psychologically, grapefruit is refreshing and reviving, helping to alleviate stress, depression, nervous exhaustion and tension. Like bergamot, it lifts the spirits in winter, and it is excellent blended in massage oils and bath oils to counteract emotional and physical exhaustion and lethargy. Grapefruit lifts self-esteem and promotes optimism.

Lime

(Citrus aurantifolia, Citrus latifolia)

Family: Rutaceae

Description: Lime is a small evergreen tree with drooping branches, oval leaves, white flowers and small green fruit. The essential oil is expressed from the peel of the nearly ripe fruit.

Countries of origin: Mexico, Peru, West Indies, America, Brazil

Characteristics: Lime has clean, fresh, green top notes with slightly bitter, citrousy undertones. It blends well with other citruses, and also with neroli, lavender, geranium, ylang ylang, rosemary, cypress and rosewood.

Main therapeutic properties: Antiseptic, anti-viral, astringent, bactericide, febrifuge, tonic.

*Lime (*Citrus aurantifolia*)*

Lime has a similar action to the other citrus essential oils, and is therefore useful for lymphatic drainage massage, oily skin and acne. Lime is also a good digestive tonic.

Psychologically, lime is refreshing and uplifting, helping to relieve fatigue, apathy and depression. It adds an interesting note to mood perfumes and massage oils.

Contraindications: Do not use if you have very sensitive skin or before exposure to sunlight. Use no more than 3 drops in the bath.

Trees and woods

Sandalwood
(Santalum album)

Family: Santalaceae

Description: Sandalwood is a small evergreen tree with pinky-purple flowers. Mysore in India is the main producer of sandalwood essential oil, which is steam- or water-distilled from the powdered heartwood and major roots.

Countries of origin: India, China, Australia, New Caledonia

Characteristics: Sandalwood's warm, heavy fragrance increases over time, and it has the longest-lasting aroma of essential oils. It has sweet, woody, roselike top notes and deep, balsamic, spicy, oriental undertones. Sandalwood blends well with most florals and resins, and also with rosewood, clove, black pepper, cypress, vetiver, patchouli and bergamot.

Main therapeutic properties: Anti-depressant, antiseptic, anti-spasmodic, aphrodisiac, astringent, bactericide, carminative, cicatrizant, demulcent, expectorant, sedative, tonic.

Sandalwood is widely used in the perfume industry and its gentle, erotic fragrance is enjoyed by women and men alike. It is excellent for urinary-tract infections and is the first choice for chronic bronchitis, soothing and alleviating the symptoms. It is wonderful in skin care for all skin types, balancing, soothing and hydrating the skin, with a possible rejuvenating effect. Overall, sandalwood is erotic, relaxing and uplifting.

Excellent for nervous tension and depression, sandalwood is also a powerful aphrodisiac, especially useful when sexual problems are caused by stress, anxiety and isolation. When used in massages and baths, sandalwood is cooling and calming, helping to prevent tense headaches and relieving insomnia.

Sandalwood (Santalum album)

Psychologically, sandalwood facilitates spiritual practice and has been used in incense as a meditation aid for centuries. It calms irritation born of frustration, quietens and stills the mind, and opens you up to your spiritual potential. Sandalwood is associated with both the crown and base chakras. Traditionally, sandalwood has been used to arouse Kundalini in tantric rituals, which means that it arouses sexual energy for the purpose of transmutation into spiritual wisdom. Sandalwood helps to balance and harmonize the chakras, thereby restoring equilibrium.

*Atlas cedarwood (*Cedrus atlantica*)*

Atlas cedarwood
(Cedrus atlantica)

Family: Pinaceae

Description: Atlas cedarwood originated from the famous biblical cedars of Lebanon. It is a tall, majestic evergreen tree that grows to more than 30 m (100 ft) and lives for more than a thousand years. The essential oil is steam-distilled from wood chips, preferably from the heartwood.

Countries of origin: Lebanon, Cyprus, Morocco, Algeria

Characteristics: Atlas cedarwood has turpentine, woody, camphorlike top notes and deep, sweet, balsamic, smoky undertones. It blends well with most other woods, and also with jasmine, black pepper, frankincense, vetiver, patchouli, rosemary and bergamot.

Main therapeutic properties: Antiseptic, anti-seborrheic, astringent, diuretic, expectorant, insecticide, sedative.

With its familiar masculine fragrance, atlas cedarwood is the first choice for men's skin and hair-care products. It improves oily skin, acne and dandruff. It is also good for treating urinary-tract infections, coughs and chronic bronchitis. Overall, atlas cedarwood is fortifying, calming and opening.

Psychologically, atlas cedarwood reduces fear and helps you discover inner strength and courage. It is good for calming nervous tension and stress, and is welcomed by those who prefer a masculine fragrance. Atlas cedarwood is good in meditations and especially helps to instil confidence. It is a good general tonic for strengthening subtle energies.

Contraindications: Avoid during pregnancy.

Virginian cedarwood
(Juniperus virginiana)

Family: Cupressaceae

Description: Virginian cedarwood is a slow-growing, majestic evergreen tree with brown cones, also commonly called red cedar. The essential oil is steam-distilled from sawdust and other timber waste.

Country of origin: America

Characteristics: Virginian cedarwood has dry, woody, pencil-shaving-like top notes and oily, sweet, balsamic undertones. It blends well with most other woods, and also with rose, vetiver, patchouli and benzoin.

Main therapeutic properties: Antiseptic, anti-seborrhoeic, astringent, diuretic, emmenagogue, expectorant, insecticide, sedative.

*Virginian cedarwood (*Juniperus virginiana*)*

Virginian cedarwood is similar in many ways to atlas cedarwood, although the latter is generally considered a finer and safer essential oil. Virginian cedarwood is a good nerve tonic, especially beneficial for chronic anxiety and nervous tension. Like atlas cedarwood, it is much used in men's toiletries and is recommended for treating oily skin, dandruff and acne. Overall, virginian cedarwood is refreshing, uplifting and restorative.

In steam inhalations, virginian cedarwood is indicated for chronic coughs and bronchitis, and in a local wash for urinary-tract infections and cystitis.

Psychologically, it is fortifying, warming and protecting. It is a powerful tonic of the subtle energies and – although sedative – is good for poor concentration and nervous debility. Virginian cedarwood assists in transforming negative emotions into their positive counterparts.

Contraindications: Avoid during pregnancy and if you have sensitive skin. Use in moderation – no more than 2 per cent.

Petitgrain
(Citrus aurantium subsp. *amara)*

Family: Rutaceae

Description: Petitgrain is the bitter orange, an evergreen tree with dark-green leaves and fragrant white flowers. The essential oil is steam-distilled from the leaves and twigs.

Countries of origin: France, Italy, Paraguay, Algeria, Haiti

Characteristics: Petitgrain shares many of the qualities of neroli and has fresh, floral, citrousy top notes and light woody, herbaceous undertones. It blends

*Petitgrain (*Citrus aurantium *subsp.* amara*)*

well with most florals and citruses, and also with rosemary, clary sage, black pepper, benzoin, patchouli, palmarosa and clove.

Main therapeutic properties: Antiseptic, anti-spasmodic, deodorant, digestive, nervine, stomachic, sedative.

Petitgrain is a traditional ingredient of eau de cologne. Its refreshing aroma is often used in skin-care products and it clears blemishes and helps to reduce over-active sebum production. Petitgrain is recommended for nervous tension and anxiety, and is similar to (but less effective than) neroli. In an evening bath it helps to prevent insomnia, especially if you are lonely. Overall, petitgrain has a relaxing, balancing, refreshing quality.

Psychologically, petitgrain is revitalizing, balancing, nourishing and clears away troubled emotions. It is good in meditation to get in touch with the rational and intellectual mind. Petitgrain's soft, gentle aroma is also useful in convalescence, especially when a stronger fragrance would be overwhelming.

Rosewood

(Aniba rosaeodora)

Family: Lauraceae

Description: Rosewood is also known as *bois de rose*, and is a tropical, evergreen tree with yellow flowers. The essential oil is steam-distilled and occasionally water-distilled from wood chips.

Countries of origin: Brazil, Peru

Characteristics: Rosewood is both subtle and powerful, with soft, floral top notes and sweet, woody undertones. It blends well with most essential oils, giving a soft, rounded note to blends.

Rosewood (Aniba rosaeodora)

Main therapeutic properties: Anti-depressant, antiseptic, aphrodisiac, bactericide, cephalic, cytophylactic, deodorant, stimulant.

Rosewood is an endangered species, so make sure you buy an essential oil that comes from a sustainable rosewood plantation. It is one of the most spiritual essential oils, with a balancing and harmonizing effect. Rosewood is a very gentle stimulant, which makes it useful for those with nervous tension and depression characterized by lethargy and apathy, and for chronic fatigue. It is a surprisingly powerful immuno-stimulant, and more pleasant to use than ti-tree. Overall, rosewood is balancing, uplifting and fortifying.

In skin care, rosewood's gentleness and healing properties make it suitable for all skin types, especially sensitive and damaged skin. A gentle aphrodisiac, rosewood is a lovely choice to use in a blend for intimate massage for lovers. Rosewood has an uplifting effect that is useful when you are tired, as it lifts your spirits and your energy. In an evening bath it also helps insomnia.

Rosewood is calming and steadying. It is one of the best essential oils to use during meditation, as it helps to clear the mind; and when blended with angelica root, it helps you to reconnect with the divine. Rosewood has an affinity with the crown chakra and is excellent for all spiritual healing.

Juniper berry
(Juniperus communis)

Family: Cupressaceae

Description: Juniper is a small tree with needle-type leaves, greenish-yellow flowers and small berries. The essential oil is steam-distilled from the crushed and partly dried berries.

Countries of origin: France, Italy, Czech Republic, Hungary, Austria, Serbia, Croatia

Characteristics: Juniper berry has clean, fresh, turpentine top notes and smoky, balsamic, woody, peppery undertones. It blends well with most other woods and citruses, and also with frankincense, clary sage, lavender, geranium, rose and benzoin.

Main therapeutic properties: Anti-rheumatic, antiseptic, anti-spasmodic, anti-toxic, aphrodisiac, astringent, carminative, cicatrizant, depurative, diuretic, emmenagogue, nervine, rubefacient.

Juniper is the purifying essential oil. On a physical level, this quality manifests as a powerful cleansing and tonic action, making juniper good in lymphatic drainage massage and in helping the body to eliminate toxins. It is also excellent when used for psychic and spiritual purifying. Overall, juniper is cleansing, tonic and restorative.

Juniper berry (Juniperus communis)

One of the best essential oils for cystitis and urinary-tract infections, juniper is good blended with bergamot in a local wash, gentle local massage and hot compresses over the lower abdomen. Juniper helps to alleviate nervous tension, intellectual fatigue and anxiety. Used in small amounts, juniper is good in skin care, especially for oily skin and when the skin is affected by toxins such as acne.

Psychologically, juniper is purifying, clearing and fortifying. Traditionally it was burned to protect from evil spirits and drive out negative energies, and this quality is still effective today. A couple of drops rubbed between the palms and brushed over the aura is purifying and protecting. Juniper is good in meditations, especially when the mind needs a spring-clean. Used in a burner, it dispels the psychic presence of other people.

Contraindications: Avoid during pregnancy and do not use if you have kidney disease. Use carefully in small amounts.

Cypress

(Cupressus sempervirens)

Family: Cupressaceae

Description: Cypress is an exceptionally long-lived evergreen tree with needle-type leaves, often grown near cemeteries. The essential oil is steam-distilled from the leaves and twigs.

Countries of origin: France, Italy, Spain, Corsica, Sardinia, Sicily

Characteristics: Cypress has spicy, resinous top notes and sweet, smoky, balsamic, woody undertones. It blends well with most other woods and citruses, and also with frankincense, clary sage, lavender, cardamom, marjoram, geranium, neroli, black pepper and benzoin.

Main therapeutic properties: Anti-rheumatic, antiseptic, anti-spasmodic, anti-sudorific, anti-toxic, astringent, deodorant, diuretic, hepatic, tonic, vasoconstrictive.

Cypress is recommended whenever there is excess fluid, because it is a powerful astringent and venous decongestant. This makes it the first choice mixed in an ointment to treat varicose veins and haemorrhoids, and in massage, baths and compresses to regulate over-heavy and painful menstruation. Cypress also helps to reduce the hot flushes associated with the menopause. In a bath or foot bath, it helps to prevent excessive sweating of the feet. Overall, cypress is warming, drying and soothing.

The clean, fresh woody aroma of cypress makes it a welcome addition to men's skin-care preparations, and it helps acne, oily and over-hydrated skin. Cypress makes a lovely deodorant when blended with bergamot and geranium, dissolved in a little vodka and mixed into orange-flower water and witch hazel. It also helps with nervous weakness and anxiety, restoring a strong, calm demeanour.

Psychologically, cypress is purifying, protecting and refreshing, and was traditionally used in purifying incense. Like juniper, it provides excellent psychic protection and, as a symbol of eternity, cypress instils strength and wisdom. It also helps the flow of stagnant subtle energies. Cypress was dedicated to Pluto, the god of the underworld, and so is associated with the base chakra. It can be used in meditations for bereavement, difficult transitions and painful changes.

Cypress (Cupressus sempervirens)

Lemon-scented eucalyptus
(Eucalyptus citriodora)

Family: Myrtaceae

Description: Lemon-scented eucalyptus is a tall evergreen tree with attractive pink and grey variegated bark. Although similar to the other eucalyptus species, it is distinguished by its aroma. The essential oil is steam-distilled from the leaves.

Countries of origin: Brazil, Indonesia, China, Morocco, Seychelles

Characteristics: Lemon-scented eucalyptus has fresh, citronella, lemon top notes and sweet, balsamic undertones. It blends well with most florals and citruses, and with some spices.

Main therapeutic properties: Antiseptic, anti-viral, bactericidal, deodorant, expectorant, insecticide.

*Lemon-scented eucalyptus (*Eucalyptus citriodora*)*

Lemon-scented eucalyptus is an excellent choice to use for colds, sore throats and flu. Steam inhalations with lemon-scented eucalyptus help clear the sinuses and relieve headaches. A couple of drops of lemon-scented eucalyptus used in the bath, perhaps blended with lavender and rosemary, is refreshing and uplifting. It is also good for athlete's foot, herpes and dandruff, and makes an excellent insect repellent. Overall, lemon-scented eucalyptus is refreshing, clearing and invigorating.

Psychologically, it dispels fatigue and debility; it also clears the mind and can assist in making decisions. Lemon-scented eucalyptus is useful in meditations if you have a cold, helping to keep the mind clear and focused.

Eucalyptus

(Eucalyptus globulus, Eucalyptus radiata, Eucalyptus smithi, Eucalyptus polybractea, etc.)

Family: Myrtaceae

Description: There are more than 600 species of eucalyptus, of which about 20 are harvested for their essential oils. They are tall evergreen tress with long, narrow leaves and white-yellow flowers. Those listed above are the main species used in aromatherapy. The essential oil is steam-distilled from the leaves and twigs.

Countries of origin: Australia, China, Spain, Portugal, Brazil, Russia, America

Characteristics: Eucalyptus has fresh, sharp, camphoraceous top notes and penetrating, woody undertones. It blends well with most other woods and herbs, and also with lavender and lemon.

Main therapeutic properties: Analgesic, anti-bacterial, anti-neuralgic, anti-rheumatic, antiseptic, anti-spasmodic, anti-viral, astringent, decongestant, deodorant, diuretic, expectorant, febrifuge.

Eucalyptus is probably the most familiar essential oil, used as a decongestant in steam inhalations to relieve colds, flu and other respiratory ailments. It clears the head wonderfully and relieves headaches and neuralgia. Eucalyptus is an excellent insect repellent and is also good at treating bites and stings. Overall, it is stimulating, refreshing and clearing.

Used in the bath or in a local wash, *Eucalyptus radiata* is reputed to relieve the pain of shingles, and when blended with bergamot it is effective against cold sores and herpes.

Psychologically, eucalyptus is piercing, stimulating and purifying. It is useful in meditations when you have a cold, to keep the mind clear.

Eucalyptus (Eucalyptus globulus)

It is a tonic of the subtle energy, especially of the lungs, and helps those who feel constricted in their lives. Eucalyptus also makes a good psychic cleaner in a burner, to cleanse rooms of negative energy.

Pine needle

(Pinus sylvestris)

Family: Pinaceae

Description: Pine is also known as Scotch pine, and is a tall evergreen tree with distinctive fissured, reddish-brown bark, needle-type leaves and pine cones. The essential oil is sometimes steam-distilled from the needles, young branches and cones, but the best oil for aromatherapy use comes from dry distillation of the needles.

Countries of origin: Austria, Hungary, America, Finland, Russia

Characteristics: Pine has fresh, turpentine, camphoraceous top notes and dry, sweet, balsamic, woody undertones. It blends well with most other woods and herbs, and also with lavender and lemon.

Main therapeutic properties: Anti-microbial, anti-neuralgic, anti-rheumatic, antiseptic, anti-viral, bactericidal, balsamic, cholagogue, deodorant, diuretic, expectorant, insecticide, rubefacient, tonic.

Pine is an excellent expectorant and is especially indicated for pulmonary complaints. It is among the best choices to clear phlegm from the lungs, and is good for sinusitis and all bronchial conditions. It is a tonic of the lungs, kidneys and nervous system. Its clear, piercing action also makes pine helpful in relieving fatigue and nervous exhaustion. Overall, pine is restorative, reviving and strengthening.

Its stimulating and analgesic properties make pine a good choice to use in compresses and massage after over-exertion and sports injuries. Pine can

*Pine needle (*Pinus sylvestris*)*

also help with cystitis and other urinary tract complaints, especially if the kidneys are weak.

Psychologically, pine is warming and cleansing. It tones subtle energy and is good burned before meditations to psychically cleanse the space. Pine instils self-confidence and allays guilt, helping to bring about acceptance, tolerance and forgiveness.

Contraindications: Do not use if you have sensitive skin. Use carefully in small amounts.

Spices

Ginger

(Zingiber officinalis)

Family: Zingiberaceae

Description: Ginger is a perennial, tropical herb with reedlike leaves, white or yellow flowers and a thick tuberous rhizome or root. The essential oil is steam-distilled from the unpeeled, dried, ground root.

Countries of origin: India, China, Thailand, Australia

Characteristics: Ginger has sharp, green top notes and fiery, woody, sweet, spicy undertones. It blends well with the citruses, and also with neroli, geranium, ylang ylang, rose, frankincense, sandalwood, vetiver, patchouli and rosewood.

Main therapeutic properties: Analgesic, antiseptic, aphrodisiac, bactericide, carminative, cephalic, febrifuge, laxative, rubefacient, stimulant, tonic.

Ginger is warming and stimulates the circulation and digestion. It is excellent used in winter to warm the body and emotions, both physically and psychologically. It is a tonic of the heart and is indicated in baths and

Ginger (Zingiber officinalis)

massage for poor circulation, cardiac fatigue and cold hands and feet. Overall, ginger is warming, comforting and fortifying.

Its stimulant properties make ginger useful for poor digestion and flatulence. It is especially good for travel sickness and morning sickness, either sniffed from a tissue or blended into a mood perfume. It is also good in massage when the muscles are tired and aching, particularly when they are cold and contracted. Ginger can be useful in a bath or inhalation when you have a cold or sore throat, as its sharp, piercing fragrance cuts through catarrh and congestion.

Psychologically, ginger is arousing, opulent and stimulating. It is indicated for use in meditation when there is debility through nervous exhaustion. It warms and strengthens the emotions, increases determination and inspires initiative and action to carry plans through to their conclusion. Ginger also helps to blow away the winter blues and is useful in combating Seasonal Affective Disorder.

Contraindications: Do not use if you have very sensitive skin. Use no more than 3 drops in the bath and no more than 2 per cent in massage oils.

*Black pepper (*Piper nigrum*)*

Black pepper
(Piper nigrum)

Family: Piperaceae

Description: Black pepper is a perennial, woody vine with heart-shaped leaves and white flowers, which turn into berries or peppercorns. The essential oil is steam-distilled from the dried, crushed, almost-ripe berries.

Countries of origin: India, Indonesia, Madagascar

Characteristics: Black pepper has hot, spicy, fiery top notes and warm, sharp, woody, oriental undertones. In small amounts, it blends well with other spices and most florals, and also with frankincense, sandalwood, marjoram and rosemary.

Main therapeutic properties: Analgesic, antiseptic, aphrodisiac, bactericide, carminative, digestive, febrifuge, laxative, rubefacient, stimulant, tonic.

Black pepper is one of the best stimulant essential oils for the digestive system. Blended with marjoram and used in firm abdominal massage, it relieves constipation. It also stimulates the appetite and helps to relieve flatulence. Black pepper stimulates the spleen so it is useful in treating anaemia. It can be used in compresses to treat bruises and chilblains. Overall, black pepper is fortifying, strengthening and stimulating.

Psychologically, it is warming, builds endurance and helps you reconnect with life whenever you feel alienated. Black pepper is full of mystery and intrigue, and fortifies both mind and spirit. Its slight aphrodisiac quality is especially useful when blended into an intimate massage oil for those whose sensual emotions lack fire and passion. Black pepper is indicated in meditations when you feel cold and aloof, and helps you move on when you feel stuck and trapped.

Contraindications: Do not use if you have very sensitive skin. Use no more than 3 drops in the bath and no more than 2 per cent in massage oils.

Clove bud

(Syzygium aromaticum, Eugenia aromatica, Eugenia caryophyllata)

Family: Myrtaceae

Description: Clove is a long-lived evergreen tree with glossy green leaves and rosy-pink buds, which become fragrant red flowers and purple fruits. The essential oil is water-distilled from the flower buds.

Countries of origin: Zanzibar, Madagascar, Indonesia

Characteristics: Clove bud has fresh, fruity top notes and deep, sweet, spicy undertones. In tiny amounts, it blends well with most citruses and florals, and also with clary sage, bay, lemongrass and sandalwood. Clove was a traditional ingredient of ancient Egyptian fragrances and adds an interesting, mysterious, oriental dimension to mood perfumes.

Main therapeutic properties: Analgesic, antiseptic, anti-spasmodic carminative, stimulant, stomachic.

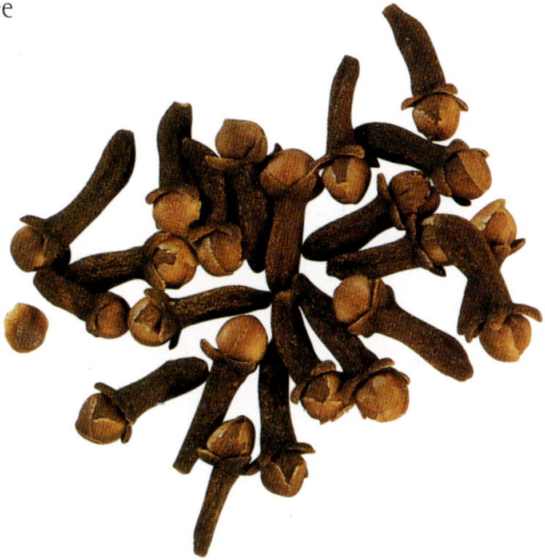

*Clove bud (*Syzygium aromaticum*)*

Clove bud is the first choice as first aid for toothache. A couple of drops of clove essential oil on a cotton wool bud, applied to the aching tooth, has a slight anaesthetic affect, relieving pain for a few hours. If the pain is caused by a lost filling, a piece of cotton wool soaked in clove oil and inserted into the cavity will have the same analgesic, anaesthetic effect. Its strong antiseptic properties make clove good at preventing colds and influenza. Overall, clove is pain-relieving, comforting and revitalizing.

Small amounts of clove blended into massage oils can help to relieve stiff, aching muscles and rheumatic joint pain. If you feel 'chilled to the bone', adding a couple of drops of clove to a bath oil blend is warming and comforting. Small amounts of clove can often enhance the fragrance of a mood perfume, massage blend or bath oil. Clove also helps to relieve flatulence, stimulate digestion and restore appetite.

Psychologically, clove is a mental, emotional and subtle energy tonic, and is both restorative and stimulating.

Contraindications: Do not use if you have sensitive or very sensitive skin. Use no more than 2 drops in the bath and no more than 1 per cent in massage oils.

Coriander

(Coriandrum sativum)

Family: Apiaceae or Umbelliferae

Description: Coriander is a fragrant annual herb with delicate white flowers turning into masses of round seeds. The essential oil is steam-distilled from the crushed ripe seeds.

Countries of origin: Russia, Romania, France, Serbia, Croatia, Bosnia

Characteristics: Coriander has fresh, sweet, spicy top notes and woody, musky undertones. It blends well with the other spices and most citruses, and also with frankincense, sandalwood, clary sage, jasmine, neroli, petitgrain, cypress, pine and melissa.

*Coriander (*Coriandrum sativum*)*

Main therapeutic properties: Analgesic, antiseptic, anti-spasmodic, bactericide, carminative, depurative, digestive, stimulant, stomachic.

Coriander is one of the more gentle spice essential oils and is a good digestive tonic, helping to relieve nausea and flatulence. It also restores and stimulates the appetite, and may be useful in treating anorexia nervosa. It lifts the spirits and is good for nervous exhaustion and general debility. Overall, coriander is revitalizing, refreshing and comforting.

Psychologically, coriander is reviving and good for stimulating low energy. It is both relaxing and stimulating – a combination of properties that inspires creativity. It adds a pleasant and interesting note to massage blends and mood perfumes, and is good for relieving stress and irritability. Coriander is also beneficial during convalescence.

Contraindications: Use in moderation.

Cardamom
(Ellettaria cardamomum)

Family: Zingiberaceae

Description: Cardamom is a perennial, reedlike herb with long, blade-shaped leaves and yellow flowers with purple tips, which are followed by oblong red-brown or green seedpods. The essential oil is steam-distilled from the dried, ripe seeds.

Countries of origin: India, Sri Lanka, Guatemala

*Cardamom (*Ellettaria cardamomum*)*

Characteristics: Cardamom has warm, sweet, spicy top notes and woody, balsamic undertones. It blends well with most other spices, citruses and florals, and also with frankincense, sandalwood, vetiver, patchouli, cedarwood and rosewood.

Main therapeutic properties: Antiseptic, anti-spasmodic, carminative, digestive, diuretic, rubefacient, stimulant, stomachic, tonic.

Cardamom is one of the best overall tonic essential oils. As well as having a general overall tonic effect on the body, it is a good tonic of the nerves and the subtle energies. Cardamom is indicated for both digestive and respiratory problems, particularly those of a damp origin or nature, such as chronic bronchitis, flatulence and colic. Overall, it is warming, gentle and penetrating.

Psychologically, cardamom is fortifying, uplifting and good for nervous exhaustion, depression of the lethargic type, and mental fatigue. It fortifies those who feel over-burdened with cares, worries and responsibilities; lifts the spirits; and inspires courage and fortitude. Cardamom is associated with the earth element and is grounding for those who tend to feel 'spaced out'.

Cinnamon leaf

(Cinnamomum zeylanicum, Cinnamomum verum)

Family: Lauraceae

Description: Cinnamon is a tropical evergreen tree with fragrant bark and oval leaves, white flowers and blue-white berries. The essential oil is steam-or water-distilled from the leaves and small twigs. A cinnamon-bark essential oil is also available, but it is a skin irritant and is best avoided in aromatherapy.

Countries of origin: Madagascar, India, Jamaica, Sri Lanka

Characteristics: Cinnamon has fiery, harsh, spicy top notes and sweet, oriental undertones. It blends well with frankincense, myrrh, orange, mandarin, benzoin and ylang ylang.

Main therapeutic properties: Anti-microbial, antiseptic, anti-spasmodic, astringent, carminative, digestive, stimulant, stomachic.

Cinnamon is used less in aromatherapy than most of the other spices, but it is excellent in a burner to ward off colds, flu and all other airborne infections and contagious diseases. Blended carefully into a local massage oil, cinnamon

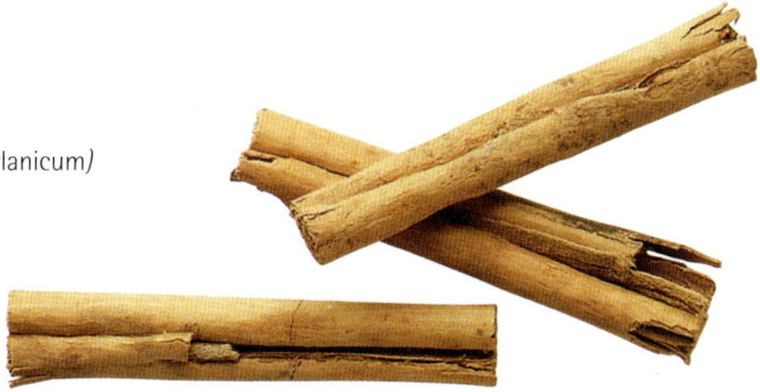

Cinnamon
(Cinnamomum zeylanicum)

is good for digestive complaints and helps a sluggish digestion, flatulence and intestinal infection. Overall, cinnamon is warming, invigorating, restorative and uplifting.

Psychologically, cinnamon is fortifying and reviving. It is indicated for general nervous debility, and for older people during winter to warm both mind and body. It is life-affirming and can help to alleviate melancholia and depression characterized by lethargy and lack of vitality. Cinnamon restores a zest for life and inspires courage.

Contraindications: Do not use if you have sensitive or very sensitive skin. Use in moderation – no more than 2 drops in the bath and no more than 1 per cent in massage oils.

Nutmeg

(Myristica fragrans, Myristica officinalis, Myristica aromatica, Myristica amboinensis)

Family: Myristicaceae

Description: Nutmeg is an aromatic, evergreen tree with dark-green leaves, yellow flowers without petals and yellowish fruits. The essential oil is steam- or water-distilled from the dried nutmegs.

Countries of origin: Indonesia, Sri Lanka, Grenada

Characteristics: Nutmeg has light, fresh, spicy top notes and deep, sweet, warm, woody undertones. It blends well with other spices, and also with clary sage, bay, mandarin, orange, geranium, lavender, rosemary, lime and petitgrain.

Main therapeutic properties: Analgesic, anti-rheumatic, antiseptic, anti-spasmodic, carminative, digestive, emmenagogue, stimulant, tonic.

*Nutmeg (*Myristica officinalis*)*

Nutmeg is reputed to have psychotropic or psychoactive properties when it is ingested orally, meaning that it can affect mental activity and perception. In large doses it is toxic, causing convulsions and possibly death. However, in small amounts nutmeg is a useful addition to the range of essential oils for all external aromatherapeutic applications. It is very good in massage blends for muscular aches and pains, and for painful joints. It is also a good digestive stimulant and helps poor digestion, nausea and diarrhoea. Overall, nutmeg is gently euphoric, comforting and elevating.

Psychologically, it is uplifting and a good nerve tonic, helping to relieve chronic fatigue. Nutmeg is good for those who feel at the end of their tether. It can be useful in meditations and mood perfumes for those who are both sleepy-tired and tired of life, and it inspires creativity and imagination.

Contraindications: Do not use during pregnancy. Use in moderation – no more than 3 drops in the bath, and no more than 1 per cent in massage oils. Do not use consistently over long periods of time.

Grasses, seeds and shrubs

Palmarosa
(Cymbopogon martinii)

Family: Gramineae

Description: Palmarosa is also known as gingergrass, russa grass and East Indian geranium oil. It is a tall, aromatic, perennial free-growing grass. The essential oil is steam-distilled from the fresh or dried grass.

Countries of origin: India, Java, Seychelles, Comoro Islands

Characteristics: Palmarosa has sweet, light, floral top notes with subtle lemon and rose-geranium undertones. Its lovely, delicate, rosy floral fragrance blends well with most other essential oils.

Main therapeutic properties: Antiseptic, bactericide, cytophylactic, digestive, febrifuge, tonic.

Palmarosa is much used in all skin-care preparations for its lovely fragrance, sebum-balancing and hydrating properties. It also helps to regenerate healthy new cells. Palmarosa is suited to all skin types, but is especially good for dry and slightly damaged skin, making it a useful addition to face creams, body lotions and hand creams. Overall, it is balancing, refreshing and soothing. A good digestive stimulant, palmarosa is recommended in local massage and

*Palmarosa (*Cymbopogon martinii*)*

baths for sluggish digestion and loss of appetite, and it may be useful for anorexia nervosa. It is also traditionally used to combat digestive infections, and is valuable during convalescence.

Psychologically, palmarosa is calming, uplifting and comforting and is good for stress, anxiety and restlessness, especially when these feelings have left you feeling vulnerable, lonely and insecure.

Lemongrass
(Cymbopogon citratus, Cymbopogon flexuosus)

Family: Gramineae or Poaceae

Description: Lemongrass is a tall, aromatic, perennial, fast-growing grass. The two varieties are distinct species, but share similar properties. The essential oil is steam-distilled from the finely chopped, fresh or partly dried grass.

Countries of origin: Guatemala, India

Characteristics: Lemongrass has pungent, fresh, lemon, hay-like top notes with earthy, green grassy undertones. It blends well with most citruses and. florals, and also with marjoram, black pepper, rosemary, angelica root and ginger.

Lemongrass (Cymbopogon citratus)

Main therapeutic properties: Analgesic, anti-depressant, anti-microbial, antiseptic, astringent, bactericide, carminative, deodorant, febrifuge, insecticidal, nervine, tonic.

Lemongrass is called the 'connective tissue essential oil', because it tightens and tones the skin and connective tissue. This makes it useful in massage and compresses after sports injuries, general strains and sprains, and after dieting when the connective tissues and skin may have lost tone and become slack. Overall, lemongrass is cooling, refreshing and stimulating.

Lemongrass has excellent antiseptic and deodorant properties, which make it a good choice to use in a burner to clear and freshen the air. Lemongrass is a powerful insecticide, and as a local wash or spray for pets it keeps fleas and bad odours at bay. It is soothing for headaches, but should be properly diluted before applying it to the temples, and it is good blended with lavender.

Psychologically, lemongrass is uplifting and energizing. It is especially useful to get you going in the morning, and a few drops sprinkled in the shower surrounds you with fresh, new energy. Lemongrass is also good for concentration and clear thinking, so it is useful in a burner when you are studying or meditating.

Contraindications: Do not use on sensitive or very sensitive skin. Use in moderation – no more than 3 drops in the bath and no more than 2 per cent in massage oils.

Carrot seed

(Daucus carota)

*Carrot seed (*Daucus carota*)*

Family: Umbellifereae or Apiaceae

Description: Carrot-seed essential oil comes from the wild carrot, not the common cultivated carrot. Wild carrot is an annual or biennial herb with a tough, inedible white root. The essential oil is steam-distilled from the dried seeds.

Countries of origin: France, America

Characteristics: Carrot seed is yellow or orange-brown and viscous, with warm, sweet but pungent, fresh herbaceous top notes and earthy, dry, woody undertones. It blends well with most spices and citruses, and also with cedarwood, geranium, patchouli and palmarosa.

Main therapeutic properties: Antiseptic, carminative, depurative, diuretic, emmenagogue, hepatic, tonic.

Carrot seed is one of the best liver tonics and when used in massage blends and bath oils, can help to regenerate liver cells after hepatitis and other liver diseases. It also has excellent blood-cleansing properties, making it useful in the treatment of eczema, psoriasis and other toxic conditions that affect the skin. Because of its excellent skin-cell regenerating properties, carrot seed is also valuable in skin care, especially for aged, mature and wrinkled skin; and it helps dermatitis and skin rashes. Overall, carrot seed is regenerative, cleansing and rejuvenating.

Psychologically, it has no particular recommendations, but its physical properties may well be mirrored in its effect on the emotions and psyche. This means that carrot seed may help to 'cleanse' the emotions of negativity, and may assist in letting go of past traumas. Its somewhat pungent aroma does not encourage carrot seed to be blended for aesthetic purposes, but it adds a grounding, earthy note to blends.

Helichrysum

(Helichrysum angustifolium, Helichrysum italicum)

Family: Compositae or Asteraceae

Description: Helichrysum is also commonly known as immortelle and everlasting. It is an aromatic herb with daisylike flowers, which dry as the plant matures and are commonly used for dried flower arrangements. The essential oil is steam-distilled from the fresh flowers and flowering tops.

Countries of origin: France, Italy, Corsica, Serbia, Croatia

Characteristics: Helichrysum has sweet, fruity, honeyed top notes with delicate tealike undertones. It blends well with most citruses and florals, and also with clove and clary sage.

Helichrysum (Helichrysum italicum)

Main therapeutic properties: Anti-inflammatory, anti-microbial, antiseptic, carminative, cholagogue, cicatrizant, diuretic, expectorant, hepatic, nervine.

Helichrysum stimulates the liver, gall bladder, kidneys and pancreas, making it a good detoxifying essential oil, useful in lymphatic drainage massage. It has anti-coagulant properties, so it is valuable in cold compresses for bruising. Its anti-inflammatory properties make it good for inflamed skin, eczema, psoriasis and rashes, and for inflamed arthritic joints. Overall, helichrysum is cleansing, calming and healing.

Psychologically, helichrysum warms and opens up repressed emotions, and is good for insight meditation. It regulates the flow of subtle energies and helps lift depression of a lethargic nature. Helichrysum is grounding and is reputed to help those who did not receive enough love as children as well as those who feel alienated and lonely.

Rock rose
(Cistus landaniferus)

Family: Cistaceae

Description: Rock rose is also commonly known as labdanum and cistus. It is a small, sticky shrub with lance-shaped leaves and fragrant white flowers that last only a few hours, but which bud anew every morning. The essential oil is steam-distilled from the gum made from boiling the twigs and leaves in water.

Countries of origin: France, Spain

Characteristics: Rock rose is dark yellow and viscous, with sweet, warm herbaceous top notes and dry, musky undertones. It blends well with clary sage, neroli, lemon, bergamot, cedarwood, jasmine, pine, juniper, lavender, cypress, vetiver, sandalwood, patchouli, orange and roman chamomile.

Rock rose (Cistus landaniferus)

Main therapeutic properties: Anti-microbial, antiseptic, astringent, emmenagogue, expectorant, tonic, vulnerary.

Rock rose is the first choice for healing minor wounds, and in a local wash or cold compress it quickly stops bleeding from open cuts, grazes and abrasions. Blended with lavender and clary sage, it is indicated for healing bed sores, and with cypress and lavender for varicose ulcers. Rock rose also heals chronic skin conditions and is especially effective when these are infected. Overall, it is cleansing, comforting and healing.

Useful in lymphatic drainage massage and in hot compresses on swollen lymph nodes on the neck, rock rose has a powerful cleansing and tonic effect on the lymphatic system. It is good in skin care for oily skins, acne, mature skin and wrinkles.

Psychologically, rock rose is warming and centring. It is valuable in meditations and mood perfumes after shock and trauma, when it warms, grounds and aids reconnection with life and soul. The essential oil mirrors the action of rock-rose flower essence and, used in combination, they provide a powerful way to deal with sudden shock. Rock rose also aids the visualization of spiritual experiences and helps to bring them into consciousness.

Contraindications: Avoid during pregnancy.

Vetiver

(Vetiveria zizanoides, Andropogon muricatus)

Family: Gramineae or Poaceae

Description: Vetiver is a tall, fragrant, densely tufted perennial grass, with an extensive network of fibrous aromatic roots. The essential oil is steam-distilled from the cleaned, washed and chopped roots and rootlets, which are first dried and then soaked in water.

Vetiver (Vetiveria zizanoides)

Countries of origin: Rèunion Islands, Indonesia, India, Sri Lanka, Malaysia

Characteristics: Vetiver is amber-brown and viscous, with deep, smoky, earthy top notes and sweet, musty, potato undertones. It blends well with orange, marjoram, sandalwood, verbena, neroli, cardamom, rose, jasmine, lavender, ylang ylang, geranium, patchouli and clary sage.

Main therapeutic properties: Antiseptic, anti-spasmodic, sedative, tonic.

Vetiver is the grounding, earthy essential oil, and is known as the 'oil of tranquillity'. It helps to centre you whenever you feel disconnected from your body, your feelings and from life itself. Its earthy fragrance is appreciated by both men and women, and it is commonly used in aftershave lotions and men's toiletries. For women, vetiver is especially recommended in baths, massage oils and skin lotions to balance hormones during the menopause. Overall, vetiver is grounding, regenerating and protecting.

Also known as moth root, vetiver repels moths and cotton wool balls sprinkled with vetiver can be placed in the wardrobe to protect clothes and linens. It is good for mature skin that has lost its tone and elasticity, as it strengthens tired, loose and undernourished skin. Vetiver is also an immuno-stimulant, and is indicated when stress and over-work are depleting the body's natural defences.

Psychologically, vetiver is valuable for nervous exhaustion, stress, chronic fatigue, depression, anxiety and insomnia. It deeply relaxes and stabilizes, and is good in bath and massage oils. Vetiver is calming, soothing and restorative; it tones subtle energies and is associated with the root chakra. It also protects against over-sensitivity and acts like a protective shield. Vetiver is good in meditations, facilitating wisdom and visionary insights.

Ti-tree

(Melaleuca alternifolia)

Family: Myrtaceae

Description: Ti-tree is also spelled tea-tree, and is a shrub or small tree with needlelike leaves, which grows best in swampy ground. Also known as paper bark, the bark of ti-tree is white and papery. The essential oil is steam- or water-distilled from the leaves and twigs.

Country of origin: Australia

*Ti-tree (*Melaleuca alternifolia*)*

Characteristics: Ti-tree has warm, spicy, camphoraceous top notes with pungent, medicinal undertones. It blends well with most spices and herbs, and also with lavender, pine and eucalyptus.

Main therapeutic properties: Anti-microbial, antiseptic, anti-viral, bactericide, cicatrizant, expectorant, fungicide, immuno-stimulant, stimulant.

Ti-tree is the most 'medicinal' of the essential oils, with powerful anti-microbial activity against all three of the infectious organisms: bacteria, viruses and fungi. When diffused in an oil burner, ti-tree is particularly helpful in preventing the spread of air-borne infections. Together with its powerful immuno-stimulant properties, ti-tree is a real ally in combating many illnesses and ailments. Overall, it is penetrating, medicinal and stimulating.

Athlete's foot, vaginal thrush, cold sores, herpes, insect bites, spots, acne and minor abrasions all respond well to local applications of ti-tree. In steam inhalations, it prevents colds and flu developing, and if they do manifest, it aids recovery and alleviates symptoms. Ti-tree in massage and bath oils can help boost those with weak immune systems, and it helps with long-term debilitating illnesses such as glandular fever. Mixed into aloe-vera gel, ti-tree helps to alleviate the pain of shingles.

Psychologically, ti-tree is strengthening and warming. Its aroma is distinctly medicinal and many people find it more palatable when it is blended. Ti-tree invigorates mind, body and spirit; inspires confidence; and dispels the doom and gloom of chronic ill health. Ti-tree also strengthens subtle energies.

Contraindications: Do not use on very sensitive skin. Use in moderation – no more than 4 drops in the bath, and no more than 2 per cent in massage oils. Avoid direct contact with the skin, except directly on spots, verrucas and cold sores.

Patchouli
(Pogostemom cablin)

Family: Labiatae or Lamiaceae

Description: Patchouli is an aromatic, perennial shrub with large green leaves and white-pink flowers. The essential oil is steam-distilled from the dried, fermented leaves.

Countries of origin: Philippines, Indonesia, Malaysia, India, China, Mauritius

Characteristics: Patchouli is dark orange and viscous with warm, rich, sweet, spicy, woody top notes and earthy, herbaceous, musky, balsamic undertones. It blends well with lavender, vetiver, sandalwood, cedarwood, rose, neroli, jasmine, ylang ylang, lemon, bergamot, geranium, clove, myrrh, frankincense and clary sage.

Main therapeutic properties: Anti-depressant, anti-inflammatory, anti-microbial, antiseptic, aphrodisiac, astringent, cicatrizant, cytophylactic, deodorant, fungicide, insecticide, sedative.

*Patchouli (*Pogostemom cablin*)*

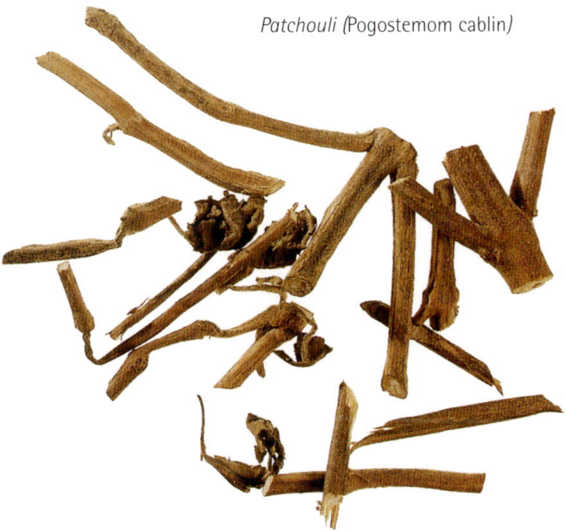

Patchouli is the 'hippy' essential oil, much used in the 1960s and early 1970s as a perfume, to mask the unpleasant odour of Afghan coats and disguise the smell of marijuana! It has always been extensively used in perfumes and deodorants, and to protect clothes and carpets from insect damage. Patchouli is a powerful aphrodisiac, and adds a sensuous, erotic, oriental note to mood perfumes, although not everyone likes its distinctive scent. Overall, patchouli is relaxing, uplifting and sensual.

Excellent in skin care, patchouli heals inflammation, dermatitis, sores, eczema and other skin conditions, and is particularly suited to mature and oily skins. It helps to regenerate healthy new skin cells and, when blended with wheatgerm oil, reduces the visibility of scar tissue. Patchouli makes a good addition to base shampoo and conditioner, helping to alleviate dandruff.

Psychologically, patchouli is soothing, stabilizing and slightly hypnotic. It is excellent for reducing stress and for alleviating anxiety and depression. It is good in massage oils, and helps those who are overly intellectual, bringing them in touch with their earthy, sensual nature. Patchouli grounds those who get lost in daydreams. It is also good in meditations for calming too many thoughts, and generally for grounding and centring.

Niaouli

(Melaleuca quinquenervia, Melaleuca veridiflora)

Family: Myrtaceae

Description: Niaouli is sometimes also called gomenol, and is a small evergreen tree with papery bark, aromatic leaves and yellow flowers. The essential oil is steam-distilled from the leaves and young twigs.

Niaouli (Melaleuca veridiflora)

Country of origin: Australia
Characteristics: Niaouli has sweet, fresh camphoraceous top notes and eucalyptus-like undertones. It blends well with lavender, pine, lemon, myrtle, orange, hyssop and eucalyptus.
Main therapeutic properties: Analgesic, antiseptic, anti-viral, bactericide, cicatrizant, decongestant, febrifuge, insecticide, stimulant, vulnerary.

Niaouli is a relative of ti-tree. It has a gentler, less effective action, but is well tolerated by the skin, making it valuable in a local wash for cleaning wounds. Its vulnerary and antiseptic properties help the wound heal cleanly and quickly. Its gentle action also makes niaouli good in a local wash for urinary-tract infections, thrush and cystitis. Overall, niaouli is healing, stimulant and refreshing.

An excellent expectorant, niaouli is good in steam inhalations and baths for coughs, colds, flu, sinusitis and bronchitis. Hot compresses of niaouli help treat boils, large painful spots and acne.

Psychologically, niaouli has no particular indications, but it is a powerful stimulant, and when vaporized in a burner it will help keep the mind clear and alert, aiding study, meditation, and so on, but avoid using niaouli in the evening.

Myrtle
(Myrtus communis)

Family: Myrtaceae

Description: Myrtle is an evergreen shrub with small, pointed leaves and fragrant white or pink flowers. The essential oil is steam-distilled from the leaves and twigs, and sometimes the flowers are also included.

Countries of origin: France, Spain, Corsica, Tunisia, Morocco, Italy

Characteristics: Myrtle has fresh, spicy, camphoraceous top notes and floral, herbaceous undertones. It blends well with spices, and also with lavender, neroli, lime, bergamot, lemon, hyssop, bay, rosemary, clary sage, pine and cypress.

Main therapeutic properties: Anti-catarrhal, antiseptic, astringent, bactericide, expectorant, sedative.

Myrtle is one of the best essential oils for children's ailments, because it is mildly sedative, has a gentle action and a soft, pleasing fragrance. It is especially recommended for respiratory ailments, and is good in back and chest massage, baths and

Myrtle (Myrtus communis)

steam inhalations. At night in a child's bedroom a burner of myrtle – placed well out of reach – is settling and alleviates irritable coughing.

Its astringent property makes myrtle useful in skin care for oily skin and open pores, and it is helpful blended into an ointment base for haemorrhoids. It can also be used in a douche to help treat urinary-tract infections. Overall, myrtle is soothing, calming and cheering.

Psychologically, myrtle is clarifying, purifying and protective. It has been recommended for addictive, self-destructive and compulsive-obsessive behaviour, especially if this manifests in drug use. Massage from an aromatherapist as part of a professional team is recommended for all serious cases. However, for minor and temporary instances, myrtle in massage, baths and mood perfumes is supportive. Myrtle carries the spirit of truth and forgiveness, and acts like a doorway to universal divine energies.

Bay

(Pimenta acris, Pimenta racemosa)

Family: Myrtaceae

Description: Bay is also known as bay rum tree or West Indian bay. This distinguishes it from the bay laurel, which is generally used less in aromatherapy. Bay is an evergreen tree, with large, leathery leaves and aromatic fruits. The essential oil is steam- or water-distilled from the leaves.

Countries of origin: West Indies, Puerto Rico, Venezuela

Characteristics: Bay has fresh, spicy, camphoraceous top notes with sweet, warm, balsamic undertones. It blends well with most spices and citruses, and also with lavender, rosemary, geranium, ylang ylang and clove.

Main therapeutic properties: Analgesic, antiseptic, astringent, expectorant, stimulant.

Bay (Pimenta racemosa)

Bay is one of the best essential oils to use as a hair tonic, and the traditional hair tonic 'bay rum' was produced by distilling rum with the bay leaves. Bay stimulates the scalp, helps to eliminate and prevent dandruff, and restores body and tone to oily and damaged, lifeless hair. Overall, bay is reviving, refreshing and clearing.

Bay gives an interesting, masculine fragrance to massage oils and is good for general body aches and pains. It is used in steam inhalations because it is an effective antiseptic for the respiratory system.

Psychologically, there are no particular indications for bay, although its masculine fragrance is often well suited to those who dislike the sweeter-smelling essential oils.

Contraindications: Do not use on very sensitive skin or directly on mucous membranes. Use in moderation and do not use for prolonged periods of time.

Manuka

(Leptospermum scoparium)

Family: Myrtaceae

Description: Manuka is a shrub or small tree, with flowers that strongly attract bees. Manuka honey – as well as being eaten – is also used for various external healing purposes, such as burns and ulcers, because it contains traces of the chemicals found in the essential oil. The oil is steam-distilled from the leaves and twigs.

Country of origin: New Zealand

Characteristics: Manuka has fresh, spicy, herbaceous top notes with sweet, warm, gentle undertones. It blends well with many other essential oils, as its delicate aroma is easily compatible with other fragrances.

Main therapeutic properties: Analgesic, anti-bacterial, anti-inflammatory, antiseptic, expectorant, fungicide, insecticide, sedative.

Manuka is a fairly recent addition to aromatherapy, although the plant has been used by the Maoris for centuries. Often compared with ti-tree, it is a possible immuno-stimulant (but not as powerful as ti-tree). Manuka is a powerful insecticide and is good for treating insect bites, athlete's foot, ringworm, cold sores, acne, and chronic wounds and ulcers.

Overall, manuka is healing, refreshing and calming. Useful in massage, manuka has a gentle analgesic effect on sore, aching muscles. It is also good

*Manuka (*Leptospermum scoparium*)*

in steam inhalations to treat coughs, colds and flu. Psychologically, manuka is protective and suited to sensitive personalities. It stabilizes and balances the nervous system, so manuka is good in meditations to maintain a healthy emotional balance.

Exotic essential oils

The directory of essential oils covers the majority of essential oils that are commonly used in aromatherapy; it also includes some essential oils that are valuable, but used less frequently. However, there are a few essential oils with minor uses that are not listed, due to lack of space. The following 'exotic' essential oils and absolutes are not widely used in professional aromatherapy, but they do add a special quality – mainly to mood perfumes, but also occasionally to massage oils and bath oils.

Safety guidelines

- Exotic essential oils need to be used with great care and discretion. Many of them are powerful absolutes, and 1–2 drops is usually sufficient to enhance a blend.

- Whereas the more frequently used essential oils have extensive safety data, some of the exotics have only minimal safety information, so you should never exceed the amounts suggested.

- Although it is unlikely, if you do experience any adverse effects - such as tingling or redness on the skin, - wash the essential oil off immediately, and do not use that particular exotic again.

These exotics are used extensively in the perfume industry for their wonderful fragrances. They are increasingly available from some suppliers of essential oils, although they tend to be expensive.

If you follow the safety guidelines (above) carefully, the exotics offer an interesting addition to your creative blending.

Exotic essential oils are sometimes used in bath oils.

Linden blossom

(Tilia vulgaris)

Linden blossom is also known as lime blossom. Linden herbal tea is commonly drunk for its relaxing and digestive properties, and the fine honey is used in liqueurs. Linden blossom is an absolute, acquired by solvent extraction of the dried flowers.

Linden blossom has sweet, herbaceous, haylike top notes with green, dry, honeyed undertones. It blends well with citruses and florals, and also with frankincense, sandalwood, myrrh and verbena.

Linden blossom is wonderful for the nerves and has a deeply calming, sedative and tonic action. It promotes a profound relaxation, and is especially

Linden blossom (Tilia vulgaris)

recommended when tiredness, stress or an over-active mind is preventing sleep. The lovely fragrance of linden blossom is soothing and, in tiny amounts, when blended with lavender, helps to relieve headaches, especially when these are caused by stress.

Use small amounts only: 1–2 drops in a bath or massage oil or in a mood perfume. Like ylang ylang, its scent can become cloying and overpowering if too much is used, or for too long or too often.

Ambrette seed
(Abelmoschus moschatus)

Ambrette seed is a tropical shrub. The seeds are used as a spice in the East, and the Arabs use them to flavour coffee. Ambrette seed is available as an essential oil, steam-distilled from the seeds, and as an absolute obtained by solvent extraction. It is aged for several months before being used.

*Ambrette seed (*Abelmoschus moschatus*)*

Ambrette seed has rich, sweet, dry, floral top notes with well-rounded, warm, musky, oriental undertones. It blends well with most florals, and also with sandalwood, clary sage, lemon, coriander, cardamom, frankincense, patchouli and cypress.

It has a calming effect on the nerves and the digestion, and a powerful effect on the adrenal glands. Ambrette seed is gently aphrodisiac and is good for stress-related conditions and depression. It is also warming and stimulant, and makes a pleasant addition to massage oils.

Use small amounts only: 1–2 drops in a bath or massage oil or in a mood perfume. Ambrette seed's fragrance is quite masculine and is well suited to those who dislike the sweeter florals.

Mimosa

(Acacia dealbata)

Mimosa is an attractive ornamental tree and its fluffy, ball-shaped yellow flowers are a familiar sight in France in early spring. The absolute is obtained by solvent extraction from the flowers and flowering twig ends. It may be viscous or a waxy solid at room temperature which melts as you hold the bottle in your hand.

Mimosa smells like a warm spring morning with sweet, delicate, green, floral top notes and fresh, deep, complex, woody undertones. It blends well with most florals, citruses and spices, and also with rosewood, sandalwood, clary sage and melissa.

Mimosa is astringent and antiseptic, with good nourishing skin-care properties, especially for oily and youthful skin. The soft, delicate fragrance of mimosa is excellent in a mood perfume for girls as they mature into

Mimosa (Acacia dealbata)

women. Like neroli, it is wonderful for alleviating anxiety, fear and depression and, with its springlike scent, may also be recommended for Seasonal Affective Disorder.

Use small amounts only: 2–3 drops in a bath or massage oil or in a mood perfume. Mimosa is well suited to shy, sensitive, impressionable, feminine and youthful personalities.

*Narcissus (*Narcissus poeticus*)*

Narcissus
(Narcissus poeticus)

Narcissus is a common spring flower, similar to (but smaller than) the daffodil. Traditionally narcissus was used as a perfume by the Arabs, and it is still used in India as an anointing oil before going into the temple to pray. Narcissus is an absolute obtained by solvent extraction of the flowers.

Narcissus has heady, herbaceous, green top notes with heavy, sweet, floral, mysterious undertones. It blends well with many essential oils and enhances blends, and is especially good with other florals, sandalwood, basil and clove.

The name comes from the Greek word *narkao*, meaning 'to be numb', and narcissus has a pronounced narcotic action and must be used with great care. Its sedative, hypnotic, earthy, languid quality is deeply calming and grounding when you are over-excited or hysterical.

Use tiny amounts only: 1 drop occasionally in a bath or massage oil or in a mood perfume. Narcissus is a gentle aphrodisiac and gives an interesting, sensual note to intimate massage blends. It is good in meditations for deep introspection.

Champaca

(Michelia champaca)

Champaca (Michelia champaca)

Champaca or champa is one of several floral absolutes from India that is gradually being introduced into aromatherapy. Champaca absolute is obtained by solvent extraction of the fragrant, yellow-orange flowers or as an attar distilled into a base of sandalwood.

Champaca has sweet, deep, exotic floral top notes with delicate, woody, sensual, roselike undertones. Champaca blends well with most florals and citruses, and also with sandalwood, rosewood, clary sage, basil, cardamom and myrtle. Champaca gives a deep, mysterious, oriental quality to all blends.

Traditionally the flowers are offered to the gods and goddesses of India, and champaca is considered an incarnation of Lakshmi, the Indian goddess of wealth. Both stimulant and anti-depressant, champaca is useful for depression characterized by lethargy. It is grounding, warming and enhances self-esteem and confidence. It is also indicated for menstrual cramps and irregularities.

Use small amounts only: 2–3 drops in a bath or massage oil or in a mood perfume. Avoid in early pregnancy. Champaca is a gentle aphrodisiac and is used extensively in perfumery. The exotic, voluptuous and gratifying fragrance is suited to mature, sensual personalities.

Oakmoss

(Evernia prunastri)

*Oakmoss (*Evernia prunastri*)*

Oakmoss is a pale-green lichen that is found growing on oak trees. Oakmoss absolute is obtained by solvent extraction from the lichen after it has been soaked in luke-warm water. There are several other moss or lichen absolutes, but oakmoss is generally considered the finest.

Oakmoss has earthy, mossy, tarlike top notes with heavy, rich, leathery undertones. It is one of the best fixatives and is much used in the perfume industry to give a full body to perfumes, and provide rich, natural undertones. It blends well with most other essential oils.

As an expectorant, oakmoss is good in massage blends for coughs and bronchitis. Excellent in mood perfumes, it gives an earthy grounding note to all types of fragrances.

Use small amounts only: 1–2 drops in a bath or massage oil or in a mood perfume. Once diluted in perfume, oakmoss has an enticing, balancing and calming effect.

Tuberose

(Polianthes tuberosa)

Tuberose is a tender perennial with large, white, fragrant flowers resembling lilies. It is among the most expensive of the floral absolutes, but is highly valued for its wonderful scent. The absolute is obtained by solvent extraction of the fresh flower buds.

Tuberose is dark orange and so viscous that it is almost a paste. It has heavy, sweet, floral, slightly spicy top notes and sensuous, radiant, honeyed undertones. It blends beautifully with the other florals and citruses, and enhances oriental and floral perfumes. The fragrance of tuberose is calming, and promotes strength and endurance. It is reputed to protect subtle energies and boundaries.

Use tiny amounts only: 1 drop occasionally in a bath or massage oil or in a mood perfume. Tuberose has a narcotic, hypnotic effect with its soporific, sensual scent.

Tuberose (Polianthes tuberosa)

Jonquil

(Narcissus jonquilla)

Jonquil is a fragrant relative of narcissus (see page 380) and is much used in the perfume industry. The absolute is obtained by solvent extraction from the flowers. Jonquil has heavy, sweet, floral, honeyed top notes and deep, green undertones. It blends easily with most florals and citruses, and also with sandalwood, rosewood, rosemary, basil, clary sage, cardamom, clove and verbena.

Jonquil is calming and relaxing. It is good for relieving anxiety and frustration, and helps you to let go of unwanted thoughts and worries. It is hypnotic and narcotic, and is reputed to help alleviate low self-esteem and bring repressed desires into consciousness.

Use tiny amounts only: 1 drop occasionally in a bath or massage oil or in a mood perfume. Jonquil is a gentle aphrodisiac, and gives an erotic, sensual note to massage and bath oils, and mood perfumes.

*Jonquil (*Narcissus jonquilla*)*

Hazardous essential oils

There are certain essential oils that are beyond the scope of this directory. Some of these are safe to use, following the usual safety guidelines, but others must *never* be used for aromatherapy. If in doubt about the safety of a particular essential oil, then don't use it. The following essential oils are hazardous and should be avoided completely.

- ajowan
- bitter almond
- boldo
- buchu
- calamus
- camphor
- cassia
- costus
- elecampane
- horseradish
- jaborandi
- mugwort (armoise)
- mustard
- oregano
- parsley seed
- pennyroryal
- rue
- sassafras
- savin
- savory
- southernwood
- tansy
- thuja
- wintergreen
- wormseed
- wormwood

Glossary of therapeutic terms

analgesic: relieves or diminishes pain

anaphrodisiac: relieves or diminishes sexual desire

anti-allergenic: relieves or reduces the symptoms of allergies

anti-bacterial/antibiotic: prevents the growth of or destroys bacteria

anti-catarrhal: relieves or reduces the production of mucus

anti-convulsive: relieves or controls convulsions

anti-depressant: uplifts and counteracts depression

anti-inflammatory: relieves or alleviates inflammation

anti-microbial: resists or destroys pathogens (agents that cause disease)

anti-neuralgic: relieves or reduces nerve pain

anti-rheumatic: relieves or reduces the symptoms of rheumatism

anti-seborrhoeic: helps to control the production of sebum

antiseptic: destroys or controls pathogenic bacteria

anti-spasmodic: relieves spasms and cramps of the smooth muscles

anti-sudorific: diminishes sweating

anti-toxic: counteracts poisoning

anti-viral: inhibits the growth of viruses

aphrodisiac: increases or stimulates sexual desire

astringent: contracts and tightens tissues

bactericidal/bactericide: prevents the growth of or destroys bacteria

balsamic: soothing and healing

carminative: settles the digestion, eases gripes and relieves flatulence

cephalic: stimulates and clears the mind

cholagogue: stimulates the flow of bile from the gall bladder into the intestines

cicatrizant: promotes healing through the formation of scar tissue

cytophylactic: stimulates the growth of healthy new skin cells

decongestant: relieves or reduces congestion, especially of mucus

demulcent: soothes, softens and alleviates irritation of the mucous membranes

deodorant: counteracts body odours

depurative: purifies and cleanses the blood

detoxifying: helps to eliminate toxins from the body

digestive: aids the digestion of food

diuretic: increases the production and secretion of urine

emmenagogue: promotes and regulates menstruation

emollient: softening and soothing, especially to the skin

expectorant: helps to expel mucus from the respiratory system

febrifuge: reduces fever

fungicidal/fungicide: resists or destroys fungal infections

galactagogue: increases the flow of breast milk

haemostatic: helps to stop bleeding

hepatic: liver tonic, stimulates and aids liver function

hypertensor/hypertensive: increases blood pressure

hypotensor/hypotensive: reduces blood pressure

immuno-stimulant: stimulates the function of the immune system

insecticidal/insecticide: destroys insects

laxative: aids bowel evacuation

nervine: nerve tonic, stimulates and strengthens the nervous system

phototoxic: causes skin discoloration by exposure to sunlight, together with certain essential oils

psychoactive/psychotropic: has a hallucinogenic, druglike effect, capable of affecting mental activity and perception

rubefacient: warms the skin and increases blood flow

sedative: calms and reduces nervousness, distress and agitation

splenic: tonic of the spleen

stimulant: stimulates the physiological functions of the body

stomachic: tonic of the stomach, aids digestion

styptic: astringent, helps to prevent external bleeding

tonic: invigorates and strengthens the body

uterine: tonic of the uterus

vasoconstrictor/vasoconstrictive: constricts and contracts the capillary walls

vasodilator: causes dilation of the capillaries

volatile: evaporates quickly and easily from a liquid (such as an essential oil) into a vapour or gas

vulnerary: promotes the healing of wounds and prevents tissue degeneration

Index

Acknowledgements

Special photography: Octopus Publishing Group Limited/Mike Prior
All other photography: Alamy/Mark Baigent 201; /Bildagentur-online.com/th-foto 377; /Mark Campbell/Photofusion Picture Library 117; /David Crausby 263; /Roger Eritja 206; /Imagebroker 382; /Kalpana Kartik 281; /Bruce Miller 186; /PBWPIX 246; /DY Riess MD 120; /Sciencephotos 203; /Shout 204; /TH Foto 376; /Moritz Wolf/Fotosonline 234. **Banana Stock** 56, 212. **Corbis UK Ltd** 226, 236; /Lester V. Bergman 138, 202; /Nancy Brown 230; /Lou Chardonnay 81, 85; /Digital Art 140; /Donna Day 238; /Michael Keller 22; /Jutta Klee 62; /Larry Williams 114; /Gail Mooney 26–27, 36; /Jose Luis Pelaez, Inc. 83, 118; /Amet Jean Pierre/Sygma 34; /Michael Porsche 124; /Steve Prezant 208; /Michael Prince 240; /Anthony Redpath 197; /Chuck Savage 105; /Thomas Schweizer 100; /Liba Taylor 8–9; /Larry Williams 148; /Elizabeth Young 111; /Jeff Zaruba 374. **Digital Vision** 23, 144. **DK Images**/Neil Fletcher and Matthew Ward 315. **Garden Picture Library**/Sunniva Harte 287. **Getty Images** 242; /Nick Clements 60; /Comstock Images 57; /Howard Kingsnorth 126; /Serge Krouglikoff 142; /Ghislain & Marie David de Losy 44; /Justin Pumfrey 70; /Roger Wright 152. **John Glover** 342, 379. **Imagesource** 244. **Imagestate** 87. **Octopus Publishing Group Limited** 20, 191, 198, 205, 228, 308, 322, 325, 327, 335, 349, 371; /Colin Bowling 1, 37, 41, 188, 193, 297, 299, 302, 304, 305, 313, 340, 347; /Michael Boys 292, 296; /Stephen Conroy 43; /Mark Gatehouse 16–17, 33; /Jerry Harpur 310; /Mike Hemsley 42, 90–91, 129, 182, 224, 352, 365; /Neil Holmes 24, 273, 276; /Alistair Hughes 107, 180; /Sandra Lane 284, 348; /William Lingwood 345; /David Loftus 355; /Zul Mukhida 32; /Peter Myers 6–7, 13, 46–47, 48, 178, 222, 255; /Ian Parsons 294, 319, 344, 351; /Lis Parsons 321, 324; /Peter Pugh-Cook 11, 21, 55, 74, 75, 76, 98, 122; /William Reavell 10, 15, 130, 218–219; /Russell Sadur 136, 146; /Gareth Sambidge 61, 108, 154, 184, 185, 210, 214, 216; /Roger Stowell 317; /Richard Truscott 171 left, 171 right; /Ian Wallace 18, 29, 58, 89, 194, 232, 248, 301; /James Young 282, 369, 380. **Jerry Harpur** 288; Longwood Gardens, Philadelphia 268–269, 372–373. **Marcus Harpur** 384. **Holt Studios** 330, 331, 337, 338, 361, 367. **Andrew Lawson** 270, 359, 383; /Torie Chugg 307, 357. **N.H.P.A.**/A.N.T. Photo Library 363; /Mike Lane 312. **Clive Nichols** 328; /Hadspen Garden, Somerset 356. **Photodisc** 12, 45, 53, 103, 151, 176. **Photos Horticultural** Horticultural 354. **Photolibrary.com**/Diaphor La Phototheque 14; /IFA-Bilderteam 275; /Ragan Romy 381. **Rubberball** 112. **Science Photo Library**/Alfred Pasieka 92; /Lino Pastorelli 290. **Tisserand Aromatherapy (++44 (0)1273 325666, www.tisserand.com)** 132–133, 134, 174. **www.ukessentialoils.com/Allovia** 333.

Executive Editor Brenda Rosen
Managing Editor Clare Churly
Executive Art Editor Sally Bond
Designer Patrick McLeavey
Picture Library Manager Jennifer Veall
Production Controller Simone Nauerth